DATE DUE

MAR 2 1 2018	
AUG 0 2 2018	

BRODART, CO. Cat. No. 23-221

American Ideals and Institutions Series

Robert P. George, series editor

Published in partnership with the James Madison Program in American Ideals and Institutions at Princeton University, this series is dedicated to exploring enduring questions of political thought and constitutional law; promoting the canon of the Western intellectual tradition as it nourishes and informs contemporary politics; and applying foundational Western principles to modern social problems.

Also available in the American Ideals and Institutions Series:

CONSCIENCE
AND ITS ENEMIES

CONSCIENCE
AND ITS ENEMIES

*Confronting the Dogmas
of Liberal Secularism*

ROBERT P. GEORGE

ISI
BOOKS

Wilmington, Delaware

Cataloging-in-Publication data is on file with the Library of Congress.
ISBN: 978-1-61017-070-3

Published in the United States by:

ISI Books
Intercollegiate Studies Institute
3901 Centerville Road
Wilmington, Delaware 19807-1938
www.isibooks.org

Manufactured in the United States of America

For Luis Tellez

Contents

Introduction

AMERICANS ARE DEEPLY divided on a range of issues—
not only as to the best means for achieving agreed-upon
goals but also as to the goals themselves. These issues centrally involve disputed fundamental values and moral principles. For
example: Should human life be protected in all stages and conditions?
Or should abortion and euthanasia be permitted and even promoted
as "best" (or "least bad") solutions to personal difficulties and social
problems? Should we preserve in our law and public policy the historic understanding of marriage as a conjugal union—the partnership
of husband and wife in a bond that is ordered to procreation and,
where the union is blessed by children, naturally fulfilled by their
having and rearing offspring together? Or should we abandon the
conjugal understanding of marriage in favor of some form of legally
recognized sexual-romantic companionship or domestic partnership
between two (or more) persons, irrespective of gender, to which the
label *marriage* is then reassigned?

Disputes such as these reflect the profound chasm that separates opposing worldviews. People on the competing sides use many

of the same words: *justice, human rights, liberty, equality, fairness, tolerance, respect, community, conscience,* and the like. But they have vastly different ideas of what those terms mean. Likewise, they have radically different views of human nature, of what makes for a valuable and morally worthy way of life, and of what undermines the common good of a justly ordered community.

There is a truth all too rarely adverted to in contemporary "culture war" debates—namely, that deep philosophical ideas have unavoidable and sometimes quite profound implications for public policy and public life. Anyone who takes a position on, say, the ethics of abortion and euthanasia, or the meaning and proper definition of marriage, is making philosophical (e.g., metaphysical and moral) assumptions—assumptions that are contested by people on the other side of the debate. The temptation, of course, is to suppose that "I'm not making any controversial assumptions; only the people on the other side are doing that." But this is absurd. All of us make philosophical assumptions—about the human good, human nature, human dignity, and many other crucial matters. One objective of this book is to show that these assumptions—our own assumptions, not just the other guy's—have important consequences, and that we should all be prepared to examine them critically.

Self-awareness is, indeed, an obligation of democratic citizenship. With so much at stake in our public debates, it becomes difficult to maintain civility and mutual respect. A spirit of self-criticism can help. People who are aware that they are making contestable assumptions are much more likely to recognize that reasonable people of goodwill can, in fact, disagree—even about matters of profound human and moral significance.

Does this mean that participants in morally charged debates should soft-pedal their arguments or keep quiet about their convictions? Certainly not. Civility and mutual respect are not inconsistent with candor and even bluntness. I daresay that the title of this book, *Conscience and Its Enemies*, is plenty blunt—blunt in a way that will perhaps strike my adversaries in the same way that the 2012 Obama campaign's claims about a "Republican war on women" struck those against whom that allegation was made. But, misguided though the allegation was, I do not object to the fact that those who sincerely believed it said so plainly. They believe that protecting unborn children against violent killing by abortion (you see, I am speaking no less plainly myself) is a violation of women's freedom and equality, and that refusing to force employers, including those with sincere moral and religious objections, to provide employees with insurance coverage that includes abortion-inducing drugs, sterilizations, and contraceptives is a denial of female employees' right to "health care."

I say, let's have a debate about these questions—a debate that goes all the way down to fundamental assumptions about human nature, the human good, and human dignity and destiny. Let's bring those assumptions, and the assumptions of contrary views, to the surface. Let's examine them closely and see how well the competing positions hold up under critical rational scrutiny.

Many people are not accustomed to such scrutiny. In formal debates and informal conversations with my friends and colleagues at Princeton University, other scholars, public intellectuals, and government officials, I have found that secular liberal views are so widespread as to go largely unquestioned. As a result, many in these elite circles yield to the temptation to believe that anyone who disagrees with them is a bigot or a religious fundamentalist. Reason and science, they confidently believe, are on their side.

With this book, I aim to expose the emptiness of that belief. I make no secret of the fact that I am a Christian or that on the most divisive moral issues I make common cause with devout Jews, Muslims, and other people of faith. But in these essays I do not base my arguments on theological claims or religious authority. As we will see, human embryology, developmental biology, and other scientific fields have established certain undeniable facts that challenge the passionately held moral convictions of secular liberals. There is also a long philosophical and moral tradition—one that extends back to ancient thinkers untouched by Jewish or Christian revelation—that supports the positions of those who supposedly have no rational basis for their views.

Increasingly, enemies of what James Madison called the "sacred rights of conscience" cloak themselves in the mantle of science to marginalize their opponents. But close scrutiny reveals that it is their own views that are thinly supported—that are, as they might say dismissively, nothing but articles of faith. In any event, that is something I hope to demonstrate in the pages that follow.

Part I

FUNDAMENTALS

1

COMMON PRINCIPLES, COMMON FOES

S OME PEOPLE THINK that the alliance of social and economic conservatives is at best a marriage of convenience. I
couldn't disagree more. Basic shared principles should lead
serious social conservatives to be economic conservatives as well. And
those same principles should lead serious economic conservatives to
be social conservatives.

A sound conservatism will, as a matter of principle, honor limited
government, restrained spending, honest money, and low taxes, while
upholding the sanctity of human life in all stages and conditions, the
dignity of marriage as the conjugal union of husband and wife, and
the protection of the innocence of children.

The Pillars of a Decent Society

Any healthy society, any decent society, will rest on three pillars. The
first is respect for the human person—the individual human being
and his dignity. Where this pillar is in place, the formal and informal

institutions of society, and the beliefs and practices of the people, will be such that every member of the human family, irrespective not only of race, sex, or ethnicity but also of age, size, stage of development, or condition of dependency, is treated as a person—that is, as a subject bearing profound, inherent, and equal worth and dignity.

A society that does not nurture respect for the human person—beginning with the child in the womb, and including the mentally and physically impaired and the frail elderly—will sooner or later (probably sooner rather than later) come to regard human beings as mere cogs in the larger social wheel whose dignity and well-being may legitimately be sacrificed for the sake of the collectivity. Some members of the community—those in certain development stages, for example—will come to be regarded as disposable. Others—those in certain conditions of dependency, for example—will come to be viewed as intolerably burdensome, as "useless eaters," as "better off dead," as *Lebensunwertes leben* ("life unworthy of life").

In their most extreme modern forms, totalitarian regimes reduce the individual to an instrument to serve the ends of the fascist state or the future communist utopia. When liberal democratic regimes go awry, it is often because a utilitarian ethic reduces the human person to a means rather than an end to which other things, including the systems and institutions of law, education, and the economy, are means. The abortion license against which we struggle today is dressed up by its defenders in the language of individual and even natural rights, and there can be no doubt that the acceptance of abortion is partly the fruit of me-generation liberal ideology—a corruption (and burlesque) of liberal political philosophy in its classical form. But more fundamentally it is underwritten by a utilitarian ethic that, in the end, vaporizes the very idea of natural rights, treating the idea (in Jeremy Bentham's famously dismissive words) as "nonsense on stilts."

In cultures in which religious fanaticism has taken hold, the dignity of the individual is typically sacrificed for the sake of tragically misbegotten theological ideas and goals. By contrast, a liberal democratic ethos, where it is uncorrupted by utilitarianism or me-generation expressive individualism, supports the dignity of the human person by giving witness to basic human rights and liberties. Where a healthy religious life flourishes, faith in God provides a grounding for the dignity and inviolability of the human person by, for example, proposing an understanding of each and every member of the human family, even someone of a different faith or professing no particular faith, as a person made in the image and likeness of the divine Author of our lives and liberties.

The second pillar of any decent society is the institution of the family. It is indispensable. The family, based on the marital commitment of husband and wife, is the original and best ministry of health, education, and welfare. Although no family is perfect, no institution matches the healthy family in its capacity to transmit to each new generation the understandings and traits of character—the values and virtues—on which the success of every other institution of society, from law and government to educational institutions and business firms, vitally depends.

Where families fail to form, or too many break down, the effective transmission of the virtues of honesty, civility, self-restraint, concern for the welfare of others, justice, compassion, and personal responsibility is imperiled. Without these virtues, respect for the dignity of the human person, the first pillar of a decent society, will be undermined and sooner or later lost—for even the most laudable formal institutions cannot uphold respect for human dignity where people do not have the virtues that make that respect a reality and give it vitality in actual social practices.

Respect for the dignity of the human being requires more than formally sound institutions; it also requires a cultural ethos in which people act from conviction to treat one another as human beings should be treated: with respect, civility, justice, compassion. The best legal and political institutions ever devised are of little value where selfishness, contempt for others, dishonesty, injustice, and other types of immorality and irresponsibility flourish. Indeed, the effective working of governmental institutions themselves depends on most people, most of the time, obeying the law out of a sense of moral obligation, not merely out of fear of detection and punishment for law-breaking. And perhaps it goes without saying that the success of business and a market-based economic system depends on there being reasonably virtuous, trustworthy, law-abiding, promise-keeping people to serve as workers and managers, lenders, regulators, and payers of bills for goods and services.

The third pillar of any decent society is a fair and effective system of law and government. This is necessary because none of us is perfectly virtuous all the time, and some people will be deterred from wrongdoing only by the threat of punishment. More important, contemporary philosophers of law tell us that the law coordinates human behavior for the sake of achieving common goals—the common good—especially in dealing with the complexities of modern life. Even if all of us were perfectly virtuous all the time, we would still need a system of laws (considered as a scheme of authoritatively stipulated coordination norms) to accomplish many of our common ends (safely transporting ourselves on the streets, to take a simple example).

The success of business firms and the economy as a whole depends vitally on a fair and effective system and set of institutions for the administration of justice. We need judges skilled in the craft of law and free of corruption. We need to be able to rely on courts to settle disputes, including disputes between parties who act in good faith, and to enforce contracts and other agreements and enforce them in a timely manner. Indeed, the knowledge that contracts will be enforced is usually sufficient to ensure that courts will not actually be called on to enforce them. A sociological fact of which we can be certain is this: where there is no reliable system to administer justice—no confidence that the courts will hold people to their obligations under the law—business will not flourish and everyone in the society will suffer.

Decency and Dynamism

If these three pillars are in place, a society can be a decent one even if it is not a dynamic one. Now, conservatives of a certain stripe believe that a truly decent society cannot be a dynamic one. Dynamism, they believe, causes instability that undermines the pillars of a decent society. So some conservatives in old Europe and even the United States opposed not only industrialism but even the very idea of a commercial society, fearing that commercial economies inevitably produce consumerist and acquisitive materialist attitudes that corrode the foundations of decency. And some, such as several Amish communities in the United States, reject education for their children beyond what is necessary to master reading, writing, and arithmetic, on the ground that higher education leads to worldliness and apostasy and undermines religious faith and moral virtue.

Although a decent society need not be a dynamic one (as the Amish example shows), dynamism need not erode decency. We can strongly support a market-based economy if we understand it correctly, and defend it, as part of a larger whole, where moral values and virtues are honored and nurtured. We can affirm the commercial economy without fearing that it will necessarily take us down the road to corruption. A dynamic society need not be one in which consumerism and materialism become rife and in which moral and spiritual values disappear.

Even some on the Left have taken up the argument that the market system and business generally tend to crowd out moral and spiritual values. Although I applaud those of my liberal colleagues who have rediscovered moral and spiritual values as something important, some of these critics seem to be giving lip service to such values as a pretext to bash an economic system that has been the greatest anti-poverty mechanism ever created. The market system is an engine of social mobility and of economic growth from which all benefit.

In fact, I venture to say that the market economy will almost certainly play a positive moral role when the conditions are in place to sustain it over the long run. So what makes social dynamism possible? The two pillars of social dynamism are, first, institutions of research and education that push back the frontiers of knowledge across the humanities, social sciences, and natural sciences and that transmit knowledge to students and disseminate it to the public at large; and, second, business firms and associated institutions that generate, widely distribute, and preserve wealth.

We can think of universities and business firms, together with respect for the dignity of the human person, the institution of the family, and the system of law and government, as the five pillars of decent and dynamic societies. The university and the business firm depend in various ways for their well-being on the well-being of the others, and they can help to support the others in turn. At the same time, ideologies and practices hostile to the pillars of a decent society can manifest themselves in higher education and in business, and these institutions can erode the social values on which they themselves depend not only for their own integrity but also for their long-term survival.

Attacks

It is all too easy to take the pillars for granted, especially for people who are living in circumstances of general affluence. So it is important to remember that each of them has come under attack from different angles and forces. Operating from within universities, persons and movements have expressed hostility to one or the other of these pillars, usually preaching or acting in the name of high ideals.

Attacks on business and the very idea of the market economy and economic freedom coming from the academic world are well known. Students are sometimes taught to hold business, and especially businesspeople, in contempt as heartless exploiters driven by greed. In my own days as a student, these attacks were often made explicitly in the name of Marxism. One notices less of that after the collapse of the

Soviet empire, but the attacks themselves have abated little. Needless to say, where businesses behave unethically, they play into the stereotypes of the enemies of the market system and facilitate their effort to smear business and the free market for the sake of transferring greater control of the economy to government.

Similarly, attacks on the family, and particularly on the institution of marriage on which the family is built, are common in the academy. The line here is that the family, at least as traditionally constituted and understood, is a patriarchal and exploitative institution that oppresses women and imposes on people forms of sexual restraint that are psychologically damaging and that inhibit the free expression of their personality. As has become clear in recent decades, there is a profound threat to the family, one against which we must fight with all our energy and will. It is difficult to think of any item on the domestic agenda that is more critical today than the defense of marriage as the union of husband and wife and the effort to renew and rebuild the marriage culture.

What has also become clear is that the threats to the family (and to the sanctity of human life) are necessarily threats to religious freedom and to religion itself—at least where the religions in question stand up and speak out for conjugal marriage and the rights of the child in the womb. From the point of view of those seeking to redefine marriage and to protect and advance what they regard as the right to abortion, the taming of religion (and the stigmatization and marginalization of religions that refuse to be tamed) is a moral imperative.

Standing—or Falling—Together

Some will counsel that economic conservatives have no horse in this race. They will say that these are moral, cultural, and religious disputes about which businesspeople and others concerned with economic freedom need not concern themselves. The reality is that the ideological movements that today seek to redefine marriage and abolish its normativity for romantic relations and the rearing of children are the same movements that seek to undermine the market-based economic system and replace it with statist control of vast areas of economic life. Moreover, the rise of ideologies hostile to marriage and the family has had a measurable social impact, and its costs are counted in ruined relationships, damaged lives, and all that follows in the social sphere from these personal catastrophes. In many poorer places in the United States, families are simply failing to form and marriage is disappearing or coming to be regarded as an optional "lifestyle choice"—one among various ways of conducting relationships and having and rearing children.

In 1965, Daniel Patrick Moynihan, a Harvard professor who was then working in the administration of President Lyndon Johnson, shocked Americans by reporting findings that the out-of-wedlock birthrate among African Americans had reached nearly 25 percent. He warned that the phenomenon of boys and girls being raised without fathers in poorer communities would result in social pathologies that would severely harm those most in need of the supports of solid family life.

His predictions were all too quickly verified. The widespread failure of family formation portended disastrous social consequences of delinquency, despair, violence, drug abuse, and crime and incarceration. A snowball effect resulted in the further growth of the out-of-wedlock birthrate. It is now over 70 percent among African Americans. It is worth noting that at the time of Moynihan's report, the out-of-wedlock birthrate for the population as a whole was almost 6 percent. Today, that rate is over 40 percent.

These are profoundly worrying statistics, with the negative consequences being borne not so much by the affluent as by those in the poorest and most vulnerable sectors of our society. When my liberal colleagues in higher education say, "You guys shouldn't be worried so much about these social issues, about abortion and marriage; you should be worrying about poverty," I say, "If you were genuinely worried about poverty, you would be joining us in rebuilding the marriage culture." Do you want to know why people are trapped in poverty in so many inner cities? The picture is complex, but undeniably a key element of it is the destruction of the family and the prevalence of out-of-wedlock pregnancies and fatherlessness.

The economic consequences of these developments are evident. Consider the need of business to have a responsible and capable workforce. Business cannot manufacture honest, hardworking people to employ. Nor can government create them by law. Businesses and governments depend on there being many such people, but they must rely on the family, assisted by religious communities and other institutions of civil society, to produce them. So business has a stake—a massive stake—in the long-term health of the family. It should avoid doing anything to undermine the family, and it should do what it can, where it can, to strengthen the institution.

As an advocate of dynamic societies, I believe in the market economy and the free-enterprise system. I particularly value the social mobility that economic dynamism makes possible. Indeed, I am a beneficiary of that social mobility. A bit over a hundred years ago, my immigrant grandfathers—one from southern Italy, the other from Syria—were coal miners. Neither had so much as remotely considered the possibility of attending a university; as a practical economic matter, such a thing was simply out of the question. At that time, Woodrow Wilson, the future president of the United States, was the McCormick Professor of Jurisprudence at Princeton. Today, just two generations forward, I, the grandson of those immigrant coal miners, am the McCormick Professor of Jurisprudence at Princeton. And what is truly remarkable is that my story is completely unremarkable. Something like it is the story of millions of Americans. Perhaps it goes without saying that this kind of upward mobility is not common in corporatist or socialist economic systems. It is very common in market-based free-enterprise economies.

Having said that, I should note that I am not a supporter of the laissez-faire doctrine embraced by strict libertarians. I believe that law and government do have important and, indeed, indispensable roles to play in regulating enterprises for the sake of protecting public health, safety, and morals, preventing exploitation and abuse, and promoting fair competitive circumstances of exchange. But these roles are compatible, I would insist, with the ideal of limited government and the principle of subsidiarity, according to which government must respect individual initiative to the extent reasonably possible and avoid violating the autonomy and usurping the authority of families, religious communities, and other institutions of civil society that play the primary role in building character and transmitting virtues.

But having said *that*, I would warn that limited government—considered as an ideal as vital to business as to the family—cannot be maintained where the marriage culture collapses and families fail to form or easily dissolve. Where these things happen, the health, education, and welfare functions of the family will have to be undertaken by someone, or some institution, and that will sooner or later be the government. To deal with pressing social problems, bureaucracies will grow, and with them the tax burden. Moreover, the growth of crime and other pathologies where family breakdown is rampant will result in the need for more extensive policing and incarceration and, again, increased taxes to pay for these government services. If we want limited government, as we should, and a level of taxation that is not unduly burdensome, we need healthy institutions of civil society, beginning with a flourishing marriage culture that supports family formation and preservation.

Advocates of the market economy, and supporters of marriage and the family, have common opponents in hard-left socialism, the entitlement mentality, and the statist ideologies that provide their intellectual underpinnings. But the union of advocates of limited government and economic freedom, on the one hand, and supporters of marriage and the family, on the other, is not, and must not be regarded as, a mere marriage of convenience. The reason they have common enemies is that they have common *principles*: respect for the human person, which grounds our commitment to individual liberty and the right to economic freedom and other essential civil liberties;

belief in personal responsibility, which is a precondition of individual liberty in any domain; recognition of subsidiarity as the basis for effective but truly limited government and for the integrity of the institutions of civil society that mediate between the individual and the centralized power of the state; respect for the rule of law; and recognition of the vital role played by the family and by religious institutions that support the character-forming functions of the family in the flourishing of any decent and dynamic society.

Paul Ryan, the 2012 Republican vice-presidential nominee, made the point when he observed:

> A "libertarian" who wants limited government should embrace the means to his freedom: thriving mediating institutions that create the moral preconditions for economic markets and choice. A "social issues" conservative with a zeal for righteousness should insist on a free-market economy to supply the material needs for families, schools, and churches that inspire moral and spiritual life. In a nutshell, the notion of separating the social from the economic issues is a false choice. They stem from the same root. . . . They complement and complete each other. A prosperous moral community is a prerequisite for a just and ordered society, and the idea that either side of this current divide can exist independently is a mirage.

The two greatest institutions ever devised for lifting people out of poverty and enabling them to live in dignity are the market economy and the institution of marriage. These institutions will stand together, or they will fall together. Contemporary statist ideologues have contempt for both of these institutions, and they fully understand the connection between them. We who believe in the market and in the family should see the connection no less clearly.

2

THE LIMITS OF CONSTITUTIONAL LIMITS

AS CITIZENS OF a liberal democratic regime, we do not refer to those who govern as "rulers." We prefer to speak of them as servants—public servants. Of course, they are nothing like the servants in *Downton Abbey* or *Upstairs Downstairs*. The extraordinary prestige and the trappings of public office would by themselves be sufficient to distinguish, say, the governor of New York or the president of the United States from Carson the butler. But that prestige also signals an underlying fact that discomfits our democratic and egalitarian sensibilities—namely, that high public officials are indeed rulers. They make rules, enforce them, and resolve disputes about their meaning and applicability. To a very large extent, what they say goes.

Of course, our rulers rule not by dint of sheer power, the way the Mafia might in a territory over which it has gained control. They rule lawfully. Constitutional rules specify public offices and settle procedures for filling them. These rules set the scope, and thus the limits, of the rulers' jurisdiction and authority. They are rulers who are subject to rules—rules they do not themselves make and cannot easily or purely on their own initiative revise or repeal.

Historically, political theorists have focused on constitutional structural constraints as the most obvious and important way to ensure that rulers do not become tyrants. Important as these constraints are, I would warn against placing too great an emphasis on them. There is a danger in ignoring the other essential features.

What Limits Government?

The U.S. Constitution is famous for its "Madisonian system" of structural constraints on the central government's powers. More than two hundred years of experience with the system gives us a pretty good perspective on both its strengths and its limitations. The major structural constraints are: (1) the doctrine of the general government as a government of delegated and enumerated, and therefore limited, powers; (2) the dual sovereignty of the general government and the states—with the states functioning as governments of general jurisdiction exercising generalized police powers (a kind of plenary authority), limited under the national constitution only by specific prohibitions or by grants of power to the general government; (3) the separation of legislative, executive, and judicial powers within the national government, creating a system of "checks and balances" that limits the power of any one branch and, it is hoped, improves the quality of government by making the legislative and policy-making processes more challenging, slower, and more deliberative; and (4) the practice (nowhere expressly authorized in the text of the Constitution, but lay that aside for now) of constitutional judicial review by the federal courts.

I often ask my students at the beginning of my undergraduate course on civil liberties how the framers of the Constitution of the United States sought to preserve liberty and prevent tyranny. It is, alas, a testament to the poor quality of civic education in the United States that almost none of the students can answer the question correctly. Nor, I suspect, could the editors of the *New York Times* or other opinion-shaping elites. The typical answer goes this way:

Well, Professor, I can tell you how the framers of the Constitution sought to protect liberty and prevent tyranny. They attached to the Constitution a Bill of Rights to protect the individual and minorities against the tyranny of the majority. And they vested the power to enforce those rights in the hands of judges who serve for life, are not subject to election or recall, cannot be removed from office except on impeachment for serious misconduct, and are therefore able to protect people's rights without fear of political retaliation.

This is about as wrong as you can get—but it is widely believed, and not just by university students. None of the American Founders, even among those who favored judicial review and regarded it as implicit in the Constitution (which not all did), believed that judicial review was the central, or even a significant, constraint on the national government's power. Nor did the Founders believe that judicial enforcement of Bill of Rights guarantees would be an important way of protecting liberty. Those who supported the proposed Constitution, the Federalists, generally opposed the addition of a Bill of Rights because they feared it would actually undermine what they regarded as the main structural constraints protecting freedom and preventing tyranny—namely, (1) the conception and public understanding of the general government as a government of delegated and enumerated powers, and (2) the division of powers between the national government and the states in a system of dual sovereignty.[1] When political necessity forced the Federalists to yield to demands for a Bill of Rights (in the form of the first eight amendments to the Constitution), they took care to add two more amendments—the ninth and tenth—designed to reinforce the delegated-powers doctrine and the principles of federalism that they feared inclusion of a Bill of Rights would obscure or weaken.

As for the way judicial review has functioned as a structural constraint in American history, suffice it to say that the practice has given Oxford University legal and political philosopher Jeremy Waldron, a fierce critic of judicial review, plenty of ammunition in making his case against permitting judges to invalidate legislation on constitutional grounds.[2] The federal courts, and the Supreme Court in particular, have had their glory moments, to be sure, such as in the racial desegregation case of *Brown v. Board of Education* in the 1950s. But they have also handed down decision after decision—from *Dred Scott v. Sandford* in the 1850s, which facilitated the expansion of slavery, to *Roe v. Wade* in the 1970s, which legalized abortion throughout the United States—in which they have plainly overstepped the bounds of their own authority and, without any warrant in the text, logic, structure, or original understanding of the Constitution, imposed their personal moral and political opinions on the entire nation under the pretext of enforcing constitutional guarantees. These usurpations are, quite apart from whatever one's views happen to be on slavery and abortion, a stain on the courts and a disgrace to the constitutional system, bringing it into disrepute and undermining its basic democratic principles.

Moreover, since the 1930s, the courts have done very little by way of exercising the power of judicial review to support the other constitutional structural constraints on central governmental power. A very small number of isolated decisions have struck down this or that specific piece of federal legislation as exceeding the delegated powers of the national government or infringing on the reserved powers of the states, but that is about it.[3] Most recently, and spectacularly, the Supreme Court found a way, by a bare majority, to uphold what seemed to many to be a rather obvious case of constitutional overreaching by the national government—the imposition of an individual mandate requiring citizens to purchase health-insurance coverage as part of President Barack Obama's signature Patient Protection and Affordable Care Act.[4]

The government defended the mandate as a legitimate exercise of the expressly delegated power to regulate commerce among the several states. The trouble is that on its face the mandate does not appear to *regulate* commerce at all; it seems to *force people into* commerce—a particular kind of commerce—on pain of a financial penalty. The Supreme Court's four liberal justices were willing to stick to what has become long-standing tradition for those in their ideological camp—namely, counting virtually anything the national government proposes to do as a legitimate exercise of the power to regulate interstate commerce if that's what the government says it is. The five more conservative justices were willing to say that whatever was going on with the imposition of a mandate to purchase health insurance, it was not regulating interstate commerce. But one of the five, Chief Justice John Roberts, decided to reinterpret the penalty as something that the Obama administration and its supporters in Congress had repeatedly and vociferously denied it was during the debate leading up to the passage of the Patient Protection and Affordable Care Act—namely, a *tax*. He then joined the four liberals to uphold the mandate and the legislation as a whole as constitutionally permissible.

It shouldn't have come to a decision by the courts at all. Congress itself, and the president, should have recognized and honored the fact that the Constitution does not empower the national government to impose a mandate on the people to purchase products, including health-care coverage. One of the problems with judicial review in general is that its practice tends to encourage the belief among legislators (and, worse still, among citizens more broadly) that the constitutionality of proposed legislation is not the concern of the people's elected representatives; if a proposed piece of legislation is unconstitutional, they say, then it is up to the courts to strike it down. But this is a travesty. For structural constraints to accomplish what they are meant to accomplish, for them to constrain the power of government as they are meant to do, the question of the constitutionality of legislation in light of those constraints is *everybody's* business—judges exercising judicial review, yes, but also legislators, executives, and the people themselves.

To its credit, the Tea Party movement—much maligned by the elite print and broadcast media, which now scarcely bothers to hide its biases in favor of larger government, socially liberal policies, and the Democratic Party—succeeded in getting people to think about the health-care individual mandate not merely as a "policy issue" but also as a constitutional question about the scope and limits of federal power. And so for the first time in my lifetime, the debate about the applicability of the doctrine of delegated and enumerated powers has spilled out of the courtrooms and into the streets, as it were. We are having a political debate about the meaning of a fundamental constitutional structural constraint—and thus a debate about limited government. I can't tell you how it will come out. But I'm glad we're having it—in particular because of what the debate says about the critical, yet oddly neglected, subject of political culture.

The Health of Political Culture

In 2008, Professor Waldron visited his native New Zealand to read his countrymen the riot act about what he condemned as the abysmal quality of that nation's parliamentary debate. He assigned the lecture the stinging title "Parliamentary Recklessness" and devoted the bulk of his talk to analyzing and critiquing a range of factors leading to the impoverishment of legislative deliberation. Waldron concluded by pointing to the possibility that the deficiencies of parliamentary debate may be at least partially compensated for by a higher quality of public debate, which could prompt the reforms necessary to begin restoring the integrity of parliamentary debate. But he warned that things could also go the other way. The corruption of parliamentary debate could "infect the political culture at large," driving public debate down to the condition of parliamentary debate—a condition he chillingly described in the following terms:

> Parliament becomes a place where the governing party thinks it has won a great victory when debate is closed down and measures are pushed through under urgency; and the social and political forum generally becomes a place where the greatest victory is

drowning out your opponent with the noise that you can bring to bear. And then the premium is on name-calling, on who can bawl the loudest, who can most readily trivialize an opponent's position, who can succeed in embarrassing or shaming or if need be blackmailing into silence anyone who holds a different view.

So, in a sense, it is up to the people to decide whether they will rise above the corruption that has demeaned parliamentary politics or permit it to "infect the political culture at large." But "the people" are not some undifferentiated mass; they are *people*, you and me, individuals. Of course, considered as isolated actors, individuals cannot do a lot to affect the political culture. Individuals can, however, cooperate for greater effectiveness in prosecuting an agenda of conservation or reform, and they can create associations and institutions that are capable of making a difference—pressure groups, think tanks, even tea parties.

Any discussion of the quality of democratic deliberation and decision making (or at least any that amounts to something more than hot air) will acknowledge the indispensable role of civil society's nongovernmental institutions, what Edmund Burke called the "little platoons." These institutions sustain a culture in which political institutions do what they are established to do, do it well, and don't do what they are not authorized to do. The danger is that bad behavior on the part of political institutions—which means bad behavior on the part of officeholders—can weaken, enervate, and even corrupt the institutions of civil society, rendering them impotent to resist the bad behavior and useless to the cause of political reform.

This is true generally, and it is certainly true with respect to the bad behavior of public officials who betray their obligations to serve by transgressing the bounds of their constitutional authority. Constitutional structural constraints are important, but they will be effective only where they are effectually supported by the political culture. The people need to understand them and value them—value them enough to resist usurpations by their rulers even when unconstitutional programs offer immediate gratifications or the relief of urgent problems. This, in turn, requires certain virtues—strengths of character—among the people.

These virtues do not just fall down on people from the heavens. They have to be transmitted through the generations and nurtured by each generation. James Madison said that "a well-instructed people alone can be permanently a free people." And that is true. It points to the fact that even the best constitutional structures, even the strongest structural constraints on governmental power, aren't worth the paper they are printed on if people do not understand them, value them, and have the will to resist the blandishments of those offering something tempting in return for giving them up. But it is also true that virtue is needed, and that's not merely a matter of improving civics teaching in homes and schools. Madison famously defended the Constitution in *Federalist* Number 51 as "supplying, by opposite and rival interests, the defect of better motives." He made this point immediately after observing that the first task of government is to control the governed, and the second is to control itself. He allowed that "a dependence on the people is, no doubt, the primary control on the government, but experience has taught mankind the necessity of auxiliary precautions"—hence the constitutional structural constraints, among other things. But even in this formulation they do not stand alone; indeed, they are presented as secondary. What is also necessary, and in fact primary, is healthy and vibrant political culture—"a dependence on the people" to keep the rulers in line.

That brings us back to the role and importance of virtue. John Adams understood as well as anyone the general theory of the Constitution. He was the ablest scholar and political theorist of the founding generation. He certainly got the point about supplying "the defect of better motives," yet he also understood that the health of political culture was an indispensable element of the success of the constitutional enterprise—an enterprise of ensuring that the rulers stay within the bounds of their legitimate authority and be servants of the people they rule. He remarked that "our Constitution is made for a moral and religious people" and "is wholly inadequate to the government of any other."[5] Why? Because a people lacking in virtue could be counted on to trade liberty for protection, for financial or personal security, for comfort, for being looked after, for being taken care of, for having their problems solved quickly. And there will always be people occupying or standing for public office who will be happy to offer the deal—an expansion of their power in return for what they can offer by virtue of that expansion.

So the question is how to form people fitted out with the virtues making them worthy of freedom and capable of preserving constitutionally limited government, even in the face of strong temptations to compromise it away. Here we see the central political role and significance of the most basic institutions of civil society—the family, the religious community, private organizations (such as the Boy Scouts) devoted to the inculcation of knowledge and virtue, private (often religiously based) educational institutions, and the like. These mediating institutions provide a buffer between the individual and the power of the central state.

It is ultimately the autonomy, integrity, and general flourishing of these institutions that will determine the fate of limited constitutional government. This is not only because of their primary and indispensable role in transmitting virtues; it is also because their performance of health, education, and welfare functions is the only real alternative to the removal of these functions to what Pope Pius XI called a "larger and higher association"—that is, to government. When government expands to play the primary role in performing these functions, the ideal of limited government is soon lost, no matter the formal structural constraints of the Constitution. The corresponding weakening of these institutions damages their ability to perform all their functions, including their moral and pedagogical ones. With that, they surely lose their capacity to influence for good the political culture that, at the end of the day, is the whole shooting match when it comes to whether the ruler can truly be a servant.

3

PRIVATE ACTS,
PUBLIC INTERESTS

THEORISTS OF PUBLIC morality—from the ancient Greek philosophers and Roman jurists on—have noticed that apparently private acts of vice, when they multiply and become widespread, can imperil important public interests. This fact embarrasses philosophical efforts to draw a sharp line between a realm of "private" morality that is not subject to law and a domain of public actions that may rightly be subjected to legal regulation.

Considered as isolated acts, someone's recreational use of narcotics or hallucinogenic drugs, for example, may affect the public weal negligibly, if at all. But an epidemic of drug abuse, though constituted by discrete, private acts of drug taking, damages the common good in myriad ways. This does not by itself settle the question whether drug prohibition is a prudent or effective policy. It does, however, undermine the belief that the recreational use of drugs is a matter of purely private choice into which public authority has no legitimate cause to intrude.

Much the same is true of pornography. Even in defending what he believed to be a moral right to pornography, the late New York

University professor Ronald Dworkin identified the *public* nature of the interests damaged in communities in which pornography becomes freely available and circulates widely. Legal recognition of the right to pornography would, Dworkin conceded, "sharply limit the ability of individuals consciously and reflectively to influence the conditions of their own and their children's development. It would limit their ability to bring about the cultural structure they think best, a structure in which sexual experience generally has dignity and beauty, without which their own and their families' sexual experience are likely to have these qualities in less degree."

In my book *Making Men Moral: Civil Liberties and Public Morality* and elsewhere, I have argued that Dworkin's efforts to derive from the principle of equality a moral right to pornography never manage to overcome the force of the public interest in prohibiting or restricting pornography that he himself identifies. That interest is *not*, fundamentally, in shielding people from shock or offense. It involves something much more substantial: the interest of every member of the community in the quality of the cultural structure that will, to a large extent, shape their experiences, their quality of life, and the choices effectively available, to themselves and their children, in a domain of human affairs marked by profound moral significance.

When we bring this reality into focus, it becomes apparent that the familiar depiction of the debate over pornography regulation as pitting the "rights of individuals" against some amorphous "majority's dislike of smut" is false to the facts. The public interest in a cultural structure—in which, as Dworkin said, "sexual experience has dignity and beauty"—is the concrete interest of individuals and families who constitute "the public." The obligations of others to respect, and of governments to respect and protect, their interests is a matter of justice.

It is in a special way a matter of justice to children. Parents' efforts to bring up their children as respecters of themselves and others will be helped or hindered—perhaps profoundly—by the cultural structure in which children are reared. Whether children themselves ever get a glimpse of pornographic images in childhood is a side issue. A decent social milieu cannot be established or maintained simply by shielding children from such images. It is the attitudes, habits, dispositions, imagination, ideology, values, and choices shaped by a culture in which pornography flourishes that will, in the end, deprive many children of what can without logical or moral strain be characterized as their right to a healthy sexuality. In a society in which sex is depersonalized, and thus degraded, even conscientious parents will have enormous difficulty transmitting to their children the capacity to view themselves and others as persons rather than objects of sexual desire and satisfaction.

There is more to the picture. We know that a more-or-less unbridled culture of pornography can result in a sexualization of children that robs them of their innocence and even places them in jeopardy of sexual exploitation by adults. Can anyone honestly deny that we have witnessed a shameful sexualization of children in our own culture? The clergy child-abuse scandal is only the tip of an iceberg. The problem of pedophile sex tourism to places like Thailand is a dirty secret that will sooner or later break upon the American consciousness and conscience. Should we be surprised at such a thing? Think about the sexualization of adolescents in contemporary music, television, movies, and commercial advertising. Consider the notorious Calvin Klein ads on New York City buses depicting young people in sexually provocative poses. Abercrombie and Fitch took things to the logical next step by peddling thong swimwear to twelve-year-old girls.

Sometimes obscenity or pornography is defined in such a way as to exclude anything qualifying as "art" from falling into the category. I see no reason for this, whether we consider the issue from the point of view of possible legal regulation or from some other perspective. Someone might argue that the artistic value of certain pornographic depictions—you may recall Robert Mapplethorpe's photograph of a bull whip in a rectum—provides a reason (or additional reason) to immunize it from legal regulation. But such depictions remain pornographic, and their negative impact on public morality cannot be denied. Moreover, it is difficult to see how any degree of artistic merit could justify the insult to morally conscientious taxpayers when they are forced to pay for pornographic depictions.

Art can elevate and ennoble. It can also degrade and even corrupt. Whatever should be done or not done by way of legal restriction of pornographic art, we ought not to make things easy on ourselves by pretending that art cannot be pornographic or that pornographic art cannot degrade. Nor ought we to avert our gaze from the peculiar insult and injustice involved in the government funding of pornography.

There are real and substantial human and personal interests competing with those desires or interests we label "freedom of expression" when it comes to the question of art and pornography. If we, as a society, are to decide against these interests—particularly if we are to do so categorically—we should face up to what we are prepared to sacrifice, particularly when it comes to the well-being of children. And if judges are to impose a decision against these interests on a public that views the matter differently, they should shoulder the burden of providing a legal and moral justification for doing so.

It will not suffice to make mere appeals to "established constitutional principles" or to the fact that a right to free speech is enumerated in the constitutional text, whereas interests competing with it in the case of pornography are not mentioned. The truth is that so-called established constitutional principles on free speech and pornography are, at best, weakly justified in the cases. A bare reliance on the mere fact of an enumeration of a right to free speech will simply confirm the validity of the arguments that Hamilton and other Founders advanced against the Bill of Rights—namely, that the enumeration of certain rights would distort the scheme of liberty established in the body of the Constitution by miseducating Americans about the nature of constitutional government and the moral substance of their rights.

4

LIBERALISM, LIBERATION, AND THE LIBERAL ARTS

WHEN MANY OF the flower children and antiwar activists of the 1960s became professors and college and university administrators in the '70s and '80s, they did not overthrow the idea, or at least *an* idea, of liberal-arts education. In a great many cases, they proclaimed themselves true partisans of liberal-arts ideals.

Now, it is true that many representatives of that generation in positions of influence and authority in the academy today believe that universities should be in the forefront of producing young men and women who will be social activists. More than a few seem to be eager to transform university education into a species of vocational training for aspiring ACLU lawyers, Planned Parenthood volunteers, and "community organizers." Some colleges and universities actually offer academic credit for social activism. Others, however, resist the idea that learning should be instrumentalized in this way. They profess allegiance to the traditional (or, in any event, traditional-sounding) idea that the point of liberal education is to enrich and even liberate the student learner. That's what is supposed to be "liberal" about liberal-arts learning—it is supposed to convey the knowledge and impart the intellectual skills and habits of mind that carry with them a certain profound form of freedom.

However traditional this may *sound*, there is nevertheless an unbridgeable chasm between the idea of liberal-arts education as classically conceived and the conception some influential academics promote today. Many academic humanists and social scientists working in contemporary higher education propose as the goal of liberal-arts learning *liberation*; the question is, liberation from *what*?

In their conception (what I call the revisionist conception), it is liberation from traditional social constraints and norms of morality—the beliefs, principles, and structures by which earlier generations of Americans and people in the West generally had been taught to govern their conduct for the sake of personal virtue and the common good. Why do they regard this form of "liberation" as desirable? Because it has become a matter of dogma that the traditional norms and structures are irrational—they are vestiges of superstition and phobia that impede the free development of personalities by restricting people's capacities to act on their desires.

In this dogmatic context, the purpose of liberal-arts learning is to undermine whatever is left of the old norms and structures. To accomplish the task, teaching and scholarship are meant either (1) to expose the texts and traditions once regarded as the intellectual treasures of our civilization—the Bible, Plato, Augustine, Dante, Aquinas, Chaucer, Shakespeare, Austen, Locke, Gibbon, the authors of *The Federalist*, etc.—as works of propaganda meant to support and reinforce unjust (racist, sexist, classist, homophobic, etc.) social orders, or yet more insidiously (2) to show how the old texts and traditions can be "reappropriated" and used to subvert allegedly unjust (racist, sexist, etc.) contemporary social orders.

Beyond this, liberal-arts learning is meant to enable students to become truly "authentic" individuals—people who are true to themselves. Here the question is: what is the "self" to which the authentic person is true? For those in the grip of the new liberationist ideology, to be true to one's *self* is to act on one's *desires*. Indeed, what one fundamentally *is*, is one's desires. So authenticity—that is, being true to oneself—is understood to consist in doing what you really want to do, in defiance, if necessary, of expectations based on putatively out-moded moral ideas and social norms.

According to this conception of personal authenticity, whatever impedes one from doing what one truly wants to do (unless, that is, what one happens to want to do would violate some norm of politi-cal correctness) is a mere hang-up—something that holds one back from being true to oneself, from being the person one truly wants to be. Such impediments, be they religious convictions, moral ideals, or what have you, are to be transcended for the sake of the free and full development of your personality. The very essence of liberation as reconceived by partisans of the revisionist conception of liberal-arts education is transcending such hang-ups by, for example, flaunting one's sexuality and acting on sexual desires that one might have been "repressing" as a result of religious and moral convictions.

Nowhere is this clearer than in freshman-orientation programs in many colleges and universities that feature compulsory events designed to undermine any lingering traditional beliefs about sexual morality and decency that the new students might bring along from home. These events are little more than catechism classes for the reli-gion of sexual liberation, however much university officials may adver-tise them as efforts to discourage date rape, unwanted pregnancy, sexually transmitted diseases, bullying, and so forth. Most are utterly one-sided—aimed solely at indoctrination. Dissenting views, such as the view that sodomy and promiscuity are immoral and affronts to human dignity, are never aired. The point seems to be to send the clearest possible message to students who may dissent from the pre-vailing sexual liberationist orthodoxy that they are outsiders who had better conform or keep their mouths shut.

A young friend of mine who attended prestigious Williams Col-lege tells a story that could be told by students and recent alumni of similar institutions, from Bates to Pomona. Shortly after arriving at the college, the new students were divided into small groups to discuss campus life. Each group was led by an official moderator. Attendance was compulsory. The moderator informed the students that it was important for each of them to understand sympathetically what it was like to come out as "gay." The presupposition, of course, was that a person who experiences strong or dominant homosexual inclinations or desires must come out as "gay" to be true to himself. No alternative view was presented, despite the fact that belief in sexual restraint and traditional sexual morality generally, not to mention reticence concerning one's personal feelings pertaining to sex, is by no means a monopoly held by "straights." But let's lay that aside for now. The moderator's next move was to direct each student to state his or her name and say, "I am gay." So around the table they went, with students, all too predictably, conforming to the moderator's absurd and offensive directive. "I'm Sarah Smith, and I am gay." "I'm Seth Farber, and I am gay." When it was my friend's turn, he politely but firmly refused. The moderator demanded an explanation. With some trepidation my friend replied by simply stating the truth: "This exercise is absurd and offensive and has nothing to do with the purposes for which I and others came to Williams College—namely, to learn to think carefully, critically, and for ourselves." Confirming the old dictum that bullies are cowards who will never stand up to people who stand up to them, the moderator backed off.

What goes on in these collegiate reeducation camps masquerading as freshman-orientation programs, and in far too many classrooms, is *radically* different from the classical understanding of what liberal-arts education is supposed to accomplish. *Formally*, the classical and the revisionist conceptions are similar. Both propose the liberal arts as liberating. Both promise to enable the learner to achieve a greater measure of personal authenticity. But in *substance* they are polar opposites. Personal authenticity, in the classical understanding of liberal-arts education, consists in *self-mastery*—in placing reason in control of desire. According to the classic liberal-arts ideal, learning promises liberation, but it is not liberation from demanding moral ideals and social norms, or liberation to act on our desires—it is, rather, liberation from slavery to those desires, from *slavery to self.*

How can it be liberating to enter into the great conversation with Plato and his interlocutors? What frees us in thinking along with Augustine, Dante, or Aquinas? Beyond being entertained by Shakespeare's charm, wit, and astonishing intellectual deftness, why should we make the effort to understand and appreciate his works? According to the classic liberal-arts ideal, our critical engagement with great thinkers enriches our understanding and enables us to grasp, or grasp more fully, great truths—truths that, when we appropriate them and integrate them into our lives, liberate us from what is merely vulgar, coarse, or base. These are soul-shaping, humanizing truths—truths whose appreciation and secure possession elevate reason above passion or appetite, enabling us to direct our desires and our wills to what is truly good, truly beautiful, truly worthy of human beings as possessors of a profound and inherent dignity. The classic liberal-arts proposition is that intellectual knowledge has a role to play in making self-transcendence possible. It can help us to understand what is good and to love the good above whatever it is we happen to desire; it can teach us to desire what is good because it is good, thus making us truly *masters of ourselves.*

The Soul vs. the Self

These contrasting views of what liberal learning is supposed to liberate us from reflect competing understandings of what human beings fundamentally are and of what it is possible for us to be or become. I have spoken of the soul-shaping power of truths, but on the revisionist view there neither is nor can be any such thing as a rational soul. There is merely a "self." And the "self" is constituted not by powers of rationality that enable us to know what is humanly good and morally right and direct our desires toward it, but rather by our desires themselves. Reason's role in our conduct can be nothing more than instrumental. It is not, and cannot be, the master of desire but only its servant. Reason can tell us not what to want but only how to obtain whatever it is we happen to want. As David Hume articulated the claim, "Reason is and ought only to be the slave of the passions, and may pretend to no office other than to serve and obey them."

Sometimes it is suggested that the convention-flouting, colorful figure of Jean-Jacques Rousseau above all others inspired the trend of belief that reached its full flower in the 1960s. I wonder, though, whether the greater blame should fall upon the staid old "conservative" David Hume. In any event, if the Humean understanding is the correct one, then the rational soul is an illusion, and belief in it, and in truths that can liberate us from slavery to our desires, is something not unlike a superstition. Although Hume himself didn't draw the conclusion, human fulfillment, such as it is, would seem to consist not in self-mastery, not in overcoming desires that run contrary to what reason identifies as good and right, but rather in freeing ourselves from "irrational" inhibitions (those "hang-ups") that impede us from doing as we please. Hence, the slogan that will ever stand as a sort of verbal monument to the me generation: "If it feels good, do it."

The true liberal-arts ideal rejects the reduction of reason to the status of passion's ingenious servant. It is an ideal rooted in the conviction that there are human goods, and a common good, in light of which we have *reasons* to constrain, to limit, to regulate, and even to alter our desires. It proposes the study of great works of the humanities and social sciences with a view to grasping more fully these goods and the reasons they provide, and to understanding them in their wholeness. What liberal-arts learning offers us is a truly audacious hope—the hope of self-mastery.

Can it really be true? What could there be in us, or about us, that could actually make it possible for human beings to be masters of their desires, feelings, emotions, and passions, not slaves to them? Only this mysterious thing that Plato's Socrates was so centrally concerned about and that so many great thinkers and writers of the Western intellectual tradition from Plato forward have sought to understand and teach us about: the soul. Soulless "selves" could have desires and even a certain form of purely instrumental rationality directed toward efficiently satisfying desires, but they could never be masters of their desires. Only by virtue of our rational souls can we exercise the more than merely instrumental form of rationality that enables us, unlike the brute animals, to be masters of our desires, not slaves to self.

Now, what if you believe in such things as reasons that have the power to constrain desire, reasons that we have access to by means of intellectual capacities—capacities that are part of an apparatus that is no slave of desire but can transcend and master desire? If you believe all those things, then what you are looking for, what you are trying to understand and know, are *virtues*. You are seeking answers to such questions as: What qualities make for an honorable, worthy, upright life? What are the habits and traits of character that we should cultivate in ourselves so as to be masters of our passions rather than slaves to desire?

A few years ago, the wonderful documentary filmmaker Michael Pack and the no-less-wonderful historian-biographer Richard Brookhiser visited us at Princeton to offer an advance viewing of their film biography *George Washington*. Some of the students were a bit perplexed when Brookhiser explained that Washington came to be who he was by imagining an ideal, truly noble individual. As a young man, the future statesman formed a picture of the kind of person he would like to be and then tried to become that person by acting the way that person would act. He "stepped into the role" he had designed for himself. He sought to make himself virtuous by ridding himself of wayward desires or passions that would have no place in the character and life of the noble individual he sought to emulate and, by emulating, to become.

For someone who understands and believes in the classical liberal-arts idea and its ideal of self-mastery, there is nothing in the least inauthentic about Washington's approach. On the contrary, this is an act of the most profound authenticity. Washington sought to be master of himself rather than a slave to his desires. But to some of the students, Washington's conduct seemed *radically* inauthentic. He was play-acting, they protested; he wasn't really being himself. He was trying to live a life that wasn't his own, because he wasn't affirming and following his desires; rather, he was trying to reshape his desires in line with standards drawn from, as one of them put it, "outside himself."

Not all the students saw things this way, but we can explain why some of them did. They had drunk deeply of the Kool-Aid of the revisionist conception of what a liberal-arts education is about—a conception rooted in a profoundly misguided notion of what a person is: a soulless self, governed by desires, whose liberation consists in freeing himself, or being freed, from constraints on those desires, be they formal or informal, external or internal. They had not so much as considered the alternative view of man that is at the core of the classical conception of liberal-arts learning—namely, the human being as a rational creature, capable of understanding reasons in light of which he can become the practitioner of virtues that enable him to master his desires. Why had they not considered it? Because, I suspect, it had never been presented to them as an option *worth* considering.

The true founder of the liberal-arts ideal was Socrates as presented by his student Plato. Socrates's method of teaching was to question. He is the great exemplar of what the late Allan Bloom labeled "the interrogatory attitude"—an attitude that even defenders of the classical liberal-arts ideal sometimes fail to exhibit and inculcate in their students. The liberal-arts ideal assumes, to be sure, that there are right answers to great moral and existential questions. It is the enemy, not the friend, of moral relativism. But liberal-arts teaching is not fundamentally about telling students what the right answers are—even when we are justifiably confident that we have the right answers. Liberal-arts learning is not just about receiving and processing information, even if it's great information, such as historical facts about the Western tradition or the American Founding. It is not just about reading Aristotle, or Chaucer, or Shakespeare, or Tocqueville and knowing what these great writers said. It is about engaging with these thinkers; indeed, it is about wrestling with them and with the questions they wrestled with. It is about considering their arguments, or arguments that can be gleaned from their work; it is about considering the best possible lines of counterargument and examining alternative points of view.

And the range of alternatives students should be invited to consider, though not limitless, needs to be wide. Liberal-arts education is not catechism class. Students should not simply be presented with officially approved views—even if they are the right views. I want my own students to consider seriously a range of possibilities, including some—Marxism, for example—that I think are not only unsound but also reprehensible, and whose record in human affairs is a record of death and abomination. I certainly want them to hear the profound arguments advanced against Marxism by people like Friedrich Hayek, Aleksandr Solzhenitsyn, and John Paul II, but I also want them to understand how it was that Marxism could have attracted the allegiance of many intelligent and even morally serious (if seriously misguided) people. I want them to know the arguments Marx and his most intelligent disciples made. In fact, I want them to consider these arguments fairly on their merits. The task of the liberal-arts teacher, as I envisage it, is not to tell students what to think; it is to teach them to think, as my young friend said, carefully, critically, and for themselves.

Now, *why*? Is it because I think there is something *intrinsically* valuable about the interrogatory attitude? Allan Bloom might have thought so. The possibility that he did is what opened him to the charge of relativism and even nihilism advanced by some culturally conservative critics of his influential book *The Closing of the American Mind*. Walker Percy, for example, faulted Bloom for allegedly holding the view that the point of an open mind is merely to have an open mind, rather than to arrive at answers that are to be affirmed and acted on. Whether or not the charge is just, the charge, if true, would be damning. The idea of a mind that never closes on a truth is antithetical to the liberal-arts ideal. The point of the interrogatory attitude, rather, is precisely to move from ignorance to truths—truths that can be affirmed and acted on. As G. K. Chesterton once said, the point of an open mind is like the point of an open mouth: to close on something solid.

The Case for Academic Freedom

We begin to understand the much misunderstood and abused concept of academic freedom when we consider the central importance of the interrogative attitude to the enterprise of liberal-arts learning. The interrogative attitude will flourish only under conditions of freedom. It can be smothered by speech codes and the like, to be sure, but also in less obvious ways. It can be smothered when well-qualified scholars, teachers, and academic administrators are denied positions in institutions that claim to be nonpartisan and nonsectarian, or when they are denied tenure or promotion or are subjected to discriminatory treatment. It can be smothered by an atmosphere of political correctness.

In 2008, Crystal Dixon, associate vice president of human resources at the University of Toledo, wrote a letter to the editor of her local newspaper. Dixon, an African-American woman and a faithful Christian, rejected the claim that "sexual orientation," as it has ambiguously come to be called, is like race and should be included alongside race, ethnicity, sex, and the like as a category in antidiscrimination and civil rights laws. When the paper published her letter online, the president of the University of Toledo, a man named Lloyd Jacobs, suspended her from her job and threatened further punishment if she did not recant and apologize for publishing a view that he evidently regarded as heretical. A few weeks later, Jacobs informed Dixon that her employment at the university had been terminated.

What is remarkable about this case is how unremarkable it is. Scarcely a week passes without some university committing an offense against intellectual or academic freedom. Given the strong leftward tilt and the manifest ideological imbalance at most of our nation's colleges and universities, it is almost always the case that the victim of the attack is a student, professor, or member of the administrative staff who has dared to write or say something (whether in a classroom, a publication, or a casual conversation) that disputes a politically correct dogma, such as the belief that there is nothing morally wrong or even questionable about homosexual conduct and that "sexual orientation" is akin to race.

Whatever his other vulnerabilities at the time, it is worth remembering that what triggered the fall of Larry Summers as president of Harvard was his merely raising an intellectual question about whether disparities between men and women in scientific achievement might have something to do with nature as well as nurture. Previous successes at enforcing political correctness made it possible to bring down even someone as powerful as a president of Harvard for asking a politically incorrect question. Summers's fall, in turn, strengthened the hand of those who wish to rule out of bounds the questioning of politically correct orthodoxies on college and university campuses around the country. And it sent a chill wind through the academy. After all, if the president of Harvard can be brought down for a thought crime, what public dissenter from the prevailing dogmas can be safe?

Yet all is not darkness. Not long ago the Department of Sociology at the University of Virginia voted against granting tenure to an outstanding young scholar of family sociology named Bradford Wilcox. Despite his extraordinary record of intellectual achievement and distinguished teaching, Professor Wilcox was punished for his conservative religious and moral opinions—opinions that his politically correct opponents were foolish enough freely to mention in discussions prior to the vote on his application for tenure. Although university administrators initially upheld Wilcox's tenure denial, the university's president, John T. Casteen, reviewed the case and reversed the decision. Wilcox was granted tenure. By rectifying a gross and manifest injustice, President Casteen struck an important blow for academic freedom, and with it, a blow for the interrogative attitude and the liberal-arts ideal—one that sent a message not only to his own faculty at the University of Virginia but also to students and faculty at institutions around the country.

It is the Larry Summers episode at Harvard in reverse: it encourages (in the literal sense of the term) those who dissent from prevailing opinions to stand up and say what they actually think, and it serves as a warning to those who would attempt to punish their dissent. The warning is that those who abuse the power of their offices by trying to enforce "politically correct" thinking or teaching may lose, and their loss will expose them for what they are—namely, enemies of free intellectual inquiry.

As we consider the appalling behavior of one university president in Crystal Dixon's case, and the encouraging conduct of another university president in the Bradford Wilcox case, perhaps it is worth pausing to ask why we care—or should care—so much about intellectual freedom in the academy. Why ought we be concerned about the rights of an administrator who is fired for stating her moral views by a university that says it is morally neutral and nonsectarian, or the freedom of an assistant professor who is denied tenure because he would not toe the party line at such a university? Why should we care about students who are punished with a bad grade for having the temerity to state views that are out of line with those of the course instructor? What is it about intellectual or academic freedom that makes it worth worrying about—and worth fighting for?

It is not—or not merely—a passion for freedom for its own sake. We want our young people and those responsible for teaching them to be free from repression or invidious discrimination, but we should fight for these freedoms for a reason that goes significantly beyond them. We should fight for freedom from oppression on our campuses because we believe that academic freedom is freedom *for* something, something profoundly important—namely, the intellectual excellence that makes self-mastery possible. We should struggle to destroy political correctness on college campuses so that students and scholars can pursue understanding, knowledge, and truth more robustly across the arts and sciences and appropriate the great goods of human intellectual striving more fully into their lives for their benefit and for the sake of the common good. We should honor academic freedom as a great and indispensable value because it serves the values of understanding, knowledge, and truth that are greater still.

Although some have depicted freedom and truth as antithetical, in reality they are mutually supportive and, indeed, dependent on each other. The defense of academic freedom and the interrogative attitude it serves and supports must, implicitly at least, appeal to the concept of truth, and any plausible case for academic freedom must present understanding, knowledge, and truth as the intrinsic values that make the intelligibility of freedom indispensable to their pursuit and meaningful appropriation. On the other side of the question, the overwhelming evidence of history, not to mention the plain evidence under our noses when we examine the contemporary situation in much of the academy, shows that freedom is as necessary to the intellectual life of man as oxygen is to his bodily life.

Should academic freedom be boundless? Of course not. And the legitimate scope of expression is obviously narrower in institutions that are founded on particular religious and moral principles than it is in institutions that proclaim themselves to be nonsectarian and nonpartisan. But the scope of freedom, as a value that is ordered to truth, must be generous—especially in the academy, where free inquiry, exploration, and experimentation are often essential to insight and richer understanding. Even within its legitimate bounds, can academic freedom not be abused? Of course it can be, and all too often it is. Academic freedom does not guarantee excellence (or even passable scholarship or teaching). Sometimes respect for it insulates abuses from correction. But, again, the lessons of history and our current situation are clear: repression of academic freedom—far from shielding us from error—undermines the very process of truth seeking.

But someone might say: "There are many truths we know. Why must we permit them to be denied and questioned? Why not take the view that error—or at least clear error—has no rights? Otherwise, doesn't the defense of academic freedom collapse into the self-stultifying denial of the possibility of truth? Doesn't it make freedom, rather than truth, the ultimate academic value?"

I have already mentioned that *some* partisans of academic freedom misguidedly depict truth as an enemy of freedom. They appeal to, or presuppose, a species of relativism or subjectivism or radical skepticism in defending freedom of inquiry. Now, it is certainly true that one reason for respecting academic freedom is that people can be mistaken about what they regard—even securely regard—as true. Indeed, even unanimity of belief does not guarantee its correctness. But I think that the possibility of error is not the primary or most powerful reason for honoring academic freedom and protecting it even in areas where we are secure in our knowledge of the truth.

The stronger and deeper reason is that freedom is the condition of our fuller appropriation of the truth. I use the term *appropriation* because knowledge and truth have their value for human beings precisely as fulfillment of capacities for understanding and judgment. The liberal arts liberate the human spirit because knowledge of truth—attained by the exercise of our rational faculties—is intrinsically and not merely instrumentally valuable. "Useful knowledge" is, of course, all to the good. It is wonderful when human knowledge can serve other human goods, such as health, as in the biomedical sciences, or economic efficiency and growth, or the constructing of great buildings and bridges, or any of a million other worthy purposes. But even "useful knowledge" is often more than instrumentally valuable, and a great deal of knowledge that wouldn't qualify as "useful" in the instrumental sense is intrinsically and profoundly enriching and *liberating*. This is why we honor—and should honor even more highly than we currently do in our institutions of higher learning—excellence in the humanities and pure science (social and natural).

Knowledge that elevates and enriches—knowledge that liberates the human spirit—cannot be merely notional. *It must be appropriated.* It is not—*it cannot be*—a matter of affirming or even believing correct propositions. The knowledge that elevates and liberates is knowledge not only *that* something is the case but also why and how it is the case. Typically such knowledge does more than settle something in one's mind; it opens new avenues of exploration. Its payoff includes new sets of questions, new lines of inquiry.

Let us return, then, to the question of why we should respect freedom even where truth is known securely. It is because freedom—freedom to inquire, freedom to assent or withhold assent as one's best judgment dictates—is a condition of the personal appropriation of the truth by the human subject, the human person for the sake of whom, for the flourishing of whom, for the liberation of whom, knowledge of truth is intrinsically valuable. And it is intrinsically valuable not in some abstract sense but precisely as an aspect of the well-being and fulfillment of human beings—rational creatures whose flourishing consists in part in intellectual inquiry, understanding, and judgment and in the practice of the virtues that make possible excellence in the intellectual question.

The freedom we must defend is freedom for the practice of these virtues. It is freedom for excellence, the freedom that enables us to master ourselves. It is a freedom that, far from being negated by rigorous standards of scholarship, demands them. It is not the freedom of "if it feels good, do it"; it is, rather, the freedom of self-transcendence, the freedom from slavery to self.

5

JUDICIAL DESPOTISM

Lessons from the "Great Emancipator"

A FTER THE SUPREME Court's landmark 1954 decision in
Brown v. Board of Education ordering the desegregation of
public schools in Topeka, Kansas, lawsuits promptly were
brought to dismantle legally sanctioned segregation in other states.
One of these was Arkansas. There, Governor Orval Faubus and other
state officials maintained that they were not bound by the Supreme
Court's ruling in *Brown*. That decision was constitutionally incorrect,
they insisted, and amounted to a federal court's usurpation of the
constitutional authority of the states. Moreover, Arkansas was not a
party in the case. Therefore, they contended, a lower federal court in
Little Rock had no constitutional authority to order the desegregation of public schools in Arkansas on the basis of the *Brown* decision.

Arkansas's appeal of the lower court's order eventually made it to
the Supreme Court of the United States in the 1958 case of *Cooper v.
Aaron*. No one had any real doubts about what the outcome of that
case would be. The justices would certainly uphold the desegregation
order. They did so, however, in a ruling that did more than merely
remind the governor and other state officials that they had "no power

to nullify a federal court order." In a unanimous opinion, the court asserted, for the first time, that "the federal judiciary is supreme in the exposition of the law of the Constitution."

The idea of judicial supremacy—or the idea that the supremacy of the Constitution entails judicial supremacy in constitutional interpretation—has come to be so widely held not only in the legal profession but also by the public at large that today it seems unremarkable. But we would do well to consider just how remarkable it is.

"The Despotism of an Oligarchy"

According to the standard account of the matter, the power of judicial review—that is, the authority of the federal judiciary to invalidate acts of Congress and the president when they are deemed to be unconstitutional—came to be entrenched in our law by the acceptance, tacit or otherwise, of the Supreme Court's ruling in the 1803 case of *Marbury v. Madison*. Of course, nowhere in the text of the Constitution is any such power granted. Rather, Chief Justice John Marshall inferred the existence of the power, or at least something like it, from the fact that the written Constitution declares itself to be the Supreme Law of the Land, combined with the evident principle that, in Marshall's language, "It is emphatically the province and duty of the judicial department to say what the law is."

Now, a lively dispute has existed from the moment the Supreme Court handed down its decision in *Marbury* as to the scope of that ruling. Even today, some scholars argue that it did nothing more than declare that the Supreme Court is within its rights in declining to exercise an authority putatively conferred on it by Congress when such authority exceeds the jurisdiction granted to the court under Article III of the Constitution. Certainly, as a technical matter, all the court did in *Marbury* was refuse to exercise original jurisdiction beyond what it was granted in Article III on the ground that the expansion of its original jurisdiction by section 13 of the Judiciary Act of 1789 was unconstitutional. So, the contemporary constitutional scholar Robert Lowry Clinton argues, it is a mistake to read the case as claiming a judicial power to tell the president or Congress what they can or cannot do under the Constitution. Clinton maintains that the *Marbury* ruling simply stands for the power of the Supreme Court, as a coequal branch of government, to act on its own interpretation of the Constitution in deciding what *it* can and cannot do. This, he observes, is entirely consistent with the recognition of a like power in the other branches.

But the conventional reading of *Marbury*—shared by the decision's friends and foes alike—has it standing for a considerably broader scope of judicial authority. Thomas Jefferson condemned the decision precisely because he viewed it as claiming for the courts the power to impose constitutional interpretations on the other branches. This, he later asserted, would have the effect of "placing us under the despotism of an oligarchy." And at the opposite extreme from Professor Clinton's reading is the reading the Supreme Court offered in *Cooper v. Aaron*. What I described as a "remarkable" claim to judicial supremacy, the *Cooper* justices presented as nothing more than a straightforward, uncontroversial, altogether logical implication of Marshall's proposition about the "province and duty of the judicial department." Indeed, the paragraph in which the justices make the claim offers nothing in its support beyond the invocation of *Marbury*.

Whatever *Marbury* was supposed to mean about the scope of the power of judicial review, it is a notable fact that the Supreme Court declined to exercise that power to declare another act of Congress unconstitutional for another half century. It did not do so until 1857, when it ruled in the case of *Dred Scott v. Sandford*. Scott was a slave in Missouri who had been taken by his master into the free state of Illinois and the free Wisconsin Territory. He then brought a suit demanding his freedom in St. Louis County Court under Missouri law, claiming that he was legally entitled to be free by virtue of having resided in a free state or territory. He won in the trial court, but the Supreme Court of Missouri reversed the ruling. Scott then brought a new case in the federal courts to consider, among other things, whether a state could reverse the "once free, always free" principle under which the St. Louis County Court had ruled in his favor.

Once the matter entered the federal courts, it became a massive political hot potato. John F. A. Sanford (a court clerk misspelled his name as *Sandford*), acting on behalf of his sister, who was Dred Scott's owner, injected into the litigation the question whether any black person, free or slave, could be a citizen of the United States. Moreover, he directly challenged the constitutionality of the Missouri Compromise of 1820, which forbade slavery in the Louisiana Territory north of latitude 36° 30'. Although the power of Congress to forbid slavery in federal territories was well established, Sanford argued that slaves were private property of the sort protected by the Constitution against deprivation without due process of law, and that therefore Congress lacked any constitutional authority to ban slavery in the territories.

When the matter reached the Supreme Court of the United States, Chief Justice Roger Brooke Taney, writing for a seven-man majority against two dissenters, accepted Sanford's major contentions, not only sending Scott back into slavery but also holding, in effect, that he had never been free. The majority ruled that blacks could not be citizens of the United States and therefore lacked the right to bring lawsuits in federal courts. Moreover, the seven justices held that Congress lacked constitutional authority to forbid or abolish slavery in federal territories. Still further, the court ruled that because slaves were personal property protected by the Constitution, the Missouri Compromise was unconstitutional.

All of this added up to a sweeping and profound ruling. The Supreme Court had massively injected itself into the most divisive and highly morally charged issue of the day. In my edited book entitled *Great Cases in Constitutional Law*, there is a most interesting exchange between Professor Cass Sunstein of the University of Chicago and Professor James McPherson, my colleague at Princeton, regarding the political impact of the *Dred Scott* decision. Sunstein defends the commonly held view that the case polarized an already dangerously divided country and made the Civil War and its toll of carnage almost inevitable. Instead of ending the conflict over slavery by definitively resolving it, as Taney apparently hoped to do, the Supreme Court, according to Sunstein, intensified the conflict and heightened emotions. McPherson holds the minority view that the case "did not really polarize the country any more than it was already polarized by the issue of slavery in the territories."

Whichever scholar has the better argument, they agree that the decision focused the debate over slavery and introduced into the already heady brew of issues involved in that debate the question of the scope of judicial power under the Constitution. McPherson points out that "so thoroughly did the *Dred Scott* decision pervade and structure the Lincoln-Douglas debates [in 1858] that in one of those debates a Douglas supporter shouted from the audience to Lincoln: 'Give us something besides *Dred Scott.*' Quick as a cat Lincoln responded: 'Yes, no doubt you want to hear something that don't hurt.'"

Lincoln on the Courts' Unchecked Power

To understand just how far our nation has traveled in its views on the legitimate scope of federal judicial power, let's consider how Lincoln understood the issue.

To the Great Emancipator, *Dred Scott* was an abomination, but for reasons of principle going even beyond those set forth by the dissenting justices in the case. That Lincoln was devoted to the Declaration of Independence and viewed its statement of principles as integral to the American scheme of constitutional government is, if anything, an understatement. But the Declaration was far from the only writing of Jefferson's of which Lincoln was mindful. In a letter of September 28, 1820, to William C. Jarvis (from which I quoted the line about judicial "despotism"), Jefferson explained his opposition to judicial supremacy in constitutional interpretation:

The Constitution has erected no such single tribunal, knowing that to whatever hands confided, with the corruptions of time and party, its members would become despots. It has more wisely made all the departments co-equal and co-sovereign within themselves. If the legislature fails to pass laws for a census, for paying the judges and other officers of government, for establishing a militia, for naturalization as prescribed by the Constitution, or if they fail to meet in Congress, the judges cannot issue their mandamus to them; if the President fails to provide the place of a judge, to appoint other civil and military officers, to issue requisite commissions, the judges cannot force him.

This language is quite shocking to us, for we live in the aftermath of an expansion of judicial power that the Supreme Court formally asserted in *Cooper v. Aaron*. Part of this, no doubt, has to do with the prestige that courts, including the Supreme Court of the United States, enjoy in elite sectors of our culture. Such elites often perceive any criticism of the scope of judicial power as, in effect, an attack on the independence of the judiciary or even the ideal of judicial independence (though in the aftermath of the *Bush v. Gore* and *Citizens United* decisions—both of which were extremely unpopular among liberal elites—this may be changing).

But Jefferson's language was not at all shocking to Lincoln. On the contrary, it was entirely in line with his own fears of the political consequences of judicial supremacy.

Like Jefferson, Lincoln believed that courts, including the Supreme Court of the United States, could violate the Constitution and even undermine constitutional government. In Lincoln's view, that judges, whenever they invalidated executive or legislative acts, purported to speak in the name of the Constitution and claimed merely to be giving effect to its commands was no guarantee against judicial despotism. He saw judges' exercising effectively unconstrained power as no less a threat to the Constitution than other governmental officers' exercising such power. His fear was not that judges would sometimes err in their constitutional rulings. Given human fallibility, that is inevitable and unremarkable. His fear, rather, was that judges, just like other government officials, were capable of exceeding the authority granted to them under the Constitution and thereby usurping the authority allocated to other branches in a delicate system of checks and balances. Indeed, Lincoln believed that judicial violations of the Constitution were in certain respects graver matters than the violations of elected officials.

Lincoln, of course, was a lawyer. He knew from experience that judges come in all shapes and sizes—competent and incompetent, conscientious and slapdash, honorable and corrupt. He wasn't a skeptic after the fashion of the legal realists who would rise to prominence in the law schools fifty years or so after his death. But his view of courts was realistic. He knew that it was essential to the success of a lawyer to know the law, but he also knew that it didn't hurt to know the judge. He believed in courts, but he didn't venerate them. Nor did he automatically identify what the courts did or said with "the law."

Lincoln's mature and most profound reflections on the scope of judicial power and the role of the judiciary in the American constitutional system came in relation to the debate over *Dred Scott*. In 1858, when Lincoln ran for Senate against Stephen Douglas, the question of how the other branches of government should respond to the ruling was far from resolved. Recall that the ruling marked the first time the court had invalidated a federal statute in more than fifty years, and only the second time in the nation's history. A politician's position on the question might well determine his electoral fate. Bound up, as it was, with the urgent and divisive issue of slavery, the issue could not be avoided—despite the best efforts of even the most agile political types, such as Douglas.

Upon his election as president, Lincoln faced the matter squarely in his Inaugural Address on March 4, 1861. With the specter of civil war looming, the new president, who had denounced the *Dred Scott* decision repeatedly in his senatorial campaign against Douglas as well as in the presidential campaign, turned attention to it in his remarks to the nation:

> I do not forget the position assumed by some that constitutional questions are to be decided by the Supreme Court, nor do I deny that such decisions must be binding in any case upon the parties to a suit as to the object of that suit, while they are also entitled to very high respect and consideration in all parallel cases by other departments of the government. And while it is obviously possible that such decision may be erroneous in any given case, still the evil effect following it, being limited to that particular case, with the chance that it may be overruled and never become a precedent for other cases, can better be borne than could the evils of a different practice. At the same time, the candid citizen must confess that if the policy of the government upon vital questions affecting the whole people is to be irrevocably fixed by decisions of the Supreme Court, the instant they are made in ordinary litigation between parties in personal actions, the people will have ceased to be their own rulers, having to that extent practically resigned their government into the hands of that eminent tribunal.

For Lincoln, then, the evil of the *Dred Scott* decision was not merely the expansion of slavery. It was also that the decision threatened to undermine the basic principles of republican government by establishing judicial supremacy in matters of constitutional interpretation. It was not only that the Supreme Court decided the suit in favor of the wrong party. It was also that the court claimed authority to decide for the other branches once and for all what the Constitution required, thus placing them in a position of inferiority and subservience. For the people to "resign their government into the hands of that eminent tribunal" would be, according to Lincoln, to abandon democratic self-government and acquiesce in oligarchic despotism. There is a not-very-faint echo of Jefferson in Lincoln's First Inaugural.

In office, Lincoln gave effect to his position against judicial supremacy by consistently refusing to treat the *Dred Scott* decision as creating a rule of law binding on the executive branch. His administration issued passports and other documents to free blacks, thus treating them as citizens of the United States despite the court's denial of their status as citizens. He signed legislation that plainly placed restrictions on slavery in the western territories, in defiance of Taney's ruling. For his critics, these actions, combined particularly with his suspension of the writ of habeas corpus, revealed him to be a lawless and tyrannical ruler, one who had no regard for the constitutional limits of his own power. But none can say that he had not made his opposition to judicial supremacy clear before assuming office.

It is ironic that the Supreme Court's 1958 declaration of judicial supremacy came in the context of the court's efforts to enforce a ruling in the cause of racial equality and civil rights. Lincoln had declared implacable opposition to judicial supremacy in response to a decision that stained the court's reputation as an institution dedicated to, as it says above the entrance to its marble temple in Washington, D.C., "equal justice under law." The popularity of the court's ruling in the *Brown* case (not, initially at least, in the South, but throughout much of the country and especially among journalists, professors, and other opinion leaders) no doubt helps to explain why the remarkable dictum in *Cooper v. Aaron* was so little remarked on at the time, and why few have noted its incompatibility with the principles of Jefferson and Lincoln.

Most of my own students are quite surprised to learn about the views of the author of the Declaration of Independence as well as those of the Great Emancipator. They, too, have drunk in the idea that courts, particularly the Supreme Court (upon which more than a few imagine themselves someday serving), are the ultimate protectors of rights and, as such, should have the ultimate say on constitutional questions. After all, they reason, somebody, or some institution, has to have the final word or else nothing is ever settled (and students want things to be settled). And the ultimate settler of things should be a nonpolitical body. Politics, my students say, is too messy. Democratic institutions are too prone to passion, prejudice, and foolishness for us to entrust to them matters of constitutional significance. We don't want to make our rights subject to voting, they say. There needs to be a higher institution to provide a check against the bigots and demagogues of politics—an institution where matters are resolved by calm and rational inquiry and judgment; an institution whose membership is drawn from a narrower, more refined, more highly educated circle; one that is not subject to political retaliation for unpopular decisions of principle. What would have happened, they ask, had the political branches felt themselves free to dispute *Brown v. Board of Education?*

One imagines Lincoln in the classroom reminding the youngsters that the unchecked power to do good is unavoidably also the unchecked power to do evil. If we like what the justices did in *Brown v. Board,* let us not forget what they did in *Dred Scott.* And there is more to the balance sheet. Was it not the Supreme Court, after all, that during the period from 1905 to 1937 repeatedly invalidated both state and federal worker protection laws and social welfare legislation? Did the justices not read into the due process clause of the Fourteenth Amendment a "right to freedom of contract" in whose name they frustrated the legislative will and usurped the constitutional authority of the elected representatives of the people? This, in any event, is the conventional reading of the history by contemporary liberals and conservatives alike.

And then there is the issue of abortion, surely the most vexing, divisive, and morally charged issue of our own time. Does the Supreme Court's ruling striking down state prohibitions of abortion in the 1973 cases of *Roe v. Wade* and *Doe v. Bolton* belong on the plus side of the court's ledger with *Brown v. Board* or on the minus side with *Dred Scott?* Does that in turn depend on whether one happens to see abortion as a woman's right or as a violation of the rights of an unborn child? If so, should one's view of the proper scope of judicial power and the legitimacy of judicial supremacy depend on the contingent fact that the court happened to come down the way it did on abortion? After all, the court could have come down, as the German Constitutional Court did in a 1975 decision interpreting Germany's Basic Law, in precisely the opposite way—invalidating a legislatively enacted liberalization of abortion. Supporters of the right to abortion who criticize the German decision make exactly the same arguments—the same Lincolnian arguments—against judicial supremacy that supporters of the right to life who criticize *Roe v. Wade* make. Their argument is that, to put it in Lincoln's language, "if the policy of the government upon vital questions affecting the whole people is to be irrevocably fixed by decisions of the Supreme Court, the instant they are made in ordinary litigation between parties in personal actions, the people will have ceased to be their own rulers, having to that extent practically resigned their government into the hands of that eminent tribunal."

6

SOME HARD QUESTIONS
ABOUT AFFIRMATIVE ACTION

A FFIRMATIVE ACTION REMAINS a contentious issue in this country. But the constitutional formula was well established as early as the 1970s: racial and ethnic classifications are suspect under the Constitution's equal protection clause, triggering strict scrutiny that places the burden on the state (or publicly funded institution) to demonstrate that a law or policy involving any such classification is narrowly tailored to secure or advance a compelling governmental interest.[1] So what happens when the U.S. Supreme Court confronts cases involving affirmative-action admissions policies at state universities? In 2003, considering two cases in conjunction, the court issued rulings on such policies—in this instance, admissions policies at the University of Michigan—that made almost no one happy but left supporters of preferences in admissions less unhappy than opponents.

In these cases—*Gratz v. Bollinger* and *Grutter v. Bollinger*—no one seriously doubted that the admissions policies in dispute involved racial and ethnic classifications.[2] Plainly, then, under prevailing constitutional doctrine, so-called strict scrutiny was the required standard for judicial review. The question was whether the policy of classifying students by race and ethnicity in order to advantage some—thus, unavoidably, disadvantaging others—was supported by something qualifying as a "compelling" governmental interest and, if so, whether the policy was "narrowly tailored" to secure or advance that interest.[3]

The Supreme Court decided that the University of Michigan's interest in racial and ethnic "diversity" qualifies as compelling.[4] The question then became whether Michigan's methods of achieving the type of diversity it desired counted as "narrow tailoring." The court judged that the admissions policy of the undergraduate college, which formally awarded valuable "points" to certain candidates based on race and ethnicity, failed the test of narrow tailoring.[5] But the court held that the law school's policy of taking race and ethnicity into account without the formal awarding of points did pass.[6]

The obvious question is whether there is a reasonable basis for the distinction. I doubt it, and so did at least six of the nine justices. Those justices most favorable to racial and ethnic preference policies (John Paul Stevens, David Souter, and Ruth Bader Ginsburg) were joined by those most opposed (William Rehnquist, Antonin Scalia, and Clarence Thomas) in suggesting that the cases are not distinguishable: either both preference schemes pass constitutional muster (as Stevens, Souter, and Ginsburg believed) or both fail (as Rehnquist, Scalia, and Thomas thought).[7] The question that the remaining justices, particularly Justice Sandra Day O'Connor, failed to address adequately is: How can it be unconstitutional to do honestly and above board what it is constitutionally permissible to do "through winks, nods, and disguises"?[8] Or, put the other way around: How can it be constitutionally permissible to do "through winks, nods, and disguises" what it is unconstitutional to do honestly and above board?

The answer Justice O'Connor offered—that the law school was doing something fundamentally different from what the college was doing, something free of the discriminatory element she found in the college's awarding of points[9]—just isn't persuasive. Racial or ethnic identity can and plainly does tip the balance in favor of some applicants for admission and against others in a significant number of cases as a result of either institution's preference scheme. Both schemes are designed to do that. The fact that one accomplishes the objective by formally awarding points to candidates of desired races or ethnicities, while the other accomplishes it by informally taking race and ethnicity into account (together with other factors), does not distinguish the schemes at the level of principle.

But let us lay this matter aside and consider an even more fundamental question. Did the Supreme Court provide any basis for its judgment that racial and ethnic diversity at the University of Michigan and like institutions constitutes a compelling governmental interest? Here, those favoring racial and ethnic preferences won a decisive victory. Should they have? This much can be said for their position: it was urged on the court in the most impassioned terms by people and institutions of enormous prestige and influence.[10] The list of amici curiae urging the court to uphold racial and ethnic preference policies was extraordinary. I cannot think of a case in which so many leading figures in the worlds of education, business, and even the military have united to protect a policy under constitutional review. The establishment left the justices in no doubt as to where the mainstream of elite opinion stood on the matter.

Yet neither the amici nor the justices who accepted the position they urged could manage to identify grounds on which racial and ethnic diversity can plausibly be said to constitute a compelling interest as a matter of constitutional law. Given that Michigan does not have anything that would qualify as a "compelling" state interest in establishing or maintaining an elite law school in the first place, how could it have a "compelling" state interest in racial and ethnic diversity at that law school? Justice Scalia, dissenting in the denial of relief to plaintiff Barbara Grutter, cut to the heart of the matter: "The allegedly 'compelling state interest' at issue here is not the incremental 'educational benefit' that emanates from the fabled 'critical mass' of minority students, but rather Michigan's interest in maintaining a 'prestige' law school whose normal admissions standards dispropor-tionately exclude blacks and other minorities. If that is a compelling state interest, everything is."[11]

Michigan wishes to maintain an elite law school. (This is some-thing it constitutionally *may* do but not something it is constitution-ally *required* to do or has a constitutionally *compelling interest* in doing.) To achieve its objective, the Michigan Law School selects students on the basis of outstanding academic achievement and professional promise as reflected in grades, LSAT scores, and other factors. This is perfectly reasonable. As a result, however, certain minority groups would be statistically underrepresented ("no critical mass") if appli-cants from those groups were not given some substantial advantage precisely on the basis of race or ethnicity.[12] Now, classifying people by race and ethnicity to advantage some and disadvantage others is, from the constitutional viewpoint, something to be avoided ("sus-pect"). It is permissible only for the gravest of reasons ("compelling"). All the justices appeared to agree on *that* point. Yet is it not clear that Michigan Law School could eliminate what it alleges to be the need to engage in the constitutionally suspect practice by abandoning a goal—namely, maintaining an elite law school—that no one contends is itself supported by a compelling state interest? If Michigan consid-ers racial and ethnic diversity on campus to be important, it could achieve diversity without discriminating against anyone simply by shifting to an open admissions policy, or by distributing slots by some fair but less competitive system of allocation.

And does the University of Michigan, or the elite colleges and uni-versities that signed on in support of its preference programs, really care about diversity on campus? Do they really cherish its educational value? If they did, would there not be concern, even steps taken, to ensure a "critical mass" of faculty representing reasonable political and religious viewpoints held by many intelligent and responsible people in our society but grossly underrepresented on elite faculties? If students and faculty are benefited by "diversity" to the point that it qualifies as a compelling interest justifying discrimination that would otherwise be unconstitutional, why the lack of concern about the absence at virtually all elite institutions of a "critical mass" of faculty who are Evangelical Protestants, devout Catholics, social conservatives, Republicans, and so forth? It is not that preference programs in faculty hiring fail to include members of these classes; it is that few people who shape university policy notice, much less care about, the absence of diversity of political and religious viewpoints and affiliations in institutions that allegedly prize the engagement of ideas.[13] It is therefore difficult to credit the claim that a desire for the intellectual benefits of diversity really motivates the defense of preference schemes.

Regardless, by ruling as it did in *Grutter*, the Supreme Court put itself on the spot to identify a principled constitutional basis for deciding what is and isn't a compelling governmental interest. The majority declared racial and ethnic diversity on campuses to qualify as such an interest without saying anything very helpful about why it is so. If "compelling state interest" is a standard less demanding than "pressing public necessity,"[14] how are the lower courts—and, for that matter, the Supreme Court itself in future cases—supposed to recognize truly compelling interests and distinguish them from interests that, though perhaps substantial, fall short of being compelling? (And when the courts do recognize such interests, how are they to decide whether the means employed to secure or advance them are sufficiently narrowly tailored to pass constitutional muster?)

The worry, of course, is that the courts will decide such questions not on the basis of preexisting legal norms but rather on the basis of the judges' personal judgments about what qualifies as a worthy or important governmental objective. In such circumstances, liberal and conservative judges, and judges in between, would vary in their judgments not because of differences of opinion about law but purely as a result of ideological differences. Judges would be acting as legislators. Courts would be functioning as political, rather than legal, forums. And, since politics naturally gravitates to the place where the political action is, the matter of judicial selection would become politicized and factions would form along ideological lines. You may well say,

"We are there already, and have been for a long time." Indeed. In that way, *Gratz* and *Grutter* reflect and reinforce the politicization of the legal system.

But is there any way to avoid the problem in the area of equal protection, short of abandoning "scrutiny analysis" altogether? Yes. It is to apply the standards of rigor clearly connoted by the phrases "compelling interest" and "narrow tailoring." On this approach, a compelling interest would indeed be a matter of pressing public necessity.[15] Narrow tailoring would require that the means used to secure the interest are, if not the only ones available, those that impinge least on the interests of anyone who is disadvantaged by the law or policy.

Prior to *Gratz* and *Grutter*, some commentators wondered whether the triggering of strict scrutiny automatically meant that a classification would be invalidated. In the case of *Adarand v. Pena* (1995), Justice O'Connor made a point of saying that it meant no such thing.[16] Plainly she was correct. Who would deny that it is constitutionally permissible for prison guards intervening to quell a brawl that has broken out between, say, Hispanic and Anglo prisoners to separate them temporarily? In such a case, the interest in restoring order and preventing violence is manifestly compelling—any reasonable person can see it—and the means used are the only ones available to those in authority. Moreover, in this situation the temporary segregation of the prisoners works no discrimination against any of them. None are disadvantaged by the ethnic classification or on the basis of ethnicity.

Gratz and *Grutter* raise the question of whether there are social goals that justify imposing disadvantages on people based on race or ethnicity (and clearly the plaintiffs, Barbara Grutter and Jennifer Gratz, were disadvantaged in the competition for admission to the University of Michigan). Because it is a competitive admissions situation, applicants who do not benefit from the preference scheme are disadvantaged by it. This disadvantage is not a side effect of the policy; the policy is designed to produce it. Those responsible for Michigan's admissions policy may regret what they take to be their policy's "necessity"—given what they say is the educational need to maintain a critical mass of certain minorities[17]—but they deliberately and directly impose disadvantages on certain applicants by granting the preferences to others.

But, then, are the University of Michigan and its supporters really interested in a critical mass of (certain) minorities? If they were, one would expect preference schemes more often than not to produce similar percentages of students representing minorities of the various types qualifying for preferences, irrespective of the representation of those minorities in the broader culture. But typically they don't. Rather, the common result, and the evident goal, of preference programs is to secure minority representation on campus more or less in line with the representation of each minority beyond the walls of the institution. As United States Civil Rights commissioner Peter Kirsanow pointedly asked, "Why does critical mass mean, e.g., 12 percent blacks, but only 8 percent Hispanics? Do Hispanics need fewer from their ethnic group to be comfortable enough to participate in class? Where is the data supporting that determination?"[18] Where, indeed.

A final question: Does the Supreme Court's decision in the Michigan cases merely preserve the status quo—that is, does it leave the law as it was after the court's landmark ruling in *Regents of the University of California v. Bakke* (1978)?[19] In *Bakke*, the court ruled unconstitutional the rigid use of racial quotas in admissions policies, but the majority did hold that race could be used as one criterion for admissions among several. As civil liberties writer Nat Hentoff pointed out, there is reason to doubt that the Michigan Law School policy could have survived review under *Bakke*.[20] Federal District Court judge Bernard Friedman, whose invalidation of the law school's preference program was reversed in *Grutter*, found that the law school in fact used "race to ensure the enrollment of a certain minimum percentage of underrepresented minority students."[21] For this reason, he ruled that the scheme was, in effect, a quota system and, as such, unconstitutional even under *Bakke*.[22] Hentoff, quoting the work of *New York Times* reporter Jacques Steinberg, observed:

In 1999, the University of Michigan Law School "accepted only one of the 61 Asian Americans, or 2 percent, who were ranked in the middle range of the applicant pools, as defined by their grades and test scores, according to court filings. The admission rate for whites with similar grades and scores was 3 percent. *But among black applicants with similar transcripts, 22 out of 27, or 81 percent, were admitted* [emphasis added]."[23]

It is hard to argue with Hentoff's conclusion: "If Justice Lewis Powell had seen undergraduate or graduate school records with those comparative numbers of the admitted and rejected—in the context of a quota system—he would, on the basis of his 'plus factor' ruling in *Bakke*, have declared those admissions policies clearly unconstitutional. And they are!"[24]

7

IMMIGRATION AND AMERICAN EXCEPTIONALISM

THAT THE UNITED States of America is an exceptional nation seems to me to be a proposition whose truth is too obvious to debate. Our nation was, as our greatest president said, "conceived in liberty and dedicated to the proposition that all men are created equal." And not only was our nation "so conceived, and so dedicated," we as a nation have proved to the world that "a nation so conceived and so dedicated can long endure." The history of our nation is the story of "We the People"—the American people—struggling (sometimes struggling against one another) to protect, and honor, and live up to the exceptional principles around which we have integrated ourselves and constituted ourselves as a people. And although our record is far from unblemished, we have not been left unblessed with success.

No one needs to be reminded that part of what is unique about the United States is that our common bonds are not in blood or even soil but in a shared moral-political creed. "We hold these truths to be self-evident, that all men are created equal, that they are endowed by their Creator with certain unalienable rights, that among these are life, liberty, and the pursuit of happiness." This is clearest in the fact that people really can, in the richest and fullest possible sense, *become* Americans. And millions upon millions of people have done so. Of course, one can become *a citizen of* Greece or France or China, but can one really *become* Greek, or French, or Chinese? An immigrant who becomes a citizen of the United States becomes, or at least can become, not merely an American citizen but an *American*. He is as American as the fellow whose ancestors arrived on the *Mayflower*.

How do immigrants become Americans? In practice, it goes beyond becoming an American citizen and even formally signing on with the American creed. The additional key ingredient, I believe, is something I know intimately from my own family's experience—namely, *gratitude*. It is, typically, an immigrant's feelings of gratitude to America for the liberty, security, and opportunity our nation affords him and his family that leads to his appreciation of the ideals and institutions of American cultural, economic, and civic life. From this appreciation comes his belief in the goodness of American ideals, as articulated above all in the Declaration of Independence, and the value of the constitutional structures and institutions by which they are effectuated. And from this belief arises his aspiration to become an American citizen together with his willingness to shoulder the responsibilities of citizenship and even to make great sacrifices for the nation, should it come to that.

My own immigrant grandfathers came to the United States a little over a hundred years ago. Like most immigrants then and now, they were not drawn here by any abstract belief in the superiority of the American political system. My father's father came from Syria, fleeing oppression visited upon him and his family as members of a relatively small ethnic and religious minority group in that troubled country. My mother's father came to escape the poverty of southern Italy. They both worked on the railroads and in the mines. My maternal grandfather settled in West Virginia, where there was a small Italian immigrant community in Clarksburg, Fairmont, and Morgantown—a trio of cities along the Monongahela River a little south of the Pennsylvania border. He was able to save enough money to start a little grocery store, which soon became a flourishing business. My paternal grandfather spent his entire life as a laborer. He died of emphysema, no doubt as a result of the pulmonary health hazards of coal mining in those days. Both men were exceedingly grateful for what America made possible for them and their families. Their gratitude was not diminished when times got hard—as they did for all Americans—in the Great Depression. Although both my grandfathers encountered ethnic prejudice, they viewed this as an aberration—a failure of some Americans to live up to the nation's ideals. It did not dawn on them to blame the bad behavior of some Americans on America itself. On the contrary, America in their eyes was a land of unsurpassed blessing. It was a nation of which they were proud and happy to become citizens. And even before they became citizens they had become patriots—men who deeply appreciated what America is and what she stands for.

Like so many other immigrants, my immigrant grandparents particularly appreciated the opportunities that America made available to their children. My father's father had a sister—she, too, an immigrant—who had a son named John Solomon, who wanted to be a lawyer. He finished college and then completed law school at West Virginia University. The law school in those days was located on University Avenue in Morgantown near the center of the campus. It was a grand building that one entered by walking up a broad set of stairs. When my cousin John's mother—we knew her as Halte Gemile—came to attend her son's graduation ceremony, she stopped to kiss each step as she ascended those stairs. Such was her gratitude. Of course, her son was thoroughly embarrassed by this display. My father, who was there, tells me that his cousin John turned to his mother at about the fourth step and pleaded, "Please, mom, you're acting like an immigrant." Indeed, she was.

My family's experience also illustrates how gratitude for liberty, security, and opportunity leads immigrants to appreciate American ideals and institutions, so much that they are willing to bear the responsibilities of citizenship and even to make great sacrifices for the country. Four of my paternal grandparents' five sons were drafted into the U.S. military to serve in the Second World War. My maternal grandparents' only son was also drafted. All these men served in combat and returned with decorations. Their immigrant parents were immensely proud of them—proud of them precisely because they fought for America and for what America stands for. They considered that their sons were fighting for *their* country—not for a country in which they were resident aliens or guests. They were fighting for a country that was not only great but also good. A country whose ideals were noble. A country to whom they were immensely grateful—and not merely because it provided a haven from poverty and oppression. *A country whose principles they believed in.*

When their boys were fighting, they knew that it was entirely possible—all too possible—that ultimately they would be called on to give what Lincoln at Gettysburg described as the "last full measure of devotion." You can imagine the anxiety this would cause in an Italian family whose one and only son had been sent into the brutal combat of the Pacific theater. But however much sleep was lost, they remained proud that their son was fighting for his country, for their country, for America. Nor did the fact that Italy under fascist rule was on the other side of the conflict give them so much as a moment's pause. The gratitude leading to appreciation leading to the conviction and commitment at the heart of true American patriotism left them in no doubt as to their loyalty.

I have the sense that my uncles' service to the nation at a time of peril was not only an expression of their Americanism, and the Americanism of their immigrant parents, but also a profound confirmation and ratification of it. If they had any doubts in their own minds about whether they were truly and fully Americans—as American as their fellow citizens whose ancestors really had arrived here on the *Mayflower*—military service erased those doubts. I daresay that the same was true any time native-born citizens had doubts about whether their immigrant neighbors really were Americans. The willingness of immigrants and their children to take the risks, and in many cases to be counted among the fallen, leaves the question of allegiance and American identity in no doubt.

Of course, some Protestant Americans wondered whether non-Protestants—and especially Catholics—could truly become Americans. They were concerned that hierarchical and nondemocratic forms of church governance would hinder the ability of non-Protestant immigrants to appreciate and fully give their allegiance to democratic institutions and principles of civic life. Some even believed that Catholic immigrants would have to be de-Catholicized by the public school system and other mechanisms in order to become patriotic Americans. The natural and understandable Catholic reaction to this—the establishment of Catholic parochial schools across the country—only heightened Protestant worries. But part of what eventually made these worries go away was the record of service and heroism of Catholic and other non-Protestant soldiers fighting for democracy and against authoritarian regimes and totalitarian ideologies in the First and especially the Second World War. Catholics saw no contradiction between their faith and their allegiance to the United States of America. On the contrary, religious commitment tended to support patriotic conviction. Faithful Catholics wanted to be, and not merely to be seen to be, the very best of good American citizens. And as they saw and see it, that doesn't require the slightest dilution of their Catholic faith.

I suspect that as you read the stories of my grandparents, you thought of stories, not at all dissimilar, of your grandparents, or great-grandparents, or great-great grandparents, and how they became Americans. The amazing and wonderful thing is that a family story like mine—of immigrant ancestors becoming Americans, sharing in the blessings of American life, and taking upon themselves their share of the nation's burdens—is not the exception; it is the norm. (Of course, the story of Africans brought to America as slaves and then subjected to segregation and discrimination after slavery was abolished is a radically different one—a story of injustice and a stain upon our nation's history. Yet the great efforts to right these wrongs and live up to our national ideals of liberty and justice for all are also part of our American heritage.)

I believe that immigration has been a great strength for America and that it will continue to be so. I certainly hope that immigrants to our land will continue to want to be Americans. Does this mean that I reject what has come to be known as "multiculturalism"? Well, it depends on what one means by that term. I certainly see no need to encourage immigrants to abandon their customs, traditions, and ethnic or religious identities; on the contrary, I think it is good for families, and good for America, for immigrants to honor their ethnic customs and identities and pass them along to the next generation. Immigrants have always done this, and it is fine and good—a source of strength. But this is to be distinguished from an ideology that promotes the rejection of a primary and central political allegiance to the United States and its ideals and institutions. And it is certainly to be distinguished from any ideology that denies the fundamental goodness of America's principles of political and civil liberty.

Now, where a culture of *opportunity* flourishes, immigrants will feel, as my grandparents felt, gratitude for the opportunities to lift themselves up and make a better life for their children by dint of hard work and determination to succeed. But it appears to be a brute fact of human psychology that where a culture of *entitlement* prevails, gratitude even for charitable assistance will not emerge. In part this is because a culture of entitlement curtails upward social mobility. This is the phenomenon known as welfare dependency. I observed its soul-destroying effects on many *nonimmigrant* families in West Virginia as I was growing up. You see, dependency is an equal-opportunity soul destroyer. Such dependency leads to resentment as people persuade themselves that they are not getting ahead because those who are already better off are manipulating the system to hold down people at the bottom of the ladder (who depend on entitlements). So the culture of entitlement impedes the gratitude that enables immigrants to become Americans.

As I said, I *want* immigrants to become Americans. I want them to believe in American ideals and institutions. I want them to "hold these truths to be self-evident, that all men are created equal, that they are endowed by their Creator with certain unalienable rights, that among these are life, liberty, and the pursuit of happiness." I want them to believe, as I believe, in the dignity of the human being, in all stages and conditions of life, and in limited government, republican democracy, equality of opportunity, morally ordered liberty, private property, economic freedom, and the rule of law. I want them to believe in these ideals and principles not because they are ours but because they are noble and good and true. They honor the profound, inherent, and equal dignity of all members of the human family. They call forth from us the best that we are capable of. They ennoble us. Our efforts to live up to them, despite our failures and imperfections, have made us a great people, a force for freedom and justice in the world, and, of course, an astonishingly prosperous nation. It is little wonder that America is, as it always has been, a magnet for people from every land who seek a better life.

But the transmission of American ideals to immigrants—or to anyone else, including new generations of native-born Americans—depends on the maintenance of a culture in which these ideals flourish. The maintenance of such a culture is a complicated business—one with many dimensions. But in this nation of immigrants, in which "We the People" have the privilege and responsibility of governing ourselves, it is every citizen's business. And it is certainly the special business of institutions of higher learning. For such institutions, civic education—education that advances the understanding of our nation's constitutional principles and institutions—is a high calling and a solemn obligation. If, as James Madison said, "a well-instructed people alone can be permanently a free people," then civic education is vital to the success of the grand experiment in ordered liberty that Madison and the other Founding Fathers bequeathed to us and our posterity.

Part II

MORALITY AND THE PUBLIC SQUARE

8

NATURAL LAW, GOD, AND HUMAN DIGNITY

ABRAHAM LINCOLN BEGAN his remarks at Gettysburg in 1863 by noting that the nation he served, and was fighting a civil war to preserve, was founded "four score and seven years ago." If one does the arithmetic, this takes us back not to the Constitution's ratification, in 1788, nor to its adoption by the constitutional convention, in 1787, but to the signing and publishing of the Declaration of Independence, in 1776. In this matter, as in so many others, Lincoln's understanding was very much in line with the nation's Founders'. They, too, believed that with the Declaration they established a new nation, albeit one whose political institutions and fundamental law were changed in significant ways by the Constitution and then by its amendments. Lincoln observed that the nation they founded was "conceived in liberty and dedicated to the proposition that all men are created equal." This "natural law" understanding of the American Founding and the American regime is, once again, something Lincoln held in common with the Founders themselves. As the Declaration itself proclaims, "We hold these truths to be self-evident, that all men are created equal, that they are endowed by their

Creator with certain unalienable Rights, that among these are Life, Liberty, and the pursuit of Happiness."

It was on this basis that America's founding statesmen launched their "experiment in ordered liberty," the experiment that would, as Lincoln said at Gettysburg, test whether a true regime of republican government "can long endure," and whether "government of the people, by the people, and for the people"—that is, republican government—would survive on the North American continent or, alas, "perish from the earth." So the experiment was a bold one. Yet Thomas Jefferson, the principal draftsman of the Declaration, had insisted that there was nothing novel about the natural-law philosophy that he and his colleagues had set forth in that document as the basis of republican liberty in the new nation. Reflecting on the Declaration in May of 1825—a little more than a year before his death (and the death of his revolutionary colleague, then political foe, then friend, John Adams), which occurred on the fiftieth anniversary of the Declaration—Jefferson said in a letter to Henry Lee that the point of the document was

> not to find out new principles or new arguments never before thought of, nor merely to say things that had never been said before, but to place before mankind the common sense of the subject. . . . It was intended to be an expression of the American mind, and to give to that expression the proper tone and spirit called for by the occasion. All its authority rests on the harmonizing sentiments of the day, whether expressed in conversations, in letters, in printed essays, or in the elementary books of public right, as Aristotle, Cicero, Locke, Sidney, etc.

Now, Jefferson, a learned man, was aware that in a vast range of particulars Aristotle's approach to practical reason and moral and political theory differs from Cicero's approach, which in turn differs from Locke's approach, and so on. So obviously Jefferson was not claiming that the United States of America was founded on a particular natural-law theory common to the four political philosophers he mentions, plus others whose influence he signals with that "etc." The claim, rather, is that a broad tradition of reflection about moral truth and its relationship to political order deeply influenced the "American mind" that produced the Declaration and the "harmonizing sentiments of the day" that prompted the bold and dangerous decision to rebel against the British crown. That tradition includes Greek philosophers and Roman jurists of antiquity and continues through the Enlightenment thinkers of the Founders' own time. It is a tradition of thought about natural law and natural rights that is broadly Aristotelian (and Thomistic) in its fundamental conceptions.

I do not claim that this account reproduces with anything approaching exactitude the thought of America's Founding Fathers. But it does emerge from the broad tradition that Jefferson identifies as among the key sources of the beliefs and sentiments that emboldened America's Founders to pledge their "lives, fortunes, and sacred honor" in the cause of a law even higher than the rules laid down by kings or parliaments.

Knowledge of Natural Law

One's knowledge of natural law, like all knowledge, begins with experience, but it does not end or even tarry there. Knowing is an activity—an intellectual activity, to be sure, but an activity nonetheless. We all have the experience of knowing. But to know is not merely to experience. Knowing is a complex and dynamic activity. The role of experience in the activity of knowing is to supply data on which the inquiring intellect works in the cause of achieving understanding. Insights are insights into data. They are, as philosopher and theologian Bernard Lonergan brilliantly demonstrated by inviting readers to observe and reflect on their own ordinary intellectual operations, the fruit of a dynamic and integrated process of experiencing, understanding, and judging.[1]

So what are the data supplied by experience that are at the foundation of practical judgments—that is to say, insights that constitute knowledge of natural law? They are the objects of intelligibly choiceworthy possibilities—possibilities that, inasmuch as they provide reasons for acting (that is, more than merely instrumental reasons), we grasp as *opportunities*.

In our experience of true friendship, for example, we grasp by what is ordinarily an effortless exercise of what Aristotle called "practical reason" the intelligible point of having and being a friend. We understand that friendship is desirable not merely for instrumental reasons—indeed, a purely instrumental friendship would be no friendship at all—but above all for its own sake. Because we grasp the intelligible point of having and being a friend, and we understand that the fundamental point of friendship is friendship itself, not goals extrinsic to friendship to which the activity of friendship is merely a means, we reasonably judge that friendship is intrinsically valuable. We know that friendship is a constitutive and irreducible aspect of human well-being and fulfillment, and that *precisely as such* friendship provides a reason for action that requires for its intelligibility no further or deeper reason or subrational motivating factor to which it is a means.

The same is true if we shift our focus to our experience of the activity of knowing itself. In our experience of wonder and curiosity, of raising questions and devising strategies for obtaining correct answers, of executing those strategies by carrying out lines of inquiry, of achieving insights, we grasp (by what is again for most people in most circumstances an effortless exercise of practical reason) the intelligible point of searching for truth and finding it. We understand that knowledge, though it may have tremendous instrumental value, is intrinsically valuable as well. To be attentive, informed, thoughtful, clearheaded, careful, critical, and judicious in one's thinking and judging is to be inherently enriched in a key dimension of human life. We reasonably judge the activity of knowing, then, to be an intrinsic (or "basic") human good—a constitutive and irreducible aspect of our flourishing as human beings. Like friendship and a number of other types of activity, knowledge provides a reason for choice and action that requires for its intelligibility no further or deeper reason or sub-rational source of motivation to which it is a means.

Knowledge of natural law, then, is not innate. It does not swing free of experience or of the data provided by experience. Even when it is easily achieved, practical knowledge (that is, knowledge of natural law) is an achievement. It is the fruit of insights into data that experience supplies. The insight—the knowledge—that friendship or knowledge itself is intrinsically humanly fulfilling is ultimately rooted in our elementary experiences of the activities of friendship and knowing. Apart from those experiences, there would be no data on which practical reason could work to yield understanding of the *intelligible point* (and, thus, of the value) of friendship or knowledge; there would be no data by which to judge that these activities are intrinsic fulfillments of the human person and, as such, objects of the primary principles of practical reason and basic precepts of natural law.

Of course, not all practical knowledge is, strictly speaking, moral knowledge (that is, knowledge of moral norms or their correct applications). But all moral knowledge is practical knowledge; it is (or centrally includes) knowledge of principles for the direction and guidance of action.[2] Knowledge of the most fundamental practical principles directing action toward the basic human goods and away from their privations, though not strictly speaking knowledge of moral norms, is foundational to the generation and identification of such norms. That is because moral norms are principles that guide our actions in line with the primary practical principles integrally conceived. Norms of morality are specifications of the directiveness of the various aspects of human well-being and fulfillment that, taken together, constitute the ideal of integral human flourishing. So if the first principle of practical reason is, as Thomas Aquinas says, "the good is to be done and pursued, and the bad is to be avoided,"[3] then the first principle of morality is that "one ought always to choose and otherwise will in a way that is compatible with a will towards integral human fulfillment."[4] And just as the first principle of practical reason is specified, as Aquinas makes clear, by identifying the various irreducible aspects of human well-being and fulfillment (namely, friendship, knowledge, aesthetic appreciation, skillful performance, religion, and so forth), so, too, the first principle of morality is specified by identifying the norms of conduct that are entailed by an openhearted love of the human good (that is, the good of human persons) taken as a whole.

Natural Law and Human Rights

A natural-law theory is a critical reflective account of the constitutive aspects of the well-being and fulfillment of human persons and the communities they form. Such a theory will propose to identify principles of right action—moral principles—specifying the first and most general principle of morality: namely, that one should choose and act in ways that are compatible with a will toward integral human fulfillment. Among these principles are respect for rights people possess simply by virtue of their humanity—rights that, as a matter of justice, others are bound to respect, and governments are bound not only to respect but also, to the extent possible, to protect.

Natural-law theorists of my ilk understand human fulfillment—the human good—as variegated. There are many irreducible dimensions of human well-being. This is not to deny that human nature is determinate. It is to affirm that our nature, though determinate, is complex. We are animals, but rational. Our integral good includes not only our bodily well-being but also our intellectual, moral, and spiritual well-being. We are individuals, but friendship and sociability are constitutive aspects of our flourishing.

By reflecting on the basic goods of human nature, especially those most immediately pertaining to social and political life, natural-law theorists propose to arrive at a sound understanding of principles of justice, including those principles we call human rights. In light of how natural-law theorists understand human nature and the human good, it should be no surprise to learn that natural-law theorists typically reject both strict individualism and collectivism. Individualism overlooks the intrinsic value of human sociability and tends mistakenly to view human beings atomistically. It fails to account for the *intrinsic* value of friendship and other aspects of human sociability, reducing all relationships to *means* by which the partners collaborate with a view to more fully or efficiently achieving their individual goals and objectives. Collectivism, meanwhile, compromises the dignity of human beings by tending to instrumentalize and subordinate them and their well-being to the interests of larger social units—the community, the state, the *volk*, the fatherland, the *führer*, the future communist utopia. Individualists and collectivists both have theories of justice and human rights, but they are, as I see it, highly unsatisfactory. They are rooted in important misunderstandings of human nature and the human good. Neither can do justice to the concept of a human *person*—that is, a rational animal who is a locus of intrinsic value (and, as such, an *end in himself* who may never legitimately treat himself or be treated by others as a mere *means*), but whose well-being intrinsically includes relationships with others and membership in communities (beginning with the family) in which he or she has, as a matter of justice, both rights and responsibilities.

Human rights exist (or obtain) if principles of practical reason direct us to act or abstain from acting in certain ways out of respect for the well-being and the dignity of persons whose legitimate interests may be affected by what we do. I certainly believe that there are such principles. They cannot be overridden by considerations of utility. At a very general level, they direct us, in Immanuel Kant's phrase, to treat human beings always as ends and never as means only. When we begin to specify this general norm, we identify important negative duties, such as the duty to refrain from enslaving people. Although we need not put the matter in terms of "rights," it is perfectly reasonable, and I believe helpful, to speak of a *right* against being enslaved, and to speak of slavery as a violation of human *rights*. It is a right that we have not by virtue of being members of a certain race, sex, class, or ethnic group but simply by virtue of our humanity.[5] In that sense, it is a *human* right. But there are, in addition to negative duties and their corresponding rights, certain positive duties. And these, too, can be articulated and discussed in the language of rights, though here we must be clear about by whom and how a given right is to be honored.

Sometimes it is said, for example, that education or health care is a human right. It is certainly not unreasonable to speak this way, but much more needs to be said if it is to be a meaningful statement. Who is supposed to provide education or health care to whom? Why should those persons or institutions be the providers? What place should the provision of education or health care occupy on the list of social and political priorities? Is it better for education and health care to be provided by governments under socialized systems or by private providers in markets? These questions go beyond the application of moral principles. They require prudential judgment in light of the contingent circumstances people face in a given society at a given point in time. Often, there is not a single, uniquely correct answer. The answer to each question can lead to further questions. The problems can be extremely complex, far more complex than the issue of slavery, where once a right has been identified, its universality and the basic terms of its application are fairly clear. Everybody has a moral right not to be enslaved, and everybody an obligation as a matter of strict justice to refrain from enslaving others; governments have a moral obligation to respect and protect that right and, correspondingly, to enforce the obligation.[6]

Human Dignity

The natural-law understanding of human rights is connected with a particular account of human dignity. Under that account, the natural human capacities for reason and freedom are fundamental to the dignity of human beings—the dignity that is protected by human rights. The basic goods of human nature are the goods of a rational creature—a creature who, unless impaired or prevented from doing so, naturally develops and exercises capacities for deliberation, judgment, and choice. These capacities are God-like—albeit, of course, in a limited way. In fact, from the theological vantage point they constitute a certain sharing—limited, to be sure, but real—in divine power. This is what is meant, I believe, by the otherwise extraordinarily puzzling biblical teaching that man is made in the very image and likeness of God. But whether or not one recognizes biblical authority or believes in a personal God, it is true that human beings possess a power traditionally ascribed to divinity—namely, the power of an agent to cause what the agent is not caused to cause. This is the power to envisage a possible reality or state of affairs that does not now exist or obtain, to grasp the intelligible point—the value—of bringing it into being, and then to act by choice (and not merely by impulse or instinct, as a brute animal might) to bring it into being. That state of affairs may involve anything from the development of an intellectual skill, to the attainment of an item of knowledge, to the creation or critical appreciation of a work of art, to the establishment of marital communion. Its moral or cultural significance may be great or, far more commonly, comparatively minor. What matters here is that it is a product of human reason and freedom. It is the fruit of deliberation, judgment, and choice.

A further question will present itself to the mind of anyone who recognizes the God-likeness of our capacities for rationality and freedom, capacities that are immaterial and spiritual in nature. That question is whether beings capable of such powers could exist apart from a divine source and ground of their being. So one finds in the affirmation of these powers a decisive ground for the rejection of materialism, and one discerns the basis of an openness to, and even the roots of an argument for, theism. But more on that point later.

What about the authority for this view of human nature, the human good, human dignity, and human rights? Natural-law theorists are interested in the intelligible *reasons* people have for their choices and actions. We are particularly interested in reasons that can be identified without appeal to any authority apart from the authority of reason itself. This is not to deny that it is often reasonable to recognize and submit to religious or secular (e.g., legal) authority in deciding what to do and not do. Indeed, natural-law theorists have made important contributions to understanding why and how people can sometimes be morally bound to submit to, and be guided in their actions by, authority of various types.[7] But even here, the special concern of natural-law theorists is with the *reasons* people have for recognizing and honoring claims to authority. We do not simply appeal to authority to justify authority.

One might then ask whether human beings are in fact rational in anything more than an instrumental sense. Can we discern any intelligible reasons for human choices and actions? Everybody recognizes that some ends or purposes pursued through human action are intelligible at least insofar as they provide means to other ends. For example, people work to earn money, and their doing so is perfectly rational. Money is a valuable means to a great many important ends. No one doubts its instrumental value. The question is whether some ends or purposes are intelligible as providing *more than merely instrumental* reasons for acting. Are there intrinsic, as well as instrumental, goods? Skeptics deny that there are intelligible ends or purposes that make possible *rationally motivated* action. Natural-law theorists, by contrast, hold that friendship, knowledge, critical aesthetic appreciation, and certain other ends or purposes are intrinsically valuable. They are intelligibly "choice worthy," not as means to other ends but as ends in themselves. They cannot be reduced to, nor can their intelligible appeal be accounted for exclusively in terms of, emotion, feeling, desire, or other subrational motivating factors. These basic human goods are constitutive aspects of the well-being and fulfillment of human persons and the communities they form, and they thereby provide the foundations of moral judgments, including our judgments pertaining to justice and human rights.

Of course, plenty of people today embrace philosophical or ideological doctrines that deny the human capacities I maintain are at the core of human dignity. They adopt a purely instrumental and essentially noncognitivist view of practical reason (e.g., Hume's view that reason is nothing more than "the slave of the passions"[8]) and argue that the human experience of deliberation, judgment, and choice is illusory. The ends people pursue, they insist, are ultimately given by nonrational motivating factors, such as feeling, emotion, or desire. "The thoughts are to the desires," Hobbes has taught them to suppose, "as scouts and spies, to range abroad and find the way to the thing desired."[9] Truly rationally motivated action is impossible for creatures like us. There are no more than merely instrumental reasons for action—no basic human goods.

If proponents of this noncognitivist and subjectivist view of human action are right, then it seems to me that the entire business of ethics is a charade, and human dignity is a myth. But I don't think they are right. Indeed, I don't think that they can give any account of the norms of rationality to which they must appeal in making the case against reason and freedom, a case that is consistent with denying that people are capable of more than merely instrumental rationality and true freedom of choice. I do not deny that emotion figures in human action—obviously it does, and on many occasions it (or other subrational factors) does the main work of motivation. But I maintain that people can have, and often do have, basic reasons for their actions—reasons provided by ends they understand as humanly fulfilling *and desire precisely as such*. These ends, too, figure in motivation.[10]

Human Imperfection and Moral Failing

Now, if I and other natural-law theorists are correct in affirming that human reason can identify human rights as genuine grounds of obligation to others, how can we explain or understand widespread failures to recognize and respect human rights and other moral principles? As human beings, we are rational animals, but we are imperfectly rational. We are prone to making intellectual and moral mistakes and capable of behaving grossly unreasonably—especially when deflected by powerful emotions that run contrary to the demands of reasonableness. Christians have a name for this: sin. And another name: fallenness. We suffer weakness of will and darkness of intellect. Even when following our consciences, as we are morally bound to do, we can go wrong. A conscientious judgment may nevertheless be erroneous.

Sometimes people fail to recognize and respect human rights because they have self-interested motives for doing so. In most cases of exploitation, for example, the fundamental failing is moral, not intellectual. In some cases, though, intellectual and moral failures are closely connected. Selfishness, prejudice, partisanship, vanity, avarice, lust, ill will, and other moral delinquencies can, in ways that are sometimes quite subtle, impede sound ethical judgments, including judgments pertaining to human rights. Whole cultures or subcultures can be infected with moral failings that blind large numbers of people to truths about justice and human rights; ideologies hostile to these truths will almost always be both causes and effects of these failings. Consider the case of slavery in the antebellum American South. The ideology of white supremacy was both a cause of many people's blindness to the wickedness of slavery and an effect of the exploitation and degradation of its victims.

Natural Law and God

Let us turn now to the question of God and religious faith in natural-law theory. Most, but not all, natural-law theorists are theists. They believe that the moral order, like every other order in human experience, is what it is because God creates and sustains it as such. In accounting for the intelligibility of the created order, they infer the existence of a free and creative intelligence—a personal God. Indeed, they typically argue that God's creative free choice provides the only ultimately satisfactory account of the existence of the intelligibilities humans grasp in every domain of inquiry.[11]

Natural-law theorists do not deny that God can reveal moral truths, and most believe that God has chosen to reveal many such truths. But natural-law theorists also affirm that many moral truths, including some that are revealed, can also be grasped by ethical reflection apart from revelation. They assert, with St. Paul, that there is a law "written on the hearts" even of the Gentiles who did not know the law of Moses—a law the knowledge of which is sufficient for moral accountability. So the basic norms against murder and theft, though revealed in the Decalogue, are knowable even apart from God's special revelation.[12] We can know the natural law, and conform our conduct to its terms, by virtue of our natural human capacities for deliberation, judgment, and choice. The absence of a divine source of the natural law would be a puzzling thing, just as the absence of a divine source of any and every other intelligible order in human experience would be a puzzling thing. An atheist's puzzlement might well cause him to reconsider the idea that there is no divine source of the order we perceive and understand in the universe. It is far less likely, I think, to cause someone to conclude that our perception is illusory or that our understanding is a sham, though that is certainly logically possible.

The question then arises: can natural law—assuming that there truly are principles of natural law—provide some measure of common moral and even political ground for people who do not agree on the existence or the nature of God and the role of God in human affairs? In my view, anybody who acknowledges the human capacities for reason and freedom has good grounds for affirming human dignity and basic human rights. These grounds remain in place whether or not one adverts to the question "Is there a divine source of the moral order whose tenets we discern in inquiry regarding natural law and natural rights?" I happen to think that the answer to this question is "yes," and that we should be open to the possibility that God has revealed himself in ways that reinforce and supplement what can be known by unaided reason. But we do not need agreement on the answer so long as we agree about the truths that give rise to the question—namely, that human beings, possessing the God-like (literally *awesome*) powers of reason and freedom, are bearers of a profound dignity that is protected by certain basic rights.

So if there is a set of moral norms, including norms of justice and human rights, that can be known by rational inquiry, understanding, and judgment even apart from any special revelation, then these norms of natural law can provide the basis for a common understanding of human rights—an understanding that can be shared even in the absence of religious agreement. Of course, we should not expect consensus. There are moral skeptics who deny that there are moral truths. There are religious fideists who hold that moral truths cannot be known apart from God's special revelation. And even among those who believe in natural law, there are differences of opinion about its precise content and implications for certain issues. So it is, I believe, our permanent condition to discuss and debate these issues, both as a matter of abstract philosophy and as a matter of practical politics.

Challenges to Natural-Law Philosophy

It is sometimes regarded as an embarrassment to natural-law thinking that some great ancient and medieval figures in the natural-law tradition failed to recognize—or denied—human rights that contemporary natural-law theorists affirm and even regard as fundamental. Consider, for example, the basic human right to religious liberty. This right was not widely acknowledged in the past, and was even denied by some prominent natural-law theorists. As Oxford professor John Finnis has observed, they wrongly believed that a wide conception of liberty in matters of faith presupposed religious relativism or indifferentism, or entailed that religious vows were immoral or nonbinding or that ecclesial communities must be subservient to the state.[13] It is interesting that when the Catholic Church put itself on record firmly in support of the right to religious freedom in the Second Vatican Council's *Dignitatis Humanae*, it presented both a natural-law argument and an argument from specifically theological sources. The natural-law argument for religious liberty is founded on the obligation of each person to pursue the truth about religious matters and to live in conformity with his conscientious judgments.[14] This obligation is, in turn, rooted in the proposition that religion—considered as conscientious truth seeking regarding the ultimate sources of meaning and value—is a crucial dimension of human well-being and fulfillment. It is among the basic human goods that provide rational motivation for our choosing. The right to religious liberty follows from the dignity of man as a conscientious truth seeker.

This right and other human rights are denied and attacked today from various quarters, and in many parts of the world they are routinely violated. The ideological justification for their denial and violation can be religious or secular. In some parts of the world, religious freedom and other basic human rights are denied in the name of theological truth. In other parts of the world, the threats come from secularist ideologies. Where secularist ideologies are liberal in form, claims to an overarching right to autonomy (or a corrupted version of the true right to have one's equal dignity respected) are often asserted to justify choices, actions, and policies that natural-law theorists believe are unjust and undermine the common good. If the natural-law view of these matters is correct, then it is moral failings conspiring with intellectual errors that sustain ideologies that compromise human rights. In a certain sense, the failings are at opposite poles. Yet from a natural-law vantage point, partisans of the competing ideologies make valid criticisms of each other. Radical Islamists, for example, harshly condemn the decadent features of cultures in which the me-generation ideology of "if it feels good, do it" flourishes. On the other side, ideological liberals denounce the subjugation of women and the oppression of religious dissenters where fundamentalist Islam holds sway.

As natural-law theorists see it, threats to human dignity and human rights exist because all of us, as human beings, are imperfectly reasonable and imperfectly moral. To put it in Christian terms, we are fallen creatures, sinners. At the same time, hope exists because we really do possess the capacities for reasonableness and virtue; truth—including moral truth—is accessible to us and has its own splendor and powerful appeal. We will never, in this vale of tears, grasp the truth completely or in a way that is entirely free from errors. Nor will we fully live up to the moral truths we grasp. But just as we made progress by abolishing the evil of slavery, by ending legally sanctioned racial segregation, by recognizing the right to religious freedom, and by turning away from the eugenics policies once favored by so many respectable people, natural-law theorists hope that we can make progress, and reverse declines, in other areas, including in protecting human life against abortion, embryo-destructive research, and euthanasia, and in protecting and revitalizing the marriage culture, beginning with the preservation of marriage as the conjugal union of husband and wife.

Of course, people who reject the natural-law understanding of human dignity and human rights will differ from natural-law theorists on questions of what constitutes progress and decline. Radical Islamists will regard the type of religious freedom defended by natural-law theorists as licensing heresy and religious irresponsibility, and they will see natural-law ideas as just a rhetorically toned-down form of Western liberal secularism. By contrast, liberal secularists will regard natural-law ideas about abortion, sexuality, and other hot-button moral issues as intolerant and oppressive—a philosophically gussied-up form of religious fundamentalism. In the end, though, natural-law ideas—like radical Islamist or liberal secularist ideas—will have to stand or fall on their merits. Anyone who wonders whether they are sound or unsound will have to consider the arguments offered in their support and the counterarguments advanced by their critics.

The "New" Natural-Law Theory

Even among people who are regarded, or who regard themselves, as natural-law theorists, there are competing accounts of natural law and natural rights. I have in various writings associated myself with what is sometimes called the "new natural-law theory" of Germain Grisez and John Finnis. But whether there is anything much that is really *new* in our approach is questionable. The core of what Grisez, Finnis, and I say at the level of fundamental moral theory is present, at least implicitly, in the writings of Aristotle, Thomas Aquinas, and other ancient, medieval, and early modern thinkers. Some commentators have insisted that what we say is fundamentally new (and, from the point of view of our critics within the natural-law camp, wrongheaded) because we are resolute about respecting the distinction between description and prescription—that is, about avoiding the fallacy (as we see it) of proposing to derive normative judgments from *purely* factual premises *describing* human nature. It would be fallacious, for example, to infer the value of knowledge from the fact that human beings are naturally curious and desire to know. But here we are being faithful to the methodological insights and strictures of Aquinas. Contrary to what is sometimes supposed, he recognized that what would later come to be called the "naturalistic fallacy" is indeed a fallacy, and he was far stricter about avoiding it than even David Hume, who is sometimes credited with "discovering" it.[15]

If, standing on the shoulders of Aristotle and Aquinas, we have been able to contribute something significant to the tradition of natural-law theorizing, it is founded on Professor Grisez's work showing how "modes of responsibility" follow as implications of the integral directiveness of the most basic principles of practical reason—principles that direct human action toward basic human goods and away from their privations. The modes of responsibility are intermediate in their generality between the first and most general principle of morality ("one ought always to choose . . . in a way that is compatible with a will towards integral human fulfillment") and fully specified moral norms that govern particular choices. The modes include the Golden Rule of fairness and the Pauline Principle, which holds that acts that are in themselves evil (*mala in se*) may not be done, even for the sake of good consequences. They begin to specify what it means to act (or to fail to act) in ways that are compatible with a will oriented positively (or, at least, not negatively) toward the well-being of all human beings in all the respects in which human beings can flourish—integral human fulfillment.

Our account of the modes of responsibility helps to make clear the ways that natural-law theories are both like and unlike utilitarian (and other consequentialist) approaches to morality, on the one hand, and Kantian (or "deontological") approaches, on the other. Like utilitarian approaches, and unlike Kantian ones, natural-law theories are fundamentally concerned with human well-being and fulfillment—and, indeed, with identifying principles that direct our choosing toward basic human goods and away from their privations—as the starting points of ethical reflection. Unlike utilitarian approaches, however, they understand the basic forms of human good (as they figure in options for morally significant choosing) as incommensurable in ways that render senseless the utilitarian strategy of trying to choose the option that overall and in the long run will bring about the net best proportion of benefit to harm (however "benefit" and "harm" may be understood and defined). Like Kantians, natural-law theorists reject aggregative accounts of morality that regard the achievement of sufficiently good consequences or the avoidance of sufficiently bad ones as justifying choices that in ordinary circumstances would be excluded by application of moral principles. Unlike Kantians, however, they do not believe that moral norms can be identified and justified apart from a consideration of the integral directiveness of the principles of practical reason directing human choice and action toward what is humanly fulfilling and away from what is contrary to human well-being. Natural-law theorists do not believe in purely "deontological" moral norms. Practical reasoning is reasoning about *both* the "right" and the "good," and the two are connected. The content of the human good shapes moral norms inasmuch as such norms entail the basic aspects of human well-being and fulfillment considered integrally.

Such a view presupposes the possibility of free choice—that is, a choice that is the pure product neither of external forces nor of inter-

nal but subrational motivating factors, such as sheer desire. So a complete theory of natural law will include an account of principles of
practical reason, including moral norms, as principles for the rational
guidance of free choices, and a defense of free choice as a genuine
possibility. This entails the rejection of strict rationalism, according
to which all phenomena are viewed as caused. It understands human
beings—some human beings, at least sometimes—as capable of causing realities that they bring into existence *for reasons by free choices*.
On the natural-law account of human action, freedom and reason
are mutually entailed. If people were not really free to choose among
options—free in the sense that nothing but the choosing itself settles
what option gets chosen—truly rationally motivated action would not
be possible. Conversely, if rationally motivated action were not possible, the experience we have of freely choosing would be illusory.[16]

Another feature of the natural-law account of human action that
"new" natural-law theorists stress is the set of distinctions between
various modes of voluntariness. We understand morality as fundamentally a matter of rectitude in willing. In sound moral judgments
and upright choices and actions, the will of the agent is oriented positively toward the human good integrally conceived. In choosing and
acting, one is not pursuing every human good—that is not possible—
but one is pursuing at least one basic human good well, and if one is
choosing and acting in a morally upright way, one is respecting the
others. Yet is it not obvious that many upright choices—choices of good
ends sought by morally good means—have some bad consequences?

For example, we know with moral certainty that by authorizing
highway drivers to operate at a speed of, say, sixty-five miles per hour,
we are permitting a circumstance to exist in which several thousand
people each year will be killed in automobile accidents. But according to the natural-law understanding of human action, there is a real
and sometimes morally critical distinction between *intending* harm to
a basic human good (and thus to a person, since human goods are
not mere abstractions but are aspects of the well-being of flesh-and-
blood human beings) and accepting foreseen harm as a *side effect* of

an otherwise morally justified choice. For instance, intending to take someone's life (whether as an end in itself or as a means to another goal) is distinct from accepting death as a side effect (even if the side effect is clearly foreseen, as we foresee the deaths of motorists and passengers on the highways in ordinary accidents).[17]

Natural Law and Moral Virtue

Let me conclude with one more proposition stressed by natural-law theorists—namely, that by our choices and actions we not only alter states of affairs in the world external to us but also determine and constitute ourselves (for better or worse) as persons with a certain character.[18] Recognition of this self-shaping or "intransitive" quality of morally significant choosing leads to a focus on virtues as habits born of upright choosing that orient and dispose us to further upright choosing—especially in the face of temptations to behave immorally.

People sometimes ask: is natural law about rules or virtues? The answer from the point of view of the "new" natural-law theory is that it is about *both*. A complete theory of natural law identifies norms for distinguishing right from wrong as well as habits or traits of character whose cultivation disposes people to choose in conformity with the norms and thus compatibly with what we might call, borrowing a phrase from Kant, a good will—a will toward integral human fulfillment.

9

WHY MORAL TRUTHS MATTER

THE OBLIGATIONS AND purposes of law and government are to protect public health, safety, and morals and to advance the general welfare—including, preeminently, protecting people's fundamental rights and basic liberties.

At first blush, this classic formulation (or combination of classic formulations) seems to grant vast and sweeping powers to public authority. Yet in truth, the general welfare—the common good—requires that government be limited. Government's responsibility is primary when the questions involve defending the nation from attack and subversion, protecting people from physical assaults and various other forms of depredation, and maintaining public order. In other ways, however, its role is *subsidiary*: to support the work of the families, religious communities, and other institutions of civil society that shoulder the primary burden of forming upright and decent citizens, caring for those in need, and encouraging people to meet their responsibilities to one another while discouraging them from harming themselves or others.

Governmental respect for individual freedom and the autonomy of nongovernmental spheres of authority is, then, a requirement of political morality. Government must not try to run people's lives or usurp the roles and responsibilities of families, religious bodies, and other character- and culture-forming authoritative communities. The usurpation of the just authority of families, religious communities, and other institutions is unjust in principle, often seriously so, and the record of big government in the twentieth century—even when it has not degenerated into vicious totalitarianism—shows that it does little good in the long run and frequently harms those it seeks to help.

Limited government is a key tenet of classic liberalism—the liberalism of people like Madison and Tocqueville—although today it is regarded as a conservative ideal. In any event, someone who believes in limited government need not embrace libertarianism. The strict libertarian position, it seems to me, goes much too far in depriving government of even its subsidiary role. It underestimates the importance of maintaining a reasonably healthy moral ecology, especially for the rearing of children, and it misses the legitimate role of government in supporting the nongovernmental institutions that shoulder the main burden of assisting those in need.

Still, libertarianism responds to certain truths about big government, especially in government's bureaucratic and managerial dimensions. Economic freedom cannot guarantee political liberty and the just autonomy of the institutions of civil society, but, in the absence of economic liberty, other honorable personal and institutional freedoms are rarely secure. Moreover, the concentration of economic power in the hands of government is something every true friend of civil liberties should, by now, have learned to fear.

There is an even deeper truth—one going beyond economics—to which libertarianism responds: law and government exist to protect human persons and secure their well-being. It is not the other way round, as communist and other forms of collectivist ideology suppose. Individuals are not cogs in a social wheel. Stringent norms of political justice forbid persons being treated as mere servants or instrumentalities of the state. These norms equally exclude sacrificing the dignity and rights of persons for the sake of some supposed "greater overall good."

What Is True?

It is a profound mistake to suppose that the principle of limited government is rooted in the denial of moral truth or a putative requirement of governments to refrain from acting on the basis of judgments about moral truth. For our commitment to limited government is itself the fruit of moral conviction—conviction ultimately founded on truths that our nation's Founders proclaimed as self-evident: namely, "that all men are created equal, that they are endowed by their Creator with certain unalienable rights, that among these are life, liberty, and the pursuit of happiness."

At the foundation is the proposition that each human being possesses a profound, inherent, and equal dignity simply by virtue of his nature as a rational creature—a creature possessing, albeit in limited measure (and in the case of some human beings in root or rudimentary form), reason and freedom, powers that make possible such human and humanizing phenomena as intellectual inquiry, aesthetic appreciation, respect for self and others, friendship, and love. This great truth of natural law, which is at the heart of our civilizational and civic order, has its theological expression in the biblical teaching that man, unlike the brute animals, is made in the very image and likeness of the divine creator and ruler of the universe.

It is critical to bear this great truth in mind. We must not adopt a merely pragmatic understanding or speak only of practical considerations in addressing the pressing issues of our day. Sound positions cannot be effectively advanced and defended by citizens and statesmen who are unwilling or unable to engage moral arguments. That is why we should, in my opinion, rededicate ourselves to understanding and making the moral argument for the sanctity of human life in all stages and conditions, and the dignity of marriage as the conjugal union of one man and one woman.

Please do not misunderstand me. I am not saying that practical considerations should or even can be left out of the argument. In a proper understanding of morality, practical considerations are not "merely" practical. The moral case for the reform of unilateral-divorce laws, for example, includes reference to the devastating, poverty-inducing, crime-promoting social consequences of the collapse of a healthy marriage culture and the role of unilateral divorce in contributing to the collapse. The moral argument for restoring legal protection to the unborn includes reference to the adverse psychological and, in some cases, physical consequences of abortion on many women who undergo the procedure. Our task should be to understand the moral truth and speak it in season and out of season. We will be told by the pure pragmatists that the public is too far gone in moral relativism or even moral delinquency to be reached by moral argument. But we must have faith that truth is luminously powerful, so that if we bear witness to the truth about, say, marriage and the sanctity of human life—lovingly, civilly, but also passionately and with determination—and if we honor the truth in advancing our positions, then even many of our fellow citizens who now find themselves on the other side of these issues will come around.

To speak of truth frightens some people today. They evidently believe that people who claim to know the truth about anything—and especially about moral matters—are fundamentalists and potential totalitarians. But, as Amherst professor Hadley Arkes has patiently explained, those on the other side of the great debates over social issues such as abortion and marriage make truth claims—moral truth claims—all the time. They assert their positions with no less confidence and no more doubt than one finds in the advocacy of pro-lifers and defenders of conjugal marriage. They proclaim that women have a fundamental right to abortion. They maintain that "love makes a family" and make other strong and controversial moral claims. The question, then, is not whether there are truths about such things as the morality of abortion and the nature of marriage; the question in each case is, what is true?

What is centrally and decisively true about human embryos and fetuses is that they are living individuals of the species *Homo sapiens*—members of the human family—at early stages of their natural development. Each of us was once an embryo, just as each of us was once an adolescent, a child, an infant, and a fetus. Each of us developed from the embryonic into and through the fetal, infant, child, and adolescent stages of our lives, and into adulthood, with his or her distinctness, unity, and identity fully intact. As modern embryology confirms beyond any possibility of doubt, we were never parts of our mothers; we were, from the beginning, complete, self-integrating organisms that developed to maturity by a gradual, gapless, and self-directed process. Our foundational principle of the profound, inherent, and equal dignity of every human being demands that all members of the human family be respected and protected irrespective not only of race, sex, and ethnicity but also of age, size, location, stage of development, and condition of dependency. To exclude anyone from the law's protection is to treat him unjustly.

And so it seems to me that justice demands our resolute opposition to the killing of human embryos for biomedical research and to elective abortion. If we would do unto others as we would have them do unto us, then we will insist that law and public policy respect the lives of every member of the human family, including those at what the late Paul Ramsey called the edges of life—the unborn, the severely handicapped, the frail, the elderly.

Of course, politics is the art of the possible. And, as Frederick Douglass reminded us in his tribute to Lincoln, public opinion and other constraints sometimes limit what can be done at the moment to advance any just cause. The pro-life movement has in recent years settled on an incrementalist strategy for protecting nascent human life. So long as incrementalism is not a euphemism for surrender or neglect, it can be entirely honorable. Many lives have been saved, and many more can be saved, by laws forbidding the public funding of abortion; requiring parental consent or at least notification for abortions performed on minors; mandating full disclosure to women contemplating abortions of factual information regarding fetal development and the possible physical and mental health consequences of submitting to abortion; forbidding late-term abortions and particularly gruesome methods of abortion, such as partial-birth abortion; and banning the production of human beings by cloning or other methods for purposes of research in which they are destroyed in the embryonic or fetal stages. Moreover, planting premises in the law whose logic demands, in the end, full respect for all members of the human family can be a valuable thing to do, even where those premises seem modest.

What Is Marriage?

Let me turn to the other great moral question we confront today: marriage. The institution of marriage is battered in our culture, but it is not lost. Much damage has been done by bad legislation and policy, almost always in the name of reform. That legislation and policy is now itself in need of reform.

If we are to restore and secure the institution of marriage, we must recover a sound understanding of what marriage is and why it is in the public interest for law and policy to take cognizance of it and support it. Marriage is a prepolitical form of association—what might be called a natural institution. It is not created by law, though law recognizes and regulates it in every culture. Nowhere is it treated as a purely private matter.

Some on the libertarian fringe toy with the idea that marriage could be privatized, and even some who are not on the fringe wonder whether that might be the best solution to the controversy over same-sex marriage. I understand why someone would consider this idea, but it strikes me as a bad one. There is a reason that all cultures treat marriage as a matter of public concern and even recognize it in law and regulate it. The family is the fundamental unit of society. Governments rely on families to produce something that governments need—but, on their own, could not possibly produce: upright, decent people who make honest, law-abiding, public-spirited citizens. And marriage is the indispensable foundation of the family. Although all marriages in all cultures have their imperfections, children flourish in an environment where they benefit from the love and care of both mother and father, and from the committed and exclusive love of their parents for each other.

Anyone who believes in limited government should strongly back government support for the family. Does this sound paradoxical? In the absence of a strong marriage culture, families fail to form, and when they do form they are often unstable. Absentee fathers become a serious problem, out-of-wedlock births are common, and a train of social pathologies follows. With families failing to perform their health, education, and welfare functions, the demand for government grows, whether in the form of greater policing or as a provider of other social services. Bureaucracies must be created, and they inexorably expand—indeed, they become powerful lobbyists for their own pres-ervation and expansion. Everyone suffers, with the poorest and most vulnerable suffering most.

Practical or pragmatic arguments are legitimate and important. But the effective defense of marriage against the current onslaught will require an understanding of marriage as a matter of moral truth. Too few pro-marriage politicians are willing to say much about what marriage actually is. This gives those who would abolish the conju-gal conception of marriage an important advantage in public debate. They hammer away with their rhetoric of "love makes a family" and demand to know how anyone's marriage would be threatened if the same-sex partners next door were also allowed to marry.

Everyone agrees that marriage, whatever else it is or does, is a relationship in which *persons* are united. But what are persons? And how is it possible for two or more of them to unite? According to the view implicit in sexual-liberationist ideology, the person is under-stood as the conscious and desiring aspect of the self. The person, thus understood, inhabits a body, but the body is regarded (if often only implicitly) as a subpersonal part of the human being—rather than part of the personal reality of the human being whose body it is. The body is viewed as serving the interests of the conscious and desiring aspect of the self by functioning as an instrument by which the individual produces or otherwise participates in satisfactions and other desirable experiences and realizes various objectives and goals.

For those who formally or informally accept this understanding of what human beings are, personal unity cannot be achieved by bodily union as such. Persons unite by uniting *emotionally* (or, as those of a certain religious cast of mind say, *spiritually*). If this is true, then persons of the same sex can unite and share sexual experiences together that they suppose will enhance their personal union by enabling them to express affection, share the uniquely intense pleasure of sex, and feel more intensely by virtue of their sex play.

The alternate view of what persons are is the one embodied in both our historic law of marriage and what Isaiah Berlin once referred to as the central tradition of Western thought. According to this view, human beings are not nonbodily persons inhabiting and using nonpersonal bodies. The body is not a mere instrument for inducing satisfactions for the sake of the conscious and desiring aspect of the self. Rather, a human person is a dynamic unity of body, mind, and spirit. The body, far from being an instrument, is intrinsically part of the personal reality of the human being. Bodily union is thus personal union, and comprehensive personal union—marital union— is founded on bodily union. What is unique about marriage is that it truly is a comprehensive sharing of life, a sharing founded on the bodily union made uniquely possible by the sexual complementarity of man and woman—a complementarity that makes it possible for two human beings to become, in the language of the Bible, "one flesh," and for this one-flesh union to be the foundation of a relationship in which it is intelligible for two persons to bind themselves to each other in pledges of permanence, monogamy, and fidelity.

So, then, how should we understand what marriage *is*? Marriage, considered not as a mere legal convention or cultural artifact, is a one-flesh communion of persons that is consummated and actualized by acts that are procreative in type, whether or not they are procreative in effect. It is an intrinsic human good, and, precisely as such, it provides a more than instrumental reason for choice and action.

The bodily union of spouses in marital acts is the biological matrix of their marriage as a comprehensive, multilevel sharing of life: a relationship that unites the spouses at all levels of their being. Marriage is naturally ordered to the good of procreation (and is, indeed, uniquely apt for the nurturing and education of children) as well as to the good of spousal unity. At the same time, it is not a mere instrumental good whose purpose is the generating and rearing of children. Marriage, considered as a one-flesh union, is *intrinsically* valuable.

To understand how it can be the case that, on the one hand, the generating and rearing of children is a perfection of marriage and not something merely incidental to it and, on the other, marriage is not simply a means to the good of generating and rearing children, it is important to see that the procreative and unitive goods of marriage are tightly bound together. The one-flesh unity of spouses is possible *because* human (like other mammalian) males and females, by mating, unite organically—they form a single procreative principle.

It is a plain matter of biological fact that reproduction is a single function, yet it is carried out not by an individual male or female human being but by a male and female as a mated pair. So in respect of reproduction, albeit not in respect of other activities (such as locomotion or digestion), the mated pair is a single organism; the partners form a single procreative principle: they become one flesh. Some people desperately want to deny this. But consider this thought experiment: Imagine a type of bodily, rational being that reproduces not by mating but by some individual performance. Imagine that for these beings, however, locomotion or digestion is performed not by individuals but only by biologically complementary pairs that unite for this purpose. Would anybody acquainted with such beings have difficulty understanding that in respect of reproduction the organism performing the function is the individual, while in respect of locomotion or digestion the organism performing the function is the united pair? Would anybody deny that the unity effectuated for purposes of locomotion or digestion is an organic unity? Precisely because of the organic unity achieved in marital acts, the bodies of persons who unite biologically are not reduced to the status of extrinsic instruments of sexual satisfaction or expression. Rather, the end, goal, and intelligible point of sexual intercourse is the intelligible good of marriage itself as a one-flesh union.

On this understanding, the body is not treated as a mere instrument of the conscious and desiring aspect of the self whose interests in satisfactions are the putative ends to which sexual acts are means. Nor is sex itself instrumentalized. The one-flesh unity of marriage is not just an *instrumental good*, a reason for acting whose intelligibility as a reason depends on other ends to which it is a means. This unity is an *intrinsic good*, a reason for acting whose intelligibility as a reason depends on no ulterior end. The central and justifying point of sex is not pleasure, however much sexual pleasure is rightly sought as an aspect of the perfection of marital union; the point of sex, rather, is marriage itself, considered as an essentially and irreducibly bodily union of persons—a union effectuated and renewed by acts of sexual congress. Because sex is not instrumentalized in marital acts, such acts are free of the self-alienating qualities that have made wise and thoughtful people from Plato to Augustine, and from the biblical writers to Kant, treat sexual immorality as a matter of the utmost seriousness.

In truly marital acts, the desire for pleasure and even for offspring is integrated with and, in an important sense, subordinated to the central and defining good of one-flesh unity. The integration of subordinate goals with the marital good ensures that such acts effect no practical dualism that separates the body from the conscious and desiring aspect of the self and treats the body as a mere instrument for the production of pleasure, the generation of offspring, or any other extrinsic goal.

But one may ask, what about procreation? On the traditional view of marriage, is not the sexual union of spouses instrumentalized to the goal of having children? It is true that St. Augustine in certain writings seems to be a proponent of this view. The conception of marriage as an instrumental good was rejected, however, by the mainstream of philosophical and theological reflection from the late Middle Ages forward, and the understanding of sex and marriage that came to be embodied in both canon law and civil law does not treat marriage as merely instrumental to having children. Western matrimonial law has traditionally and universally understood marriage as consummated by acts fulfilling the behavioral conditions of procreation, whether or not the nonbehavioral conditions of procreation happen to obtain.

By contrast, the sterility of spouses—so long as they are capable of consummating their marriage by fulfilling the behavioral conditions of procreation (and, thus, of achieving true bodily, organic unity)—has never been treated as an impediment to marriage, even where sterility is certain and even certain to be permanent. Children who may be conceived in marital acts are understood not as ends extrinsic to marriage but rather as gifts—fulfilling for the couple as a marital unit and not merely as individuals—that supervene on acts whose central defining and justifying point is precisely the marital unity of spouses. I and others have elsewhere developed more fully the moral case for the conjugal conception of marriage as the union of one man and one woman pledged to permanence and fidelity and committed to caring for children who come as the fruit of their matrimonial union. I have argued that acceptance of the idea that two persons of the same sex could actually be married to each other would make nonsense of key features of marriage and would necessarily require abandoning any ground of principle for supposing that marriage is the union of only two persons, as opposed to three or more. Only a thin veneer of sentiment, if it happens to exist (and only for as long as it exists), can prevent acceptance of polyamory as a legitimate marital option once we have given up the principle of marriage as a male-female union.

To those arguments, I will here add an additional reason to reject the idea of same-sex marriage: the acceptance of the idea would result in a massive undermining of religious liberty and family autonomy, as supporters of same-sex marriage would, in the name of equality, demand the use of governmental power to whip others into line. The experience of Massachusetts as well as foreign jurisdictions is that once marriage is compromised or formally redefined, principles of nondiscrimination are quickly used as cudgels against religious communities and families who wish to uphold true marriage by precept and example.

Part of the trouble pro-marriage politicians and others have in defending marriage follows from the fact that these pathologies that afflict the marriage culture are widespread, and supporters of marriage, being human, are not immune to them. This is not to excuse anyone from personal responsibility.

But the fact is that sustaining a marriage despite the collapse of many of its social supports is difficult. In trying to stand up for marriage, political leaders, intellectuals, and activists who have had marital problems of their own are subjected to charges of hypocrisy. Many therefore censor themselves. As a result, the pro-marriage movement loses the leadership of some of its most talented people. The question of same-sex marriage is critically important, but rebuilding and renewing the marriage culture goes far beyond it. By abolishing the basic understanding of marriage as an inherently conjugal union, legal recognition of same-sex marriage would be disastrous. But many would say that such recognition would simply ratify the collapse of marriage that followed from widespread divorce, nonmarital sexual cohabitation, and other factors having nothing to do with homosexual conduct. It is certainly true that the origins of the pathologies afflicting marriage lie in such factors. Rebuilding the marriage culture will require careful, incremental legal reforms to roll back unilateral divorce, accompanied by herculean efforts on the part of nongovernmental institutions—especially churches and other religious bodies—to prepare couples more adequately for marriage, help them nurture strong marital relationships, and assist those who are dealing with marital problems. Public-private partnerships will be essential, in my view, to cutting the divorce rate. This won't be easy. If marriage weren't so important, it wouldn't be worth trying.

Like abortion, same-sex marriage has been advanced in some

cases by socially liberal activist judges who exercise creative powers of constitutional interpretation. That gives us reason to pursue with new dedication the larger fight against the judicial usurpation of democratic legislative authority—another profound abuse of governmental power.

Despite extraordinarily broad support for same-sex marriage in the universities and the media, initiatives to preserve marriage as the union of one man and one woman have prevailed, usually by decisive margins, when they have been put on the ballot. Even in the deep blue state of Wisconsin, a marriage initiative prevailed in a near-landslide on Election Day in November 2006—in the course of what was around the country a big night for liberals and Democrats. With the Federal Marriage Amendment stalled, state marriage initiatives and constitutional amendments are vitally important. The issue should be taken to the people at every possible opportunity. Even in the bluest states, marriage will have a stronger chance with the people than with the judges or even with the legislators.

Some people have wondered whether the best way to handle the conflict over marriage in our politics is a federalist solution, one that eschews a national policy on marriage and leaves it to each state to define marriage as it sees fit. This, too, I think is a bad idea. Just as the nation could not endure half slave and half free but eventually had to go all one way or all the other, we will not be able to get by with a situation in which some couples are "married" in one state, not married when they move to or travel through the next, and married again when they reach a third. If same-sex "marriage" is legally recognized in a small number of states, it will spread throughout the nation, either through judicial action under the Constitution's full faith and credit clause or by the working of informal cultural pressures. Some states may try to hold out, but they will sooner or later be forced into line. That is why we need a national resolution of the issue, and probably a constitutional one. Believers in marriage did not start this fight, and we are loath to interfere with traditional state powers—precisely because we view federalism as serving limited government and embodying our belief in the principle of subsidiarity. But judicial usurpation has triggered a chain of events that will result in the radical redefinition of marriage unless action is taken at the national level—going beyond the Defense of Marriage Act (which the courts may yet strike down)—to preserve the conjugal conception of marriage.

Finally, there is the question of civil unions. Some politicians and others say that they are against same-sex marriage but in favor of legal recognition of same-sex partnerships, with all or most of the rights and responsibilities of marriage, only falling under a different rubric. If law and policy are at least to do no harm to marriage, it is critical that they avoid treating nonmarital conduct and relationships as if they were marital. There are clear moral lines—and not merely semantic ones—between what is marital and what is not, and the law should respect them. If they are blurred or erased, the public understanding of the meaning of marriage will erode. Some of the benefits traditionally associated with marriage may legitimately be made more widely available in an effort to meet the needs of people who are financially interdependent with a person or persons to whom they are not married. Private contracts between such people should be sufficient to accomplish all or most of what they consider desirable. If, however, a jurisdiction moves in the direction of creating a formalized system of domestic partnerships, it is morally crucial that the privileges, immunities, and other benefits and responsibilities contained in the package offered to nonmarried partners *not* be predicated on the existence or presumption of a sexual relationship between them. Benefits should be made available to, for example, a grandparent and adult grandchild who are living together and caring for each other. The needs that domestic-partnership schemes seek to address have nothing to do with whether the partners share a bed and what they do in it. The law should simply take no cognizance of the question of a sexual relationship. It should not, that is, treat a nonmarital sexual relationship as a public good.

Urgent Causes

The defense of life against abortion and embryo-destructive research calls America back to the founding principles of our regime and to reflection on the justifying point and purposes of law and government. The defense of marriage, meanwhile, shores up the cultural preconditions for a regime of democratic republican government dedicated to human equality, fundamental human rights, and principled limits on governmental powers. These causes should not be regarded as distractions from other pressing goals, such as economic growth, assistance to the needy, environmental protection, and the defense of the nation against terrorism. They are, rather, causes that spring from the foundational moral purposes of law and the state. They are today among the most urgent causes.

10

TWO CONCEPTS OF LIBERTY
... AND CONSCIENCE

ONE OF THE dubious achievements of the Obama administration has been to put the issue of religious freedom and the rights of conscience back on the agenda in American politics. Most notoriously, the administration has sought to impose upon private employers, including religious people and even religious institutions, a requirement to provide health insurance coverage for abortion-inducing drugs, sterilizations, and contraceptives, even if the employer cannot, as a matter of conscience, comply. The administration's mandates have been challenged on statutory and constitutional grounds in federal courts around the country, and there is a high likelihood that the Supreme Court, pursuant to the Religious Freedom Restoration Act (RFRA), will require exemptions for religious employers and others who conscientiously object.

Of course, the administration contends that its mandates do not violate religious freedom or the rights of conscience, properly understood. Indeed, its defenders argue that the mandates—which contain only the narrowest of exemptions—are necessary to protect the freedom and rights of conscience of women who wish to use contraceptives and abortifacient drugs such as "Ella" (some of which they deny are actually abortion-inducing) or to avail themselves of sterilization procedures. So we find people on both sides of the debate claiming to be the defenders of liberty and conscience. It would be well for us, then, to pause to reflect in a philosophically rigorous way on the moral foundations of competing concepts of liberty and conscience. To that end, we might consider the ideas of two of modern intellectual history's most distinguished thinkers—John Stuart Mill and John Henry Newman.

Mill and Newman were the greatest English intellectuals of the nineteenth century. They were men of deep and wide learning and formidable intelligence. Both wrote powerful defenses of freedom. Mill's was in the form of an essay entitled simply "On Liberty" (1859). There he defended what he described as "one very simple principle [that is] entitled to govern absolutely the dealings of society with the individual in the way of compulsion and control, whether the means used be physical force in the form of legal penalties, or the moral coercion of public opinion." That principle has been dubbed Mill's "harm principle":

> The only purpose for which power can be rightfully exercised over any member of a civilized community, against his will, is to prevent harm to others. His own good, either physical or moral, is not a sufficient warrant. He cannot rightfully be compelled to do or forbear because it will be better for him to do so, because it will make him happier, because, in the opinions of others, to do so would be wise, or even right.[1]

Mill's principle is frequently invoked in cocktail party conversations and in freshman class discussions. It has, however, been sharply criticized even by philosophers of a generally liberal persuasion, such as the late H. L. A. Hart of Oxford University, who argue that it is too sweeping in ruling out paternalistic reasons for limiting certain forms of liberty.[2] More conservative philosophers, I myself among them, have been even more skeptical and critical. For present purposes, though, I am less interested in the scope or breadth of Mill's principle, or in its content, than in its *ground*. What, for Mill, provides the moral basis for respecting people's liberty? What is the basis of the obligation?

Mill doesn't hide the ball:

> It is proper to state that I forego any advantage which could be derived to my argument from the idea of abstract right, as a thing independent of utility. I regard utility as the ultimate appeal on all ethical questions; but it must be utility in the largest sense, grounded on the permanent interests of man as a progressive being.[3]

Mill grounds his principle of liberty and the obligation to respect it in the belief that respect for liberty will, in its consequences, on the whole be beneficial to . . . well, to whom? Or to what?

To the community? Which community? Local? National? Imperial? International? Mill doesn't exactly say. As we've seen, he does, however, say this: the concept of utility that must govern as the criterion of morality in our choosing, and as the ground of moral obligation, including the obligation to respect and protect liberty, must be utility "in the largest sense, as grounded on the permanent interests of man as a progressive being."

Note two things about Mill's defense of liberty, whether it is freedom of speech (which Mill treats as central) or freedom of religion (which interests him less) or any other freedom. First, the ultimate basis of the moral claims of freedom is social benefit: "utility." It is not "abstract right." Second, Mill's view of humanity is imbued with nineteenth-century optimism and belief in progress. Man is naturally good—a "progressive being." He therefore will, in his cultural and personal maturity, do well by himself and others if only he is left free of paternalistic and moralistic constraints to engage in experiments in living from which he, corporately and individually, will learn what conduces to happiness and what does not. Freed from the old moralisms and religious and other superstitions—liberated to be the progressive being that, by nature, he is—he will flourish. Those old moralisms and superstitions—far from preventing him from descending into vice and degradation, or even assisting him in that project—tie him down and wound his spirit. They profoundly impede (and have impeded) his full flourishing and self-realization. Free to do as they please, free to do what they want to do so long as they do not harm others, mature persons in mature cultures will, on the whole, want to do good and productive—i.e., utility-enhancing—things. (And there is no danger of regression to the former condition of things in barbarian societies and in small threatened communities, in both of which cases Mill's defense of liberty did not, he thought, hold good.)

I have been severely critical of Mill's concept and defense of liberty.[4] His naive optimism and progressivism—they were wrong, to be sure. And the utilitarianism, that was wrong too. The Christian philosophical anthropology Mill regarded as a relic of superstitious ages has proved to be far more plausible and reliable than the alternative that Mill, quite uncritically, accepted. And utilitarian and other forms of consequentialism in ethics are in the end unworkable and even incoherent. They presuppose a kind of commensurability of human values and their particular instantiations that simply does not square either with reality or with conditions of deliberation and choice. The basic aspects of human well-being and fulfillment that together constitute the ideal of integral human flourishing are reducible neither to each other nor to some common substance or factor they share. These basic human goods, though they provide more than merely instrumental reasons for action and partially constitute our all-around well-being (which is how and why they are intrinsic, rather than merely instrumental, goods), are good not in a univocal sense, as if they were constituted by the same substance but merely manifested it differently, but only in an analogical sense. They differ substantially as distinct dimensions of our flourishing and fulfillments of our capacities as human persons (rational animals); they are, as such, incommensurable in a way that renders hopeless the utilitarian project of identifying an option for choice—or even a rule for choosing—that promises "the greatest happiness of the greatest number."[5]

But Mill was by no means completely wrong. He was right, in my opinion, in forgoing an appeal to "abstract right" and looking for the moral ground of liberty in a consideration of the well-being and fulfillment—in a word, the flourishing—of human beings (what he calls "the end of man" and characterizes as "bringing human beings themselves closer to the best they can be"). People have rights, including rights to liberties, because there are basic human goods—that is, ends or purposes that not only conduce to but actually *constitute* their flourishing. The full defense of any particular liberty, including the freedom of religion, requires the identification and defense of those human goods, those basic aspects of human well-being and fulfillment, that the liberty secures, protects, or advances.

The trouble was that Mill had something of a tin ear for religion, at least in its traditional manifestations. His "harm principle" would, of course, extend to religious activities and practices, but I doubt that he viewed those as having much real value. They would, I suspect he believed, soon wither away in an age of freedom (since man is a "progressive being," and freedom brings "enlightenment").

By contrast, John Henry Newman was a religious genius. And his understanding of religion enabled him to produce an account of freedom—in particular the freedom of conscience—that was profoundly superior to Mill's, and from which we today have much to learn. Like Mill, Newman does not appeal to "abstract right" as the ground of liberty, but instead he locates the foundation of honorable freedoms in a concern for human excellence and human flourishing. Newman has the immense advantage over Mill of believing in human fallenness (what Christian faith knows as original sin), and so he is spared naive optimism and faith in human progress. Moreover, as a serious Christian, he sees no appeal whatsoever in a utilitarian approach to moral decision making (and all that it presupposes and entails). He is cognizant of both the need for *restraints* on freedom, lest men descend into vice and self-degradation, and the supreme importance of central freedoms as conditions for the realization of values that truly constitute the integral flourishing of men and women as free and rational creatures—creatures whose freedom and rationality reflects their having been made in the very image and likeness of God.

Newman's dedication to the rights of conscience is well known. Even long after his conversion from Anglicanism to Catholicism, he famously toasted "the Pope, yes, but conscience first," as he put it in his *Letter to the Duke of Norfolk* (1875). Our obligation to follow conscience was, he insisted, in a profound sense primary and even overriding. Is there a duty to follow the teachings of the pope? Yes, to be sure. As a Catholic, he would affirm that with all his heart. If, however, a conflict were to arise, such that conscience (formed as best one could form it) forbade one's following the pope, well, it is the obligation of conscience that must prevail.

Of course, many a contemporary dissenting Catholic would be tempted right there to shout, "Right on, Brother Newman!" But that's only if they didn't know the rest of the story. Newman, though the most powerful defender of freedom of conscience, held a view of conscience and of freedom that could not be more deeply at odds with the liberal ideology that is dominant (even, dare one say, orthodox?) in the contemporary secular intellectual culture and in those sectors of religious culture that have fallen under its influence. Let's permit Newman to speak for himself, for he had already identified in the nineteenth century the tendency of thought about rights, liberty, and conscience that have become the secular liberal orthodoxy today:

Conscience has rights because it has duties; but in this age, with a large portion of the public, it is the very right and freedom of conscience to dispense with conscience. Conscience is a stern monitor, but in this century it has been superseded by a counterfeit, which the eighteen centuries prior to it never heard of, and could not have mistaken for it if they had. It is the right of self-will.[6]

Conscience, as Newman understood it, is the very opposite of "autonomy" in the modern liberal sense. It is not a writer of permission slips. It is not in the business of licensing us to do as we please or conferring on us (in the words of the U.S. Supreme Court) "the right to define one's own concept of existence, of meaning, of the universe, and of the mystery of human life."[7] Rather, conscience is one's last best judgment specifying the bearing of moral principles one grasps, yet in no way makes up for oneself, on concrete proposals for action. Conscience identifies one's *duties* under the moral law. It speaks of what one must do and what one must not do. Understood in this way, conscience is indeed what Newman said it is: a stern monitor.

Contrast this understanding of conscience with what Newman condemns as its counterfeit. Conscience as "self-will" is a matter of feeling or emotion, not reason. It is concerned not so much with identifying what one has a duty to do or not do, one's feelings and desires to the contrary notwithstanding, but rather with sorting out one's feelings. Conscience as self-will identifies permissions, not obligations. It licenses behavior by establishing that one doesn't feel bad about doing it—or at least one doesn't feel so bad about doing it that one prefers the alternative of not doing it.

I'm with Newman. His key distinction is between conscience, authentically understood, and self-will—conscience as the permissions department. His core insight is that conscience has rights *because it has duties.* The right to follow one's conscience and the obligation to respect conscience—especially in matters of faith, where the right of conscience takes the form of religious liberty of individuals and communities of faith—obtain not because people as autonomous agents should be able to do as they please; they obtain, and are stringent and sometimes overriding, because people have duties and the obligation to fulfill them. The duty to follow conscience is a duty to do things or refrain from doing things not because one wants to follow one's duty but even if one strongly does *not* want to follow it. The right of conscience is a right to do what one judges oneself to be under an obligation to do, whether one welcomes the obligation or must overcome strong aversion to fulfill it. If there is a form of words that sums up the antithesis of Newman's view of conscience as a stern monitor, it is the imbecilic slogan that will forever stand as a verbal monument to the so-called me generation: "If it feels good, do it."

Let me conclude with a few words about the centrality and one might even say *priority* of religious freedom among the basic civil liberties. Observed from a certain perspective, any basic liberty might be assigned a kind of priority: free speech, for example, which is so essential to the enterprise of republican government (and, in truth, good government of any kind); or freedom of association and assembly; or the right of self-defense and defense of one's family and community. The collapse of any of these rights would place all the others in jeopardy.

Still, there is a special sense in which freedom of religion has priority or at least a sort of pride of place. It is rightly labeled in America "the first freedom," not only because it is listed first in our Bill of Rights and because of its foundational historical role in establishing free institutions but even more significantly because it protects an aspect of our flourishing as human persons that is architectonic to the way we lead our lives. Religion concerns ultimate things. In the focal cases, it represents our efforts to bring ourselves into a relationship of friendship with transcendent sources of meaning and value. Our religious questioning, understanding, judging, and practicing shape what we do not only in the specifically "religious" aspects of our lives (prayer, liturgy, fellowship, and so forth) but in every aspect of our lives. It helps us to view our lives as a whole and to direct our choices and activities in ways that have *integrity*—both in the moral sense of that term and in the broader sense of having a life that hangs together.

Religion is not the only basic human good; nor are the other basic human goods mere means to the fuller realization of the good of religion. But religion *is* an intrinsic and constitutive aspect of our integral flourishing as human persons and also a good that shapes and integrates all the other intrinsic and constitutive aspects of human well-being and fulfillment.[8]

Finally, there is the critical role of religion, and thus of religious freedom, in civil society in the carrying out of essential health, education, and welfare functions, and thus in limiting the scope of government and checking the power of the state. Religion provides authority structures and, where it flourishes and is healthy, is among the key institutions of civil society providing a buffer between the individual and the state. This is a vital way in which religion and religious institutions, when they respect the legitimate autonomy of the secular sphere and avoid illiberalism, time-serving subservience to the state, and theocracy, serve the common good. In the face of tyrannical regimes, they can, if they avoid corruption and co-option, serve the common good even more dramatically by doing, for example, what the Catholic Church did in the face of communist tyranny in Poland.[9]

Religion can, in other words, contribute to both the theory and the practice of resistance—but only where it is basically healthy (that is, uncorrupted) and capable of providing, or providing resources for, prophetic witness. This is one more reason to cherish religious freedom and to push back hard against forces that threaten to erode or diminish it—especially when the threats come from overreaching governments.

11

RELIGIOUS LIBERTY

A Fundamental Human Right

T HE STARTING POINTS of all ethical reflection are those fundamental and irreducible aspects of the well-being and fulfillment of human persons that some philosophers refer to as "basic human goods."[1] These goods—as more than merely instrumental ends or purposes—are the subjects of the very first principles of practical reason that control all rational thinking with a view to acting, whether the acts performed are, in the end, properly judged to be morally good or bad.[2] The first principles of practical reason direct our choosing toward what is rationally desirable because it is humanly fulfilling (and therefore intelligibly available to choice), and away from the privations of these basic human goods.[3] It is, in the end, the integral directiveness of these principles that provides the criterion (or, when specified, the set of criteria—the moral norms) by which it is possible rationally to distinguish right from wrong—what is morally good from what is morally bad—including what is just and unjust.[4] Morally good choices are choices that are in line with the various fundamental aspects of human well-being and fulfillment integrally conceived; morally bad choices are choices that are not.

To make these very abstract statements is simply to spell out philosophically the point Martin Luther King made in his *Letter from Birmingham Jail* about just and unjust laws—laws that honor people's rights and those that violate them. The great civil rights champion anticipated a challenge to the moral goodness of the acts of civil disobedience that landed him behind bars in Birmingham. He anticipated his critics asking: How can you, Dr. King, engage in willful lawbreaking when you yourself stressed the importance of obedience to law in demanding that officials of the southern states conform to the Supreme Court's desegregation ruling in *Brown v. Board of Education*? Here is King's response to the challenge:

> The answer lies in the fact that there are two types of laws: just and unjust. I would be the first to advocate obeying just laws. One has not only a legal but a moral responsibility to obey just laws. Conversely, one has a moral responsibility to disobey unjust laws. I would agree with St. Augustine that "an unjust law is no law at all."
>
> Now, what is the difference between the two? How does one determine whether a law is just or unjust?
>
> A just law is a man-made code that squares with the moral law or the law of God. An unjust law is a code that is out of harmony with the moral law. To put it in the terms of St. Thomas Aquinas: An unjust law is a human law that is not rooted in eternal law and natural law.
>
> Any law that uplifts human personality is just. Any law that degrades human personality is unjust. All segregation statutes are unjust because segregation distorts the soul and damages the personality. It gives the segregator a false sense of superiority and the segregated a false sense of inferiority.[5]

So just laws elevate and ennoble the human personality, or what King in other contexts referred to as the human spirit; unjust laws debase and degrade it. His point about the morality or immorality of laws is a good reminder that what is true of what is sometimes called "personal morality" is also true of "political morality." The choices and actions of political institutions at every level, like the choices and actions of individuals, can be right or wrong, morally good or morally bad. They can be in line with human well-being and fulfillment in all its manifold dimensions, or they can fail to respect the integral flourishing of human persons. In many cases when laws, policies, and institutions fail to fulfill the requirements of morality, we speak intelligibly and rightly of a violation of human rights. This is particularly true when the failure is properly characterized as an injustice—failing to honor people's equal worth and dignity, failing to give them, or even actively denying them, what they are due.

But, contrary to the teaching of the late John Rawls and the extraordinarily influential stream of contemporary liberal thought of which he was the leading exponent,[6] I wish to suggest that good is prior to right and, indeed, to rights. To be sure, human rights, including the right to religious liberty, are among the moral principles that demand respect from all of us, including governments and international institutions (which are morally bound not only to respect human rights but also to protect them). To respect people, to respect their dignity, is to, among other things, honor their rights, including the right to religious freedom. Like all moral principles, however, human rights (including the right to religious liberty) are shaped, and given content, by the human goods they protect. Rights, like other moral principles, are intelligible as rational, action-guiding principles because they entail and at some level specify the integral directiveness of principles of practical reason that directs our choosing toward what is humanly fulfilling and enriching (or, as Dr. King would say, uplifting) and away from what is contrary to our well-being as the kind of creatures we are—namely, human persons.

So, for example, it matters to the identification and defense of the right to life—a right violated by abortion, the infanticide of handicapped newborns and the killing of other physically or mentally disabled persons, the euthanizing of persons suffering from Alzheimer's disease and other dementias, and all other acts of direct killing of innocent human beings—that human life is no mere instrumental good but is an intrinsic aspect of the good of human persons, an integral dimension of our overall flourishing.[7] And it matters to the identification and defense of the right to religious liberty that religion is yet another irreducible aspect of human well-being and fulfillment—a basic human good.[8]

The Good of Religion

But what is religion?

In its fullest and most robust sense, religion is the human person's being in right relation to the divine—the more than merely human source or sources, if there be such, of meaning and value. Of course, even the greatest among us fall short of perfection in various ways. But in the ideal of perfect religion, the person would understand as comprehensively and deeply as possible the body of truths about spiritual things and would fully order his or her life, and share in the life of a community of faith that is ordered, in line with those truths. In the perfect realization of the good of religion, one would achieve the relationship that the divine—say God himself, assuming for a moment the truth of monotheism—wishes us to have with Him.

Of course, different traditions of faith have different views of what constitutes religion in its fullest sense. There are different doctrines, different scriptures, different structures of authority, different ideas of what is true about spiritual things and what it means to be in proper relationship to the more than merely human sources of meaning and value that different traditions understand as divinity.[9]

For my part, I believe that reason has a very large role to play for each of us in deciding where spiritual truth most robustly is to be found. And by reason here, I mean not only our capacity for practical reasoning and moral judgment but also our capacities for understanding and evaluating claims of all sorts: logical, historical, scientific, and so forth. But one need not agree with me about this to affirm with me that there is a distinct basic human good of religion—a good that is uniquely architectonic in shaping one's pursuit of and participation in all the basic human goods—and that one begins to realize and participate in this good from the moment one begins the quest to understand the more than merely human sources of meaning and value and to live authentically by ordering one's life in line with one's best judgments of the truth in religious matters.

If I am right, then the existential raising of religious questions, the honest identification of answers, and the fulfilling of what one sincerely believes to be one's duties in the light of those answers are all parts of the human good of religion—a good whose pursuit is an indispensable feature of the comprehensive flourishing of a human being. If I am right, in other words, then man is, as Becket Fund founder Seamus Hasson says, intrinsically and by nature a religious being—*homo religiosus*, to borrow a phrase from Eliade—and the flourishing of man's spiritual life is integral to his all-around well-being and fulfillment.

But if that is true, then respect for a person's well-being, or more simply respect for the person, demands respect for his or her flourishing as a seeker of religious truth and as a man or woman who lives in line with his or her best judgments of what is true in spiritual matters. And that, in turn, requires respect for his or her liberty in the religious quest—the quest to understand religious truth and order one's life in line with it. Because faith of any type, including religious faith, cannot be authentic—it cannot be *faith*—unless it is free, respect for the person (that is, respect for his or her dignity as a free and rational creature) requires respect for his or her religious liberty. That is why it makes sense, from the point of view of reason, and not merely from the point of view of the revealed teaching of a particular faith, to understand religious freedom as a fundamental human right.

Tragically, regard for persons' spiritual well-being has sometimes been the premise, and motivating factor, for *denying* religious liberty or conceiving of it in a cramped and restricted way. Before the Catholic

Church embraced the robust conception of religious freedom that honors the civil right to give public witness and expression to sincere religious views (even when erroneous), in the Second Vatican Council's *Dignitatis Humanae*, some Catholics rejected the idea of a right to religious freedom on the theory that "only the truth has rights." The idea was that the state, under favoring conditions, should not only publicly identify itself with Catholicism as the true faith but also forbid religious advocacy or proselytizing that could lead people into religious error and apostasy.

The mistake here was not in the premise: religion is a great human good, and the truer the religion, the better for the fulfillment of the believer. That is true. The mistake, rather, was in the supposition that the good of religion was not being advanced or participated in outside the context of the one true faith, and that it could be reliably protected and advanced by having agencies of the state enforce civil restrictions on the advocacy of religious ideas. In rejecting this supposition, the fathers of the Second Vatican Council did not embrace the idea that error has rights; they noticed, rather, that *people* have rights, and they have rights even when they are in error.[10] And among those rights, integral to authentic religion as a fundamental and irreducible aspect of the human good, is the right to express what one believes to be true about spiritual matters, even if one's beliefs are, in one way or another, less than fully sound, and, indeed, even if they are false.[11]

When I have assigned the document *Dignitatis Humanae* in courses addressing questions of religious liberty, I have always stressed to my students the importance of reading another document of the Second Vatican Council, *Nostra Aetate*, together with it. Whether one is Catholic or not, I don't think it is possible to achieve a rich understanding of the Declaration on Religious Freedom, and the developed teaching of the Catholic Church on religious freedom, without considering what the council fathers proclaim in the Declaration on Non-Christian Religions. In *Nostra Aetate*, the fathers pay tribute to all that is true and holy in non-Christian faiths, including Hinduism and Buddhism, and especially Judaism and Islam. In so doing, they give recognition to the ways in which religion enriches, ennobles, and fulfills the human person in the spiritual dimension of his being, even where it does not include the defining content of what the fathers, as Catholics, believe to be religion in its fullest and most robust sense—namely, the Incarnation of Jesus Christ. This is to be honored and respected, in the view of the council fathers, because the dignity of the human being requires it. Naturally, the nonrecognition of Christ as the Son of God must count for the fathers as a shortcoming in the non-Christian faiths—just as the proclamation of Christ as the Son of God must count as an error in Christianity from a Jewish or Muslim point of view. But, the fathers teach, this does not mean that Judaism and Islam are simply false and without merit (just as neither Judaism nor Islam teaches that Christianity is simply false and without merit); on the contrary, these traditions enrich the lives of their faithful in their spiritual dimensions, thus contributing vitally to their fulfillment.

What Religious Freedom Demands

Now, the Catholic Church does not have a monopoly on the natural-law reasoning by which I am explicating and defending the human right to religious liberty.[12] But the church does have a deep commitment to such reasoning and a long experience with it. And in *Dignitatis Humanae*, the fathers of the Second Vatican Council present a natural-law argument for religious freedom—indeed, they begin by presenting a natural-law argument before supplementing it with arguments appealing to the authority of God's revelation in sacred scripture. So the key Catholic texts, as the teachings of an actual faith, offer a useful illustration of how religious leaders and believers, and not just statesmen concerned to craft policy in circumstances of religious pluralism, can incorporate, into their understanding of the basic human right to religious liberty, principles and arguments available to all men and women of sincerity and goodwill by virtue of what John Rawls once referred to as "our common human reason."[13]

Let me quote at some length from *Nostra Aetate* to give you an appreciation of the rational basis of the Catholic Church's affirmation of the good of religion as manifested in various different faiths. I do this to show how one faith, in this case Catholicism, can root its defense of a robust conception of freedom of religion not in a mutual nonaggression pact with other faiths, or in what the late Judith Shklar labeled a "liberalism of fear," or, much less, in religious relativism or indifferentism. Rather, such a defense can be, and is, rooted in a rational affirmation of the value of religion as embodied and made available to people in and through many traditions of faith. Here is what *Nostra Aetate* says:

> Throughout history even to the present day, there is found among different peoples a certain awareness of a hidden power, which lies behind the course of nature and the events of human life. At times there is present even a recognition of a supreme being or still more of a Father. This awareness and recognition results in a way of life that is imbued with a deep religious sense. The religions which are found in more advanced civilizations endeavor by way of well-defined concepts and exact language to answer these questions. Thus in Hinduism men explore the divine mystery and express it both in the limitless riches of myth and the accurately defined insights of philosophy. They seek release from the trials of the present life by ascetical practices, profound meditation and recourse to God in confidence and love. Buddhism in its various forms testifies to the essential inadequacy of this changing world. It proposes a way of life by which men can with confidence and trust, attain a state of perfect liberation and reach supreme illumination either through their own efforts or by the aid of divine help. So, too, other religions which are found throughout the world attempt in their own ways to calm the hearts of men by outlining a program of life covering doctrine, moral precepts and sacred rites.
>
> *The Catholic Church rejects nothing of what is true and holy in these religions.* She has a high regard for the manner of life and conduct,

the precepts and doctrines which, although differing in many ways from her own teaching, nevertheless often reflect truths which enlighten all men. Yet she proclaims and is in duty bound to proclaim without fail Christ, who is the way, the truth and the life (Jn. 1:6). In him, in whom God reconciled all things to himself (2 Cor. 5:18–19), men find the fullness of their religious life.

The Church, therefore, urges her sons to enter with prudence and charity into discussion and collaboration with members of other religious. Let Christians, while witnessing to their own faith and way of life, acknowledge, preserve and encourage the spiritual and moral truths found among non-Christians.

The Church has also a high regard for the Muslims. They worship God, who is one, living and subsistent, merciful and almighty, the Creator of heaven and earth, who has also spoken to men. They strive to submit themselves without reserve to the decrees of God, just as Abraham submitted himself to God's plan, to whose faith Muslims link their own. Although not acknowledging Jesus as God, they revere him as a prophet; his virgin Mother they also honor, and even at times devoutly invoke. Further, they await the Day of Judgment and the reward of God following the resurrection of the dead. For this reason they highly esteem an upright life and worship God, especially by way of prayer, almsgiving, and fasting.

Over the centuries many quarrels and dissensions have arisen between Christians and Muslims. The sacred Council now pleads with all to forget the past, and urges that a sincere effort be made to achieve mutual understanding; for the benefit of all men, let them together preserve and promote peace, liberty, social justice and moral values.

Sounding the depths of the mystery which is the Church, this sacred Council remembers the spiritual ties which link the people of the New Covenant to the stock of Abraham.

The Church of Christ acknowledges that in God's plan of salvation the beginning of her faith and election is to be found in the patriarchs and in Moses and the prophets. She professes that all Christ's faithful, who as men of faith are sons of Abraham (cf. Gal. 3:7), are included in the same patriarch's call and that the salvation of the Church is mystically prefigured in the exodus of God's chosen people from the land of bondage. On this account the Church cannot forget that she received the revelation of the Old Testament by way of that people with whom God in his inexpressible mercy established the ancient covenant. Nor can she forget that she draws nourishment from that good olive tree onto which the wild olive branches of the Gentiles have been grafted (cf. Rom. 11:17-24). The Church believes that Christ who is our peace has through his cross reconciled Jews and Gentiles and made them one in himself (cf. Eph. 2:14-16).[14]

Respect for the good of religion requires that civil authority respect (and, in appropriate ways, even nurture) conditions or circumstances in which people can engage in the sincere religious quest and live lives of authenticity reflecting their best judgments as to the truth of spiritual matters. To compel an atheist to perform acts that are premised on theistic beliefs that he cannot, in good conscience, share is to deny him the fundamental bit of the good of religion that is his—namely, living with honesty and integrity in line with his best judgments about ultimate reality. Coercing him to perform religious acts does him no good, since faith really must be free, and dishonors his dignity as a free and rational person. The violation of liberty is worse than futile.

Of course, there are limits to the freedom that must be respected for the sake of the good of religion and the dignity of the human person as a being whose integral fulfillment includes the spiritual quest and the ordering of one's life in line with one's best judgment as to what spiritual truth requires. Gross evil—even grave injustice—can be committed by sincere people for the sake of religion. Unspeakable wrongs can be done by people seeking sincerely to get right with God or the gods or their conception of ultimate reality, whatever it is. The presumption in favor of respecting liberty must, for the sake of the human good and the dignity of human persons as free and rational creatures—creatures who, according to Judaism and Christianity, are made in the very image and likeness of God—be powerful and broad. But it is not unlimited. Even the great end of getting right with God cannot justify a morally bad means, even for the sincere believer. I don't doubt the sincerity of the Aztecs in practicing human sacrifice, or the sincerity of those in the history of various traditions of faith who used coercion and even torture in the cause of what they believed was religiously required. But these things are deeply wrong and need not (and should not) be tolerated in the name of religious freedom. To suppose otherwise is to back oneself into the awkward position of supposing that violations of religious freedom (and other injustices of equal gravity) must be respected for the sake of religious freedom.

Still, to overcome the powerful and broad presumption in favor of religious liberty, to be justified in requiring the believer to do something contrary to his faith or in forbidding the believer to do something his faith requires, political authority must meet a heavy burden. The legal test in the United States under the Religious Freedom Restoration Act is one way of capturing the presumption and burden: to justify a law that bears negatively on religious freedom, even a neutral law of general applicability must be supported by a compelling state interest and represent the least restrictive or intrusive means of protecting or serving that interest. We can debate, as a matter of American constitutional law or as a matter of policy, whether it is, or should be, up to courts or legislators to decide when exemptions to general, neutral laws should be granted for the sake of religious freedom, or to determine when the presumption in favor of religious freedom has been overcome. But the substantive matter of what religious freedom demands from those who exercise the levers of state power should be something on which reasonable people of goodwill across the religious and political spectrums should agree on—precisely because it is a matter capable of being settled by our common human reason.

12

WHAT MARRIAGE IS— AND WHAT IT ISN'T

MARRIAGE IS AN all-encompassing sharing of life. It involves, like other bonds, a union of hearts and minds— but also, and distinctively, a bodily union made possible by the sexual-reproductive complementarity of man and woman. Hence it is ordered to the all-encompassing goods of procreation and family life, and it calls for all-encompassing commitment, one that is pledged to permanence and sexual exclusivity and fidelity. Marriage unites a husband and wife holistically, not merely in an emotional bond but also on the bodily plane in acts of conjugal love and in the children such love brings forth—for the whole of life. Marriage is a form of relationship—indeed, *the* form of relationship—in which a man and a woman unite in a bond that is naturally ordered to, and would be fulfilled by, their conceiving and rearing children together. And those who enter into this form of relationship—the human good of marriage—are truly and fully participants in it even where their bond is not blessed with the gift of children.

To be in such a relationship—a bodily as well as emotional union whose distinctive features and norms are shaped by its orientation to, and aptness for, procreation and the rearing of children—is intrinsically, not merely instrumentally, valuable. So marriage, though it bears an inherent (rather than incidental) link to procreation, is not properly understood as having its value merely as a means to the good of conceiving and rearing children. That is why, historically and rightly, infertility is not regarded as an impediment to marriage. True bodily union in acts fulfilling the behavioral conditions of procreation is possible even where the nonbehavioral conditions of procreation happen not to obtain. Such union can provide the foundation and matrix of the multilevel sharing of life that marriage is.

These insights into the nature of marriage as a human good require no particular theology. They are, to be sure, consistent with Judeo-Christian faith, yet ancient thinkers untouched by Jewish or Christian revelation—including Aristotle, Plato, Socrates, Musonius Rufus, Xenophanes, and Plutarch—also distinguished conjugal unions from all others, as do many nonbiblical faiths to this day. Nor did animus against particular persons or categories of persons produce this conclusion, which arose in various cultures long before the modern concept of "sexual orientation."

Nevertheless, today many are demanding the redefinition of marriage as something other than a conjugal partnership. Indeed, several jurisdictions in the West, including a number of European nations and several American states, have redefined marriage to eliminate the norm of sexual complementarity. In truth, what they have done is abolish marriage as a legal category and replace it with something quite different—legally recognized sexual-romantic companionship or domestic partnership—to which the label *marriage* has been reassigned. So, strictly speaking, we are talking not so much about a redefinition as an abolition of marriage.

When marriage is understood as a conjugal relationship—that is, as a comprehensive (emotional *and* bodily) union oriented toward procreation and the providing of children with both a mother and a father—it is easy to make sense of its core features as historically understood in Western and other cultures. But eliminating the norm of sexual complementarity removes any ground of principle for these features. After all, if two men or two women can marry, then what sets marriage apart from other bonds must be emotional intensity or priority. But nothing about emotional union or intensity requires it to be permanent, as opposed to deliberately temporary. Nothing beyond mere sentiment or subjective preference would require it to be sexually "closed" as opposed to "open," or limited to relationships of two persons, as opposed to three or more in "polyamorous" sexual ensembles. There would be no ground for understanding marriage as a sexual partnership, as opposed to one integrated around any of a range of possible nonsexual shared interests or commitments (for example, playing tennis, reading novels, supporting a certain sports team). Nor would there be any basis for understanding marriage as a relationship that is inherently enriched by family life and shaped by its demands. Yet these have always been defining features and norms of marriage—features and norms that make marriage unlike other forms or companionship or friendship (and unlike in *kind*, not just in degree of emotional intensity).

These considerations buttress my point that what is at stake in contemporary debates about the definition and meaning of marriage is not whether to "expand" marriage to enlarge the pool of people "eligible" to participate in it. What is at stake is whether to retain and support marriage in our law and culture or to jettison it in favor of a different way of organizing human relationships.

Marriage law shapes our actions by promoting a vision of what marriage is and, therefore, what its norms and requirements are. In almost all Western jurisdictions, marriage has been deeply wounded by a culture of divorce, the widespread practice of nonmarital sexual cohabitation, the normalization of nonmarital childbearing, and other practices. None of these had to do with same-sex partnerships or homosexual conduct, nor were or are people who are attracted to persons of the same sex responsible for them. It was the impact of these practices on the public understanding of marriage that weakened people's grasp of marriage as a conjugal union and made the otherwise inconceivable idea of same-sex "marriages" conceivable. Still, abolishing marriage as a legal category and reassigning the label *marriage* to sexual-romantic domestic partnerships would complete the rout, making it all but impossible to carry out the reforms needed to restore the conjugal understanding of marriage and with it a vibrant and healthy marriage culture. The more we equate marriage with what amounts to a form of sexual-romantic companionship or domestic partnership, the more difficult it will be for people to live by the stabilizing norms specific to true marriage. This is the lesson of the past forty-five years. Unless we restore a sound understanding of marriage and rebuild the marriage culture, the erosion of marriage ideals will continue to harm everyone—children, spouses, societies as a whole—but especially the poorest and most vulnerable. By rewriting the parenting ideal, abolishing conjugal marriage as the legal norm would undermine in our mores and practice the special value of biological mothers and fathers. Moreover, by marking support for the conjugal view as "bigotry," it would, as we are already seeing in Europe, the United States, and elsewhere, damage religious liberty and freedom of speech and association.

It is important to bear in mind that under *any* marriage policy some bonds, some types of intimate relationship, will remain unrecognized, and thus some people will remain legally unmarried (however much they would like their relationships to count as marriages under law). So we need to be able (and ought) to meet people's concrete needs apart from civil marriage. Moreover, if we reject equating marriage with companionship—and marriage licenses with generic approval—we will see that conjugal marriage laws deprive no one of companionship or its joys and mark no one as less worthy of fulfillment. True compassion means extending authentic community to everyone, especially the marginalized, while using marriage law for the social goal it serves best—the goal that justifies regulating such intimate bonds in the first place: to ensure that children know the committed love of the mother and father whose union brought them into being.

Just as compassion for same-sex-attracted people does not require redefining marriage, neither does preserving the conjugal view mean making them scapegoats for its erosion. It certainly isn't about legalizing (or criminalizing) anything. In all fifty of the United States, two men or women can have a wedding (if they happen to believe in same-sex marriage) and share a domestic life. Their employers and religious communities are legally free to recognize their unions. At issue here is whether governments will effectively coerce many other actors in the public square to do the same. And also at issue is whether government will expand. Robust support for marital norms serves children, spouses, and hence our whole economy, especially the poor. Family breakdown thrusts the state into roles for which it is ill-suited: parent and discipliner to the orphaned and neglected, and arbiter of disputes over custody and paternity.

A Comprehensive Sharing of Life

Let me now address the issue at a deeper, more philosophical level. Everyone agrees that marriage, whatever else it is or does, is a relationship in which *persons* are *fully* united. But what are *persons*? And how is it possible for two (or more) of them to *fully* unite?

The view typically (if often only implicitly) held by advocates of liberal positions on issues of sexuality and marriage is that the person is the conscious and desiring aspect of the self. The "person" (that is, the mind, the center of consciousness or emotion) inhabits (or is somehow associated with) a body, certainly. But the body is regarded, if often only implicitly, as a *subpersonal* reality—a mere physical vessel—rather than a part of the personal reality of the human being whose body it is. The body is viewed as an extrinsic *instrument* by which the individual produces or otherwise participates in satisfactions and other desirable experiences and realizes various goals.

For those who formally or informally accept this dualistic understanding of what human beings are, personal unity cannot be achieved by bodily union. And this takes us to the very crux of the debate about the nature and meaning of marriage. According to this view, persons instead unite *emotionally* (or, as those of a certain religious cast of mind say, *spiritually*). Of course, if this is true, then persons of the same sex can unite (that is, form an intense emotional bond), and they can share erotic experiences that they suppose will enhance their personal union by enabling them to express affection, share pleasure, and feel more intensely by virtue of their sex play. (By the same token, ensembles of three or more persons can unite by forming an intense emotional bond and can share erotic experiences that they suppose will enhance their polyamorous union.)

The alternative to the dualistic view of what persons are (and therefore of how persons can be united) is the one embraced in both the historic law of marriage and what Sir Isaiah Berlin described as the central tradition of Western thought. According to this anti-dualistic view, human beings are *bodily persons*, not consciousnesses, minds, or spirits inhabiting and using nonpersonal bodies. A human person is a dynamic unity of body, mind, and spirit. Far from being an extrinsic instrument of the person, the body is intrinsically part of the personal reality of the human being. Organic bodily union is thus *personal* union, and comprehensive personal union—marital union—includes, and is indeed founded on, bodily union.

The bodily union we are here considering is possible because human males and females unite organically when they mate—though two, they become one as the single, unified subject performing the act that fulfills the behavioral conditions of procreation. That is why mating is something distinct from simply rubbing together, even erotic rubbing together. And mating remains mating, and no mere rubbing together, even when the nonbehavioral conditions of procreation happen not to obtain. That is why zoologists or farmers can distinguish acts of mating even in nonhuman animals from failures to mate, no matter how much rubbing together has gone on, without the need to wait to see whether conception has occurred. Conception itself, though a consequence of mating (where the nonbehavioral conditions of reproduction obtain), is distinct from the act of mating itself. Whether mating has occurred is one thing; whether it has resulted in conception is something else.

This leaves the question of the existential and moral significance of human mating. Given that humans become one in the bodily sense by mating—the body being, in the nondualistic view, part of the personal reality of the human being, not just a vessel or subpersonal instrument—what follows about the meaning of marriage as a distinctive human good?

To move toward answers, let us explore a bit more the concept of bodily union as personal union. In the bodily union made possible by the sexual-reproductive complementarity of male and female, partners, while remaining distinct persons, together form a single reproductive principle. Although reproduction is a single act, in humans (as in many other species) the reproductive act is performed not by individual members of the species but by a mated pair as an organic unit. Germain Grisez has carefully explained the point:

> Though a male and a female are complete individuals with respect to other functions—for example, nutrition, sensation, and locomotion—with respect to reproduction they are only potential parts of a mated pair, which is the complete organism capable of reproducing sexually. Even if the mated pair is sterile, intercourse, provided it is the reproductive behavior characteristic of the species, makes the copulating male and female one organism.

What is unique about marriage is that it truly is a comprehensive sharing of life—a union not only of hearts and minds (as friendships and other types of relationships also are) but of bodies as well. Indeed, this comprehensive sharing is founded on the bodily union made uniquely possible by the sexual-reproductive complementarity that allows a man and woman to become, in the language of the Bible, "one flesh." This one-flesh union is the foundation of a relationship in which it is intelligible (not a matter of subjective preference) for two persons to bind themselves to each other in pledges of permanence, monogamy, and sexual fidelity.

People who reject this understanding of sex and marriage say that "love makes a family." And it does not matter whether the love is between two people of opposite sexes or the same sex. (Those who are clearheaded and candid acknowledge that, by the same token, it would not matter if the love were among three or more people.) Nor does the form of sexual expression of that love make any difference.

Arguments that true marriage is something other than or broader than the union of two sexually complementary spouses necessarily suppose that the value of sex must be instrumental either to procreation or to pleasure, considered as an end in itself or as a means of expressing affection, tender feelings, and so forth. Critics of traditional norms of marriage and sexuality say that sexual acts of same-sex partners, for example, are indistinguishable from the acts of coitus of spouses whenever the motivation for coitus is something other than procreation. That is to say, the sexual acts of same-sex partners are indistinguishable in motivation, meaning, value, and significance from the marital acts of spouses who know that at least one spouse is temporarily or permanently infertile. Thus, the argument goes, the traditional understanding of marriage is guilty of unfairness in treating sterile persons of opposite sexes as capable of marrying while treating same-sex partners as ineligible to marry.

My friend and colleague Professor Stephen Macedo has accused the traditional view and its defenders of precisely this "double standard." He asks: "What is the point of sex in an infertile marriage? Not procreation: The partners (let us assume) know that they are infertile. If they have sex, it is for pleasure and to express their love, or friendship, or some other good. It will be for precisely the same reason that committed, loving gay couples have sex."

Many people find this sort of criticism impressive, and even some conservatively oriented people seem to find themselves stumped by it. Once the core of the traditional view is brought into focus, however, it is clear that the criticism straightforwardly fails because it presupposes that the point of sex in marriage can only be instrumental. In fact, a central tenet of the traditional view is that the point of sex is the good of marriage itself, consummated and actualized in and through sexual acts that unite spouses as one flesh—their bodily communion being integrally and constitutively part of their comprehensive marital unity as embodied persons. Thus, the traditional view rejects the instrumentalizing of sex (and, thus, of the bodies of sexual partners) to extrinsic ends *of any sort*. Procreation and pleasure are rightly sought, but they are integrated with the basic good and justifying point of marital intercourse—namely, the one-flesh union of marriage itself.

Critics of the traditional understanding of marriage who grasp this point must therefore argue that the apparent one-flesh unity that distinguishes marital intercourse from other types of sexual conduct is illusory. The apparent bodily communion of spouses in acts that fulfill the behavioral conditions of procreation is not really possible, they say.

Macedo, for instance, claims that "the 'one-flesh communion' of sterile couples would appear . . . to be more a matter of appearance than reality." Because of their sterility, such couples cannot really unite biologically: "Their bodies . . . can form no 'single reproductive principle,' no real unity." Indeed, Macedo argues that even fertile couples who conceive children in acts of sexual intercourse do not truly unite biologically, because, he says, "penises and vaginas do not unite biologically; sperm and eggs do."

John Finnis has aptly replied that "in this reductivist, word-legislating mood, one might declare that sperm and egg unite only physically and only their pronuclei are biologically united. But it would be more realistic to acknowledge that the whole process of copulation . . . is biological through and through." Moreover, as Finnis points out, "The organic unity which is instantiated in an act of the reproductive kind is not," as Macedo reductively imagines, "the unity of penis and vagina. It is the unity of the persons in the intentional, consensual act of sexual intercourse."

The unity to which Finnis here refers—unity of body, sense, emotion, reason, and will—is central to our understanding of humanness. Yet it is a unity of which Macedo and others who deny the possibility of true bodily communion in marriage can give no account. For this denial presupposes a dualism of *person* (as conscious and desiring self), on the one hand, and *body* (as instrument of the conscious and desiring self), on the other hand, which is flatly incompatible with this unity. The dualism of person and body is implicit in the idea, central to Macedo's denial of the possibility of one-flesh marital union, that noncoital sexual acts differ from what law and philosophy have traditionally regarded as chaste and honorable marital acts only as a matter of the arrangement of the "plumbing." According to this idea, the genital organs of an infertile woman or man are not really "reproductive organs" any more than, say, mouths, rectums, tongues, or fingers are reproductive organs. Thus, the intercourse of a man and a woman where at least one partner is infertile cannot really be an act of the reproductive type.

But the plain fact is that the genitals of men and women are reproductive organs all the time—even during periods of sterility. Acts that fulfill the behavioral conditions of procreation are acts of the procreative kind even where the nonbehavioral conditions of procreation do not obtain. Insofar as the point of sexual intercourse is marital union—a point central to the historical understanding of marriage as a conjugal relationship—the spouses achieve the desired unity (they unite biologically, they become "two in one flesh") precisely insofar as they *mate*. Or, to put the same point another way, they perform the type of act on which the gift of a child may supervene—what traditional law and philosophy have always referred to as "the act of generation" and "the conjugal act."

These days, the views Macedo advances are hardly considered radical. On the contrary, many consider his views about sex and marriage to be too conservative, even old-fashioned. He and other defenders of this "moderate liberal" position have been taken to task by those to their left for affirming the principle of sexual fidelity and criticizing, if usually only implicitly, promiscuity and sexually "open" marriages. They have an admirable commitment to the notion of marriage as a permanent and exclusive sharing of life integrated around (but certainly not reducible to) sexual activity. But they think that the *nature* of the sexual activity just does not matter. Sex is sex. It cannot, in their view, truly unite people as one flesh, but it can enable them to express their affection in a special way.

Once marriage and marital intercourse are reduced to the status of instrumental goods, the only intelligible point of entering into marriage will be the achievement of some other end or ends. For some, certainly, the end of marriage will be procreation, but whether a particular marriage is a "reproductive alliance" or an alliance for purposes entirely unrelated to reproduction is purely a matter of the *subjective preferences* of the parties entering into the alliance. In no way is marriage considered to be naturally ordered to the coming to be and nurturing of children. Nor are the contours of the marital state or the terms of the marital relationship understood to be established or shaped by a natural orientation toward child rearing.

Marriage, on this revised understanding, is marked by a plasticity or malleability that sharply distinguishes it from the conception of marriage it is proposed to replace. In this revisionist understanding, marriage is also unnecessary—even for child rearing. If two (or perhaps more) people find, or suppose, that the state of being married works for them, then they have a reason to marry. If not, then marriage is not as a matter of principle understood to be a uniquely, or even especially, apt context for them to structure their lives together.

What about sex? What is the point of that in the revised conception of marriage? The worldview sometimes referred to as "expressive individualism" or "lifestyle liberalism" rejects the belief that sex is properly to be restricted to the marital relationship. It certainly has no ground of principle to object to sexual cohabitation outside of marriage. And even with regard to sex apart from stable relationships, lifestyle liberalism is "nonjudgmental." Its main principle of rectitude in sexual matters is the principle of consent, not, as in the traditional view, the principle of marriage. So long as there is no coercion or deceit in the procurement of sex, sexual choices—as Frederick Elliston, for example, insists—do not raise moral questions.

Even adultery is unproblematic under the expressive individualist conception of marriage if, as in so-called "open marriages," there is no deception of a spouse involved. Indeed, under the expressive individualist conception it is impossible to identify any *reason*—there are only subjective preferences—for spouses to demand fidelity of each other. Why should they "forsake all others"? What is the point of sexual fidelity? There is no *reason*, strictly speaking, not to have an "open marriage"—only emotions or purely subjective preferences that some people happen to have and others do not have. This is why people who reject the traditional terms of marriage—even those, like Macedo, who do so for putatively conservative reasons, such as to make the good of marriage available to people who prefer erotic experiences with partners of their own sex—find it impossible, in the end, to condemn promiscuity and the like, except, occasionally, on pragmatic grounds.

Redefining Means Undermining

Advocates of redefining "marriage" as sexual-romantic companionship or domestic partnership to accommodate same-sex relationships are increasingly confirming the point that this shift erodes the basis for permanence and exclusivity in *any* relationship.[1]

University of Calgary philosophy professor Elizabeth Brake, for example, supports what she calls "minimal marriage," in which "individuals can have legal marital relationships with more than one person, reciprocally or asymmetrically, themselves determining the sex and number of parties, the type of relationship involved, and which rights and responsibilities to exchange with each."[2]

Judith Stacey, a prominent New York University professor who is in no way regarded as a fringe figure, testified before Congress against the Defense of Marriage Act. During her testimony, she expressed hope that the redefinition of marriage would give marriage "varied, creative, and adaptive contours . . . [leading some to] question the dyadic limitations of Western marriage and seek . . . small group marriages."[3]

In their statement "Beyond Same-Sex Marriage," more than three hundred "LGBT and allied" scholars and advocates called for legally recognizing sexual relationships involving more than two partners.[4] Such relationships are by no means unheard of: *Newsweek* reported in 2009 that there were more than five hundred thousand in the United States alone.[5] In Brazil, a public notary has recognized a trio of people as a civil union.[6] Mexico City has considered expressly temporary marriage licenses.[7] The Toronto District School Board has taken to promoting polyamorous relationships among its students.[8]

What about the connection to family life? Writer E. J. Graff celebrates the fact that recognizing same-sex unions would change the "institution's message" so that it would "ever after stand for sexual choice, for cutting the link between sex and diapers."[9] Enacting same-sex marriage "does more than just fit; it announces that marriage has changed shape."[10]

What about sexual exclusivity? Andrew Sullivan, a self-styled proponent of the conservative case for same-sex marriage, has now gone so far as to extol the "spirituality" of "anonymous sex." He welcomes the fact that the "openness" of same-sex unions might erode sexual exclusivity among those in opposite-sex marriages.[11]

Similarly, in a *New York Times Magazine* profile, same-sex-marriage activist Dan Savage encourages spouses to adopt "a more flexible attitude" about sex outside their marriage. A piece in *The Advocate*, a gay-interest newsmagazine, supports my point still more candidly: "Anti-equality right-wingers have long insisted that allowing gays to marry will destroy the sanctity of 'traditional marriage,' and, of course, the logical, liberal party-line response has long been 'No, it won't.' But what if—for once—the sanctimonious crazies are right? Could the gay male tradition of open relationships actually alter marriage as we know it? And would that be such a bad thing?"[12]

Other advocates of redefining marriage have explicitly proclaimed the goal of weakening the institution. Former president George W. Bush "is correct," writes journalist Victoria Brownworth, "when he states that allowing same-sex couples to marry will weaken the institution of marriage. . . . It most certainly will do so, and that will make marriage a far better concept than it previously has been."[13] Michelangelo Signorile, another prominent advocate of redefining marriage, urges people in same-sex relationships to "demand the right to marry not as a way of adhering to society's moral codes but rather to debunk a myth and radically alter an archaic institution." He says they should "fight for same-sex marriage and its benefits and then, once granted, redefine the institution of marriage completely, because the most subversive action lesbians and gay men can undertake . . . is to transform the notion of 'family' entirely."[14]

Those wishing to overturn the traditional understanding of marriage as a male-female partnership increasingly agree that redefining marriage would undermine its stabilizing norms.

A Culture of Marriage

A standard revisionist response to the defense of conjugal marriage like the one I am here proposing is the claim that, even if the traditional position is, from the moral viewpoint, true, it is nevertheless unfair for the law to embody it. Stephen Macedo, for example, argues that if disagreements about the nature of marriage "lie in . . . difficult philosophical quarrels, about which reasonable people have long disagreed, then our differences lie in precisely the territory that John Rawls rightly marks off as inappropriate to the fashioning of our basic rights and liberties." So Macedo and others claim that law and policy must be neutral with regard to competing understandings of marriage and sexual morality.

This claim is deeply unsound. The true meaning, value, and significance of marriage are fairly easily grasped (even if people sometimes have difficulty living up to its moral demands) in a culture—including, critically, a legal culture—that promotes and supports a sound understanding of marriage. Furthermore, ideologies and practices that are hostile to a sound understanding and practice of marriage in a culture tend to undermine the institution of marriage in that culture. Hence it is extremely important that governments eschew attempts to be neutral with regard to marriage and embody in their laws and policy the soundest, most nearly correct, understanding.

The law is a teacher. Either it will teach that marriage is a reality in which people can choose to participate but whose contours people cannot make and remake at will, or it will teach that marriage is a mere convention that is malleable in such a way that individuals, couples, or, indeed, groups can choose to make of it whatever suits their desires, goals, and so on. The result, given the biases of human sexual psychology, will be the development of practices and ideologies that truly tend to undermine the sound understanding and practice of marriage, together with the development of pathologies that tend to reinforce the very practices and ideologies that cause them.

The Oxford philosopher Joseph Raz, a liberal who does not share my views regarding sexual morality, is rightly critical of forms of liberalism, including Rawlsianism, that suppose law and government can and should be neutral among competing conceptions of moral goodness. He has noted, for example, that "monogamy, assuming that it is the only valuable form of marriage, cannot be practiced by an individual. It requires a culture which recognizes it, and which supports it through the public's attitude and through its formal institutions."

Of course, Raz does not suppose that, in a culture whose law and public policy do not support monogamy, a man who happens to believe in it somehow will be unable to restrict himself to having one wife or will be required to take additional wives. His point, rather, is that, even if monogamy is a key element in a sound understanding of marriage, large numbers of people will fail to understand that or why that is the case—and therefore will fail to grasp the value of monogamy and the point of practicing it—unless they are assisted by a culture that supports, formally by law and policy, as well as by informal means, monogamous marriage. What is true of monogamy is equally true of the other elements of a sound understanding of marriage.

In short, marriage is the kind of good that can be chosen and meaningfully participated in only by people who have at least an elementary understanding of it and who choose it with that understanding in mind. Yet people's ability to understand it, at least implicitly, and thus to choose it, depends crucially on institutions and cultural understandings that both transcend individual choice and are constituted by a vast number of individual choices.

13

THE MYTH OF A "GRAND BARGAIN" ON MARRIAGE

I T WAS ONLY yesterday, was it not, that we were being assured
that the redefinition of marriage to include same-sex partnerships
would have no impact on persons and institutions that hold the
traditional view of marriage as a conjugal union? It won't affect your
marriage or your life, we were told, if the law recognizes Henry and
Herman or Sally and Sheila as "married."

Those offering these assurances also claimed that redefining
marriage would not influence the public understanding of marriage
as a monogamous and sexually exclusive partnership. No one, they
insisted, wanted to alter those traditional marital norms. On the contrary, the redefinition of marriage would promote and spread those
norms more broadly.

When some of us warned that all of this was nonsense, and pointed
out the myriad ways that Catholics, Evangelicals, Mormons, Eastern
Orthodox Christians, Orthodox Jews, Muslims, and others would be
affected and their opportunities and liberties restricted, the proponents of marriage redefinition accused us of "fearmongering." When
we observed that reducing marriage to a merely emotional union

(which is what happens when sexual-reproductive complementarity is banished from the definition) removes all principled grounds for understanding marriage as a sexually exclusive and faithful union of two persons, not an "open" partnership or polyamorous sexual ensemble, we were charged with invalid slippery-slope reasoning. Remember?

No one, they assured us, would require Catholic or other foster-care and adoption services to place children in same-sex-headed households. No one, they said, would require religiously affiliated schools and social-service agencies to treat same-sex partners as spouses, or would impose penalties or disabilities on those that dissent. No one would be fired from his or her job (or suffer employment discrimination) for voicing support for conjugal marriage or criticizing same-sex sexual conduct and relationships. And no one was proposing to recognize polyamorous relationships or normalize "open marriages"; nor would redefinition undermine the norms of sexual exclusivity and monogamy in theory or practice.

That was then; this is now.

I must say, though, that I still can't fathom why anybody believed any of it—even then. The whole argument was and is that the idea of marriage as the union of husband and wife lacks a rational basis and amounts to nothing more than "bigotry." Therefore, no reasonable person of goodwill can dissent from the liberal position on sex and marriage, any more than a reasonable person of goodwill could support racial segregation and subordination. And this, because marriage, according to the redefiners, consists principally of the emotional union of people committed to mutual affection and care. Any distinctions beyond this one they condemn as baseless.

Since most liberals and even some conservatives, it seems, apparently have no understanding at all of the conjugal conception of marriage as a one-flesh union—not even enough of a grasp to consciously consider and reject it—they uncritically conceive of marriage as sexual-romantic companionship or domestic partnership, as if it couldn't possibly be anything else. This is despite the fact that the conjugal conception has historically been embodied in our marriage laws and explains their content (not just the requirement of spousal sexual complementarity but also rules concerning consummation and annulability, norms of monogamy and sexual exclusivity, and the pledge of permanence of commitment) in ways that the sexual-romantic domestic-partnership conception simply cannot. Still, seeing no possible alternative conception of marriage to the sexual-romantic domestic-partnership idea, they assume (and it is an assumption—a gratuitous one) that no actual reason exists for regarding sexual-reproductive complementarity as integral to marriage. After all, two men or two women can have a romantic interest in each other, live together in a sexual partnership, care for each other, and so forth. So why can't they be married? Those who support "traditional norms" of marriage, having no rational basis for their arguments, discriminate invidiously.

Thus, advocates of redefinition are increasingly open in saying that they do not see disputes about sex and marriage as honest disagreements among reasonable people of goodwill. They are, rather, battles between the forces of reason, enlightenment, and equality, on one side, and those of ignorance, bigotry, and discrimination, on the other. The "excluders" are to be treated just as racists are treated—since they are the equivalent of racists. Of course, we (in the United States, at least) don't put racists in jail for expressing their opinions—we respect the First Amendment. But we don't hesitate to stigmatize them and impose various forms of social and even civil disability on them and their institutions (in such areas as tax policy, professional licensing, and educational accreditation).

In the name of "marriage equality" and "nondiscrimination," liberty—especially religious liberty and the liberty of conscience—and genuine equality are undermined.

A fundamental error some supporters of conjugal marriage have made is to imagine that a grand bargain could be struck with their opponents: "We will accept the legal redefinition of marriage; you will respect our right to act on our consciences without penalty, discrimination, or civil disabilities of any type. Same-sex partners will get marriage licenses, but no one will be forced for any reason to recognize those marriages or suffer discrimination or disabilities for declining to recognize them." *There was never any hope of such a bargain being accepted.* Perhaps liberal forces would accept *parts* of such a bargain *temporarily* for strategic or tactical reasons, as part of the political project of getting marriage redefined. But guarantees of religious liberty and nondiscrimination for people who cannot in conscience accept same-sex marriage could then be eroded and eventually removed.

There is, in my opinion, no chance—*no chance*—of persuading champions of sexual liberation (and it should be clear by now that this is the cause they serve) that they should respect, or permit the law to respect, the conscience rights of those with whom they disagree. Look at it from their point of view: Why should we permit "full equality" to be trumped by bigotry? Why should we respect religions and religious institutions that are "incubators of homophobia"? Bigotry, religiously based or not, must be smashed and eradicated. The law should not give it recognition or lend it any standing or dignity.

The lesson for those of us who believe that the conjugal conception of marriage is true and good, and who wish to protect the rights of our faithful and of our institutions to honor that belief in carrying out their vocations and missions, is that there is no alternative to winning the battle in the public square over the legal definition of marriage. The "grand bargain" is an illusion we should dismiss from our minds.

Of course, with sexual liberalism now so powerfully entrenched in the established institutions of the elite sector of our culture (and, let us not kid ourselves, fully embraced by the leadership of the Democratic Party), some view the defense of marriage as a lost cause. I think that is another mistake—one that sexual liberals have every reason to encourage and ample resources to promote. We've all heard the argument (or taunt): "The acceptance of same-sex marriage on a national scale is inevitable. It's a done deal. You had better get on the right side of history."

But this is what we were told about a "woman's right" to abortion in the mid-1970s. And yet a greater percentage of Americans are pro-life today than in the 1970s, and young people are more pro-life than people of their parents' generation. The idea promoted by the abortion lobby when its cause seemed to be a juggernaut—that "the American people will inevitably accept abortion as a matter of women's rights and social hygiene"—proved spectacularly false.

Or, speaking of "social hygiene," think back to the 1920s and '30s when eugenics was embraced by elite institutions of American society—from wealthy philanthropic foundations, to the mainline Protestant denominations, to the Supreme Court of the United States. Affluent, sophisticated, "right-minded" people were on board with the eugenics program. It, too, seemed like a juggernaut. Only those retrograde Catholics, joined by some other backward religious folk, resisted; the thought was that their resistance would soon be broken by the sheer *rationality* of the eugenics idea. The eugenicists were certain that their adversaries were on "the wrong side of history." The full acceptance of eugenics was "inevitable." But, of course, things didn't quite turn out that way. (My point here is *not* to say or imply that redefining marriage is morally equivalent to abortion or eugenics. There are obvious and important differences. My point involves the claim that the triumph of each cause was "inevitable" and that those who declined to go along were "against progress" and had placed themselves on the "wrong side of history.")

Does this mean that, instead, the conjugal conception of marriage will inevitably prevail in law and culture? No. There is nothing inevitable in this domain. As the left-wing—but anti-Hegelian—Brazilian legal theorist Roberto Unger used to preach to us in courses at Harvard Law School, the future will be the fruit of human deliberation, judgment, and choice; it is not subject to fixed laws of history and forces of social determinism. As the Marxists learned the hard way, the reality of human freedom is the permanent foiler of "inevitability" theses. Same-sex marriage and the assaults on liberty and equality that follow in its wake are "inevitable" only if defenders of marriage make their adversaries' prophecies self-fulfilling ones by buying into them.

14

GOD AND GETTYSBURG

THE DECLARATION OF Independence, the Gettysburg Address, and the Constitution of the United States of America—those were the three texts in the blue pamphlet I found on the table in front of me as I took my seat at a conference at Princeton.

On the cover was the logo of the American Constitution Society for Law and Policy, an influential organization whose board members include former *New York Times* Supreme Court reporter Linda Greenhouse, controversial Obama judicial nominee Goodwin Liu, former New York governor Mario Cuomo, former solicitors general Drew Days and Walter Dellinger, and former attorney general Janet Reno. Before being appointed to the Supreme Court, Elena Kagan was a speaker at the society's annual conventions in 2005, 2007, and 2008. And inside the pamphlet was a page saying, "The printing of this copy of the U.S. Constitution and of the nation's two other founding texts, the Declaration of Independence and the Gettysburg Address, was made possible through the generosity of Laurence and Carolyn Tribe."

How nice, I thought. Here is a convenient, pocket-sized version of our fundamental documents, including Lincoln's great oration at Gettysburg on republican government. Although some might question the idea that a speech given more than eighty years after the Declaration qualifies as a founding text, its inclusion seemed to me entirely appropriate. By preserving the Union, albeit at a nearly incalculable cost in lives and suffering, Lincoln completed, in a sense, the American Founding. Victory at Gettysburg really did ensure that government "by the people" and "for the people"—republican government—would not "perish from the earth."

I recalled that in sixth grade I was required to memorize the address, and as I held the American Constitution Society's pamphlet in my hands, I wondered whether I could still recite it from memory. So I began, silently reciting: "Four score and seven years ago . . . ," until I reached "the world will little note nor long remember what we say here, but it can never forget what they did here." Then I drew a blank. So I opened the pamphlet and read the final paragraph:

> It is rather for us, the living, we here be dedicated to the great task remaining before us—that, from these honored dead we take increased devotion to that cause for which they here, gave the last full measure of devotion—that we here highly resolve these dead shall not have died in vain; that this nation shall have a new birth of freedom, and that government of the people by the people and for the people shall not perish from the earth.

Deeply moving—but, I thought, something isn't right. Did you notice what was omitted? What's missing is Lincoln's description of the United States as a nation under God. What Lincoln actually said at Gettysburg was: "that this nation, *under God*, shall have a new birth of freedom." The American Constitution Society had omitted Lincoln's reference to the United States as a nation under God from the address he gave at the dedication of the burial ground at Gettysburg.

At the time, staring at the text, I wondered whether it was an innocent, inadvertent error. It seemed more likely, though, that here was the apex of the secularist ideology that has attained a status not unlike that of religious orthodoxy among liberal legal scholars and political activists. Nothing is sacred, as it were—not even the facts of American history, not even the words spoken by Abraham Lincoln at the most solemn ceremony of our nation's history.

When the atheist Michael Newdow was challenging in court the inclusion of the words "under God" in the Pledge of Allegiance, he and his supporters pointed out that the words were not in the original pledge created in the 1920s. Congress added them in the 1950s in the midst of the Cold War, in response to a campaign led by the Catholic men's organization the Knights of Columbus. The words were introduced into the pledge to highlight the profound difference between the United States, whose political system is founded on the theistic proposition that all men are "endowed by their Creator with certain unalienable rights," and the atheistic premises of Soviet Marxism.

What Newdow and his supporters avoided mentioning is that the pledge's words *under God* were not pulled from a sermon by Billy Graham or a papal encyclical. They were taken from Lincoln's Gettysburg Address. The pledge, as amended, simply quotes one of our nation's founding texts.

This fact is more than a little inconvenient for those who hold that government must be neutral not only among competing traditions of religious faith but also between religion and atheism—or, as it is sometimes put, "between religion and irreligion." The constitutional basis for their claim is the religion clause of the First Amendment, which states that "Congress shall make no law respecting an establishment of religion, or prohibiting the free exercise thereof." They allege that these words were intended to forbid such things as descriptions of America as a nation "under God" in official government documents because the Founders sought "strict separation" of church and state.

But this puts the American Constitution Society in a sticky position. In assembling its pamphlet, the society was eager to include Lincoln as a Founder—the author of one of America's founding documents, the Gettysburg Address. But the Great Emancipator's characterization of the United States as a nation under God appears to undermine the strict separationism that the American Constitution Society wishes to promote. What to do?

The answer the society hit on was simply to make Lincoln's inconvenient words disappear. Now you are thinking: how did this group imagine it could get away with that? The Gettysburg Address is the opposite of an obscure document. Millions of Americans can recite it by heart.

Well, here the plot thickens. First, the society knows that it gets a certain level of immunity because its liberal secularist viewpoint is overwhelmingly the viewpoint of American legal academics and, indeed, academics generally. Even if the society were to be exposed, it would not be treated the way, say, the conservative Federalist Society would be treated if caught altering historical documents for ideological reasons. Second, the society knew that in a pinch it could muddy the waters by asserting that, in fact, five copies of the Gettysburg Address in Lincoln's hand exist, and two of them do not include the words "under God."

But that won't wash. The two drafts not containing the words are known as the Nicolay draft and the Hay draft. They are held in the Library of Congress. The other three, all containing the words, are known as the Everett, Bancroft, and Bliss copies. The Everett copy is held in the Illinois State Historical Society Library in Springfield. The Bancroft is in the Kroch Library at Cornell University. The Bliss is on display at the White House.

The Bliss copy is generally regarded as the authoritative one, mainly because it is the last—and the only one to which Lincoln attached his signature. The Nicolay draft is thought to be the earliest. It gets its name from the custodian of Lincoln's papers, John Nicolay, one of the president's private secretaries. The Hay draft was found about forty years after Lincoln's death among the papers of John Hay, Lincoln's other private secretary. It seems to have the greatest number of deviations from the other drafts and from what Lincoln is known to have said at Gettysburg. The Everett copy was sent to Edward Everett by Lincoln at Everett's request in 1864. (Everett was the famed orator who was actually the main speaker at the Gettysburg ceremony the day Lincoln spoke.) The Bancroft copy got its name because Lincoln produced it for George Bancroft, a historian and secretary of the navy. The Bliss copy is named for the publisher Alexander Bliss, Bancroft's stepson.

Of course, none of these copies is actually the Gettysburg Address. The Gettysburg Address is the set of words Lincoln spoke at Gettysburg. As it happens, we know what those words are. (The Bliss copy nearly perfectly reproduces them.) Three entirely independent reporters, including a reporter for the Associated Press, telegraphed their transcriptions of Lincoln's remarks to their editors immediately after the president spoke. All three transcriptions include the words "under God," and no contemporaneous report omits them. There isn't really room for equivocation or evasion: Abraham Lincoln's Gettysburg Address—one of the founding texts of the American republic—expressly characterizes the United States as a nation under God.

I was clearly not the first to notice the omission. When I went to the American Constitution Society's website, I found that the version of the pamphlet available as a PDF download had been amended to introduce the words "Hay Draft," albeit with no explanation of its meaning, as a subtitle for the Gettysburg Address. This tail-covering maneuver makes the society's intellectual dishonesty manifest. It is now impossible to suppose that the society's presentation of the Hay draft as the actual Gettysburg Address was an innocent error—the product, one might otherwise have thought, of a summer intern's overly hasty Internet search for the text of Lincoln's remarks at Gettysburg. The society's decision to exclude the words from Lincoln's Gettysburg Address must have been deliberate.

In short, a liberal legal advocacy organization omitted the words "under God" from a document the group characterizes as a founding text, this in the context of debates over the role of religion in American public life and the meaning of the Constitution's provisions pertaining to religion. These groups know exactly what they are doing, and, to achieve the result they want, they are willing to violate scholarly consensus, common sense, and the memorization of generations of schoolchildren.

Perhaps the American Constitution Society can provide some evidence to show that it did not have an ideological purpose in omitting words that, if included in a founding text, are so damaging to liberal orthodoxy on church-state issues. If so, we can look forward to a correction of the pamphlet's text on the society's website and in the next edition. We might then send the pamphlet, with the American Constitution Society's imprimatur, to the Supreme Court for its consideration when another case like Michael Newdow's reaches the justices.

Part III

LIFE AND DEATH

15

CONSCIENCE AND ITS ENEMIES

O VER THE PAST few years, we have become all too aware of the threats to conscience rights in various domains, especially those having to do with issues pertaining to the sanctity of human life and to sexual morality, marriage, and the family. These specific threats reflect and manifest attitudes and ideologies that are now deeply entrenched in the intellectual world and in the elite sector of the culture more generally. President Barack Obama, Secretary of Health and Human Services Kathleen Sebelius, and many, many other federal and state officials are advancing and supporting policies trampling conscience rights, such as the notorious Department of Health and Human Services (HHS) contraception and abortion drug mandate, because they have deeply absorbed me-generation dogmas that make nonsense of the very idea of conscience rights.

Secretary Sebelius and her closest collaborators, especially the Planned Parenthood Federation of America, insist that opponents of the HHS mandate oppose both women's health and science itself. There is rich irony here; neither HHS nor the White House has responded substantively to the flood of evidence submitted by experts demonstrating the lack of scientific support for the medical, demographic, or economic claims associated with the HHS mandate. This practice—refusing to grapple with the relevant evidence while using the mantle of "science" to silence or marginalize objectors—is commonly used by enemies of conscience.

The practice was not new to the Obama administration. In fact, an important example of these tactics emerged in 2008 when the American College of Obstetricians and Gynecologists (ACOG) issued a report that recommended denying meaningful conscience protection to medical professionals on the grounds of a nonscientific, ideologically dictated preference for widely available abortion.

Personal Opinions and Ideology, Not "Science"

On September 11, 2008, the President's Council on Bioethics heard testimony by Anne Lyerly, MD, chair of ACOG's Committee on Ethics. Dr. Lyerly appeared in connection with the council's review of her committee's opinion (No. 385) entitled "Limits of Conscientious Refusal in Reproductive Medicine." That opinion proposes that physicians in the field of women's health be *required as a matter of ethical duty* to refer patients for abortions and sometimes even to perform abortions themselves.

I found the ACOG Ethics Committee's opinion shocking and, indeed, frightening. One problem was its lack of regard—bordering on contempt, really—for the sincere claims of conscience of Catholic, Evangelical Protestant, Orthodox Jewish, and other pro-life physicians and health-care workers. But beyond that, it treated feticide—the deliberate destruction of a child in the womb—as if it were a matter of health care, rather than what it typically is: namely, a decision based on *nonmedical* considerations (such as whether a woman or her husband or boyfriend happens to want a child). On the understanding of medicine implicit in the report, the ends of medicine are fundamentally not about the preservation and restoration of health considered as an objective reality and human good but rather about satisfying the personal preferences or lifestyle desires of people who come to physicians requesting surgeries or other services, irrespective of whether these services are in any meaningful sense medically indicated.

Let's say that a woman conceives a child and is unhappy about it. Is she sick? Does she need an abortion for the sake of her health? Not on any reasonable understanding or definition of health, even if we mean mental health. Pregnancy is not a disease. It is a natural process. In the normal case, a pregnant woman is not sick. Nor in the overwhelming majority of cases does pregnancy pose a threat to a woman's health. This is clear enough, but to make it still clearer let's imagine that a woman who is initially unhappy to be pregnant changes her mind. On reflection, she's content to be pregnant and happy to have a baby on the way. Did she suddenly shift from being sick and in need of "health care" in the form of an abortion to being well? Now let's consider that a couple of months later, she changes her mind again. It turns out that the baby is a girl, and she really wants a boy. So she is once again unhappy about the pregnancy and she reverts to wanting an abortion. Did knowledge of the baby's sex transform her from being a healthy pregnant woman to being sick? The question answers itself.

Now let us consider the ACOG committee report. What jumped off the page at me when I first read it is that it is an exercise in moral philosophy—bad moral philosophy, but lay that aside for now—not medicine. It proposes a definition of conscience, something that cannot be supplied by science or medicine, then proposes to instruct its readers on "the limits of conscientious refusals, describing how claims of conscience should be weighed in the context of other values critical to the ethical provision of health care."

Again, knowledge of these limits and values, or of what should count as the ethical provision of health care, is not and cannot possibly be the product of scientific inquiry for medicine as such. The proposed instruction offered by those responsible for the ACOG

committee report represents a philosophical and ethical opinion—
their philosophical and ethical opinion.

The report goes on to "outline options for public policy" and
propose "recommendations that maximize accommodation of the
individual's religious and moral beliefs while avoiding imposition
of these beliefs on others or interfering with the safe, timely, and
financially feasible access to reproductive health care that all women
deserve." Yet again notice that every concept in play here—the putative balancing, the judgment as to what constitutes an "imposition"
of personal beliefs on others, the view of what constitutes health care
or reproductive health care, the judgment about what is deserved—is
philosophical, not scientific or, strictly speaking, medical.

To the extent that they are "medical" judgments even loosely
speaking, they reflect a concept of medicine informed, structured,
and shaped by philosophical and ethical judgments—bad ones, by the
way, such as the implicit judgment that pregnancy, when unwanted,
is in effect a disease.

Those responsible for the report purport to be speaking as physicians and medical professionals. The report's supposed authority
derives from their standing and expertise *as physicians and medical professionals*, yet at every point that matters, the judgments offered reflect
their philosophical, ethical, and political judgments, not any expertise they have by virtue of their training and experience in science and
medicine.

At the meeting of the President's Council, the chairman,
Dr. Edmund Pellegrino, asked me to offer a formal comment on
Dr. Lyerly's presentation of her committee's report. I was happy for
the opportunity to call her and her colleagues out on their attempt to
use their special authority as physicians to force fellow physicians to
practice medicine in accord with their contestable—and contested—
philosophical, ethical, and political judgments. And make no mistake
about it: at every key point in the report, their judgments are contestable and contested. Indeed, they are contested by the very people on
whose consciences they seek to impose—the people whom they would,

if their report were adopted and made binding, force into line with their philosophical and ethical judgments *or drive out of their fields of medical practice.* Many others contest the committee's judgments too. In each of these contests a resolution one way or the other cannot be determined by scientific methods; rather, the debate is *philosophical, ethical, or political.*

That is the key thing to see: the issues in dispute are philosophical and thus can be resolved only by philosophical reflection and debate; they cannot be resolved by science or methods of scientific inquiry. Lay aside for the moment the question of *whose* philosophical and political judgments are right and whose are wrong. The point is that the committee's report reflects and promotes a particular moral view and vision, and particular understandings of health and medicine shaped by that moral view and vision.

The report, in other words, in its driving assumptions, reasoning, and conclusions, is not morally neutral. It represents a partisan position among the possible positions debated by people of goodwill in the medical profession and in society generally. For me, the partisanship of the report is its most striking feature. It represents a sheer power play on behalf of pro-abortion individuals who happen to have acquired power in their professional association. This is not about medicine. It is about ideology. It is about politics and political power.

The greatest irony of the report is its stated worry about physicians allegedly imposing their beliefs on patients by, for example, declining to perform or refer for abortions—or at least declining to perform abortions or provide other services in emergency situations. The assumption here is the philosophical one that abortion, even elective abortion, is "health care," and that deliberately killing babies in their mother's wombs is morally acceptable and even a woman's right.

The truth is that the physician who refuses to perform abortions or the pharmacist who declines to dispense abortifacient drugs coerces no one. He or she simply refuses to participate in the destruction of human life—the life of the child in utero. Such a physician is not "imposing" anything on anyone, just as a sports shop owner who refuses to stock hollow-point "cop killer" bullets, even if he or she may legally sell them, is not imposing anything on anyone. By contrast, those responsible for the report evidently *would* use coercion against physicians and pharmacists who have the temerity to dissent from the philosophical and ethical views of those who happen to have acquired power in ACOG—by forcing them either to get in line or to go out of business.

If the committee's advice were followed, the medical field would be cleansed of pro-life physicians whose convictions required them to refrain from performing or referring for abortions. Faithful Catholics, Evangelicals and other Protestants, and many observant Jews and Muslims would be excluded from or forced out of obstetrics and gynecology. The entire field would be composed of people who agreed with, or at a minimum went along with, the moral and political convictions of the report's authors.

So, in truth, who in this debate is guilty of intolerance? Who is trampling on freedom? Who is imposing values on others? These questions, too, answer themselves.

It won't do to say that what the committee seeks to impose on dissenters is not a morality but merely good medical practice, for it is not science or medicine that is shaping the report's understanding of what counts as good medical practice. It is, rather, a moral opinion doing the shaping. The opinion that abortion is good medicine is a philosophical, ethical, and political opinion; it is a judgment *brought to* medicine, not a judgment *derived from* it. It reflects a view that abortion is morally legitimate and no violation of the rights of the child who is killed. It also reflects the view that medicine is rightly concerned with facilitating people's lifestyle choices even when they are neither sick nor in danger of being injured, and even when the "medical" procedure involves the taking of innocent human life.

Whether an elective abortion—or an in vitro fertilization procedure, or what have you—counts as health care, as opposed to a patient's desired outcome, cannot be resolved by the methods of science or by any morally or ethically neutral form of inquiry or reasoning. One's view of the matter will reflect one's moral and ethical convictions either way.

So the report's constant use of the language of "health" and "reproductive health" in describing or referring to the key issues giving rise to conflicts of conscience is *at best* question begging. No, that's too kind. The report's use of this language amounts to a form of rhetorical manipulation. The question at issue in abortion is not "reproductive health" or health of any kind, precisely because direct abortions are not procedures designed to make sick people healthy or to protect them against disease or injury. Again, pregnancy is not a disease. The goal of direct abortions is to cause the death of a child because a woman believes that her life will be better without the child's existing than it would be with the child's existing. In itself, a direct (or elective) abortion—deliberately bringing about the death of a child in utero—does nothing to advance maternal health (though sometimes the death of the child is an unavoidable side effect of a procedure, such as the removal of a cancerous womb, that is designed to combat a grave threat to the mother's health). That's why it is wrong to depict elective abortion as health care.

There is yet another irony worth noting. The report, in defending its proposal to compel physicians at least to refer for procedures that many physicians believe are immoral, unjust, and even homicidal, states that such referrals "need not be conceptualized as a repudiation or compromise of one's own values, but instead can be seen as an acknowledgment of both the widespread and thoughtful disagreement among physicians and society at large and the moral sincerity of others with whom one disagrees."

Suddenly it's the case that the underlying issues at stake, such as abortion, are matters of widespread and thoughtful disagreement. I agree with that. And it becomes clear from the report that we should show respect for the moral sincerity of those with whom we disagree. But it follows from these counsels that thoughtful and sincere people need not agree that abortion is morally innocent or acceptable, or that there is a "right" to abortion, or that the provision of abortion is part of good health care or is health care at all, at least in the case of elective abortions.

But then what could possibly justify *compelling* thoughtful, morally sincere physicians who believe that abortion is a homicidal injustice to perform or refer for the procedure, or else leave the practice of medicine? The report's "my way or the highway" view is anything but an acknowledgement of the widespread, thoughtful disagreement among physicians and society at large and the moral sincerity of those with whom one disagrees. Indeed, it is a repudiation of it.

Abortion and Conscience

Needless to say, the enemies of conscience in the medical establishment now have powerful friends in the highest realms of government. It has become all too clear that these friends share the desire to eradicate conscience protection for pro-life physicians and other healthcare workers and pharmacists. The Obama administration formally abrogated the conscience-protection regulations the Bush administration promulgated in 2008. The Bush regulations were long-overdue rules needed for the effective implementation and enforcement of conscience-protective federal laws that had been in place since the 1970s. They strengthened conscience protections for pro-life medical professionals and medical students in a variety of ways. For example, they very clearly prohibited any form of discrimination against practitioners and medical students who refused to undergo training for abortions, or to perform abortions, or to refer for abortions. Moreover, they proscribed discrimination in credentialing or licensing on grounds related to the refusal to be involved in the practice of abortion.

I suspect that the Obama administration's goal in abrogating conscience-protection regulations was to establish a policy very much in line with the ACOG Ethics Committee's proposed "ethics" rules on conscientious refusal in "reproductive" medicine.

This is no surprise. President Obama's fervent support for abortion is a matter of public record extending over his entire political career. To my knowledge, he has never supported a restriction on abortion or opposed an effort to expand its availability. He famously said that if one of his daughters "made a mistake," he would not want to see her "punished" with a baby.[1] He usually does not claim even to be "personally opposed" to abortion, as most "pro-choice" politicians claim to be. He opposed legislation prohibiting partial-birth abortions (a procedure in which the infant is killed after he or she is partially delivered outside the mother's body) and even fought against laws to protect children born alive after an unsuccessful attempt at abortion. As president, he revoked the Mexico City Policy, which prohibited the U.S. government from funding organizations that perform or promote abortions overseas, and he promised to fight for repeal of the Hyde Amendment, which forbids the federal funding of abortions in the United States. During the 2008 presidential campaign, he promised to give priority to enacting the provisions of the so-called Freedom of Choice Act, which would, in the words of the abortion lobby, overturn hundreds of state and federal anti-abortion laws, such as parental-notification requirements for minors seeking abortions and informed-consent laws requiring women contemplating abortions to be informed of the facts of fetal development and the physical and emotional risks of abortion. (So far, the president has not made good on this promise, though he is likely to be pressed by the abortion lobby to make good on it in his second term.) And, of course, President Obama is attempting to *require* religious employers (and everybody else) to provide health-care coverage not only for contraceptives and sterilization but also for abortion-inducing drugs such as Ella.

And so it falls to us to resist, and to do so not only for the sake of defending the lives of our most vulnerable brothers and sisters—children in the womb—but also in defense of what James Madison called "the sacred rights of conscience." Today, many of those who would sanction and support the taking of human life by abortion or in embryo-destructive research have also made themselves the enemies of conscience. We who are the friends of life must also be the friends of conscience. Indeed, we must be conscience's best friends. For many of us, standing up for conscience means defending the principles of our faith. For all of us, standing up for conscience means defending principles on which our nation was founded.

16

WHEN LIFE BEGINS

WHEN DOES THE life of a human individual begin? Although the question is of obvious importance for our public policy debates over abortion and embryonic-stem-cell research, politicians have usually avoided it like the plague. Things may be changing, however. In recent years some of our nation's most prominent political leaders have weighed in on the question.

Faced with the complicated and not very widely known facts of human embryology, most people are inclined to agree with the sentiment expressed by Nancy Pelosi, the Democratic leader in the House of Representatives, who stated, "I don't think anybody can tell you when . . . human life begins."

But is Pelosi correct? Is it actually the case that no one can tell you with any degree of authority when the life of a human being actually begins?

No, it is not. Treating the question as some sort of grand mystery, or expressing or feigning uncertainty about it, may be politically expedient, but it is intellectually indefensible. Modern science long ago resolved the question. We actually know when the life of a new human individual begins.

The facts of human embryogenesis and early development make the conclusion inescapable: from a purely biological perspective, *scientists can identify the point at which a human life begins.* The relevant studies are legion. The biological facts are uncontested. The method of analysis applied to the data is universally accepted.[1]

Your life began, as did the life of every other human being, when the fusion of egg and sperm produced a new, complete, living organism—an embryonic human being. You were never an ovum or a sperm cell; those were both functionally and genetically parts of other human beings—your parents. But you *were* once an embryo, just as you were once an adolescent, a child, an infant, and a fetus. By an internally directed process, you developed from the embryonic stage into and through the fetal, infant, child, and adolescent stages of development and ultimately into adulthood with your determinateness, unity, and identity fully intact. You are the same being—the same *human* being—who once was an embryo.

It is true that each of us, in the embryonic and fetal stages of development, were dependent on our mothers, but we were not maternal body parts. Though dependent, we were distinct individual human beings. That is why physicians who treat pregnant women know that they are caring not for one patient but for two (or more than two, in cases of twins and triplets).

Why, then, do we seem so far from a consensus on questions of abortion and embryo-destructive research?

Perhaps because the debate over when human life begins has never been about the biological facts. It has been about the *value* we ascribe to human beings at the dawn of their lives. When we debate questions of abortion, assisted reproductive technologies, human embryonic stem-cell research, and human cloning, we are not really disagreeing about whether human embryos are human beings. The scientific evidence is simply too overwhelming for there to be any real debate on this point. What is at issue in these debates is the question of whether we ought to respect and defend human beings in the earliest stages of their lives. In other words, the question is not about scientific facts; it is about the nature of human dignity and the equality of human beings.

On one side are those who believe that human beings have dignity and rights *by virtue of their humanity*. They believe that all human beings, irrespective not only of race, ethnicity, and sex but also of age, size, and stage of development, are equal in fundamental worth and dignity. The right to life is a human right, and therefore all human beings, from the point at which they come into being (conception) to the point at which they cease to be (death), possess it.

On the other side are those who believe that those human beings who have worth and dignity have them *in virtue of having achieved a certain level of development*. They deny that all human beings have worth and dignity and hold that a distinction should be drawn between those human beings who have achieved the status of "personhood" and those (such as embryos, fetuses, and, according to some, infants and severely retarded or demented individuals) whose status is that of human nonpersons.

A common error is for people to convert the question of when a human life begins from a matter of biology to a matter of religious faith or personal belief. Both as a senator and as vice president of the United States, Joe Biden has asserted that although he believes life begins at the moment of conception, this is a "personal" belief deriving from his religion that may not legitimately be imposed on others.[2]

Biden is perfectly correct about when a life begins—at conception. But he is wrong to suppose that this is a mere matter of personal opinion or a position deriving only from religion. It is a matter of biological fact. Politics should not be permitted to trump it.

In view of the established facts of human embryogenesis and early intrauterine development, the real question is not whether human beings in the embryonic and fetal stages are human beings. *Plainly they are.* The question is whether we will honor or abandon our civilizational and national commitment to the equal worth and dignity of all human beings—even the smallest, youngest, weakest, and most vulnerable.

17

EMBRYO ETHICS

What Science Tells Us,
What Justice Demands of Us

WHEN PRESIDENT BARACK Obama permitted federal taxpayer dollars to be used for research involving the destruction of human embryos, the decision dramatically revived the debate over the moral status of the human embryo. There are reasonable people of goodwill on both sides of this debate. Such people recognize that the question is difficult and that their opponents are neither knaves nor fools.

This does not mean that there is no right answer, or that the right answer cannot be known. But getting to the right answer requires careful reflection and argumentation—argumentation that attends to the facts of human embryogenesis and early development, and applies sound philosophical principles in light of the facts. Responsible people on both sides of the debate know, and do not hesitate to admit, that their opponents have advanced serious arguments and that these arguments must be thoughtfully engaged and answered. I believe it is necessary to engage the very best arguments in support of the position opposed to my own.

At the heart of the debate are two fundamental questions. The first is scientific, and it is to be answered by appeal to the facts that modern human embryology and developmental biology have established: Are human embryos human beings in the earliest stages of their natural development, or are they entities of another sort—say, mere clumps of cells, or prehuman organisms? The second question is philosophical: If human embryos are, as I argue, embryonic human beings, do they have the same right as human beings at other developmental stages to be treated with respect and not as raw material for scientific research in which they are deliberately killed?

The Irrelevance of the Theology of "Ensoulment"

I will say almost nothing here about religion or theology. That is not a tactical decision; rather, it reflects my view on how to think about the dispute over human embryo killing. It is sometimes said that opposition to embryo-destructive research is based on a controversial theology of "ensoulment." But I don't think the question has anything to do with "ensoulment" or whether a human being who dies in the embryonic stage will have spiritual remains in the form of an immaterial soul.

Questions of whether human beings have immortal spiritual souls needn't be engaged in arguments about whether human embryos are human beings. And one need not appeal to any theology of ensoulment to assert that there is a rational basis for treating all human beings—including those at the embryonic stage—as creatures possessing intrinsic worth and dignity. Question of ensoulment and the eternal fate of human beings who die before birth are, to be sure, interesting *theological* questions, but they are not necessary to the *moral* debate and the question of *public policy*.[1]

My view is that we should resolve our national debate over embryo-destructive research on the basis of the best scientific evidence as to when the life of a new human being begins and the most careful philosophical reasoning as to what is owed to nascent human life. Faith can, I believe, motivate us to stand up and speak out in defense of human life and dignity. And religious people should never hesitate to do that. But we need not rely on religious faith to tell us whether a human embryo is a new human life or whether all human beings—irrespective not only of race, ethnicity, and sex but also of age, size, stage of development, and condition of dependency—possess full moral worth and dignity. The application of fundamental philosophical principles in light of facts established by modern embryological science is more than sufficient for that task.[2]

Human Embryos Are Embryonic Humans

The adult human being that is now you or I is the same human being who, at an earlier stage of his or her life, was an adolescent, and before that a child, an infant, a fetus, and an embryo.[3] Even in the embryonic stage, you and I were undeniably whole, living members of the species *Homo sapiens*. We were then, as we are now, distinct and complete human organisms (though in the beginning we were, of course, developmentally immature); we were not mere parts of other organisms.

A human embryo is not something different *in kind* from a human being, like a rock, or a potato, or a rhinoceros. A human embryo is a human individual in the earliest stage of his or her natural development.[4] Unless severely damaged or deprived of a suitable environment, an embryonic human being will, by an internally directed process of integral organic functioning, develop to each more mature developmental stage along the gapless continuum of a human life. The embryonic, fetal, infant, child, and adolescent stages are just that: *stages* in the development of a determinate and enduring entity—a human being—who comes into existence as a single-cell organism (zygote) and develops, if all goes well, into adulthood many years later.[5]

By contrast, the gametes whose union brings into existence the embryo are not whole or distinct organisms. They are functionally (and genetically) identifiable as *parts* of the male or female (potential) parents. Each has only half the genetic material needed to guide the development of an immature human being toward full maturity. They are destined either to combine with an oocyte or spermatozoon to generate a new and distinct organism, or simply to disintegrate. Even when fertilization occurs, they do not survive; rather, their genetic material enters into the composition of a new organism.

But none of this is true of the human embryo, from the zygote and blastula stages onward. The combining of the chromosomes of the spermatozoon and of the oocyte generates what human embryology identifies as a new, distinct, and enduring organism. Whether produced by fertilization or by somatic-cell nuclear transfer (SCNT) or some other cloning technique, the human embryo possesses all the genetic material needed to inform and organize its growth. [6] The direction of its growth *is not extrinsically determined* but is in accord with the genetic information *within* it.[7] Nor does it merely possess organizational information for maturation; rather, if left to itself in a suitable environment, it will develop using that information. The human embryo is, then, a whole and distinct human organism—an embryonic human being.

If the embryo were not a complete organism, then what could it be? Unlike the spermatozoa and the oocytes, it is not simply a part of a larger organism—namely, the mother or the father. Nor is it a disordered growth or gamete tumor such as a complete hydatidiform mole or teratoma.

Perhaps someone will say that the early embryo is an intermediate form, something that regularly emerges into a whole human organism but is not one yet. But what could cause the emergence of the whole human organism, and cause it with regularity? As I have already observed, it is clear that from the zygote stage forward the major development of this organism is *controlled and directed from within*—that is, by the organism itself. After the embryo comes into being, no event or series of events occurs that could be construed as the production of a new organism; that is, nothing extrinsic to the developing organism itself acts on it to produce a new character or new direction in development.[8]

Do Embryonic Human Beings Deserve Respect?

A supporter of embryo-destructive research might concede that a human embryo is a human being, in a biological sense, yet deny that human beings in the early stages of their development are due full moral respect such that they may not be killed to benefit more fully developed human beings suffering from afflictions.[9]

But to deny that embryonic human beings deserve full respect, one must suppose that not every human being deserves full respect. And to do that, one must hold that those human beings who deserve full respect deserve it in virtue not of the kind of entity they are but rather of some acquired characteristic that some human beings (or human beings at some stages) have and others do not have and that some human beings have in greater degree than others.

In my judgment, this position is untenable. It is clear that one need not be actually or immediately conscious, reasoning, deliberating, making choices, etc., to be a human being who deserves full moral respect, for plainly people who are asleep or in reversible comas deserve such respect. So if one denies that human beings are intrinsically valuable in virtue of what they are, and holds instead that they require an additional attribute, the additional attribute has to be a capacity of some sort, and obviously a capacity for certain mental functions.

Of course, human beings in the embryonic, fetal, and early-infant stages lack immediately exercisable capacities for mental functions that most human beings carry out at later stages of maturity. Still, they possess in radical form these very capacities—radical in the original sense of going to the root. Precisely by virtue of *the kind of entity they are*, they are from the beginning actively developing themselves to the stages at which these capacities will (if all goes well) be immediately exercisable. Although, like infants, they have not yet developed themselves to the stage at which they can perform intellectual operations, it is clear that they are *rational animal organisms*.[10] That is the *kind* of entity they are.

Defining Capacities

It is important, then, to distinguish two senses of the "capacity" (or what is sometimes referred to as the "potentiality") for mental functions: an immediately exercisable capacity, and a basic natural capacity, which develops over time. And there are good reasons for believing that the second sort of capacity, not the first, provides the justificatory basis for regarding human beings as ends in themselves, not as means only—as bearers of inherent dignity and subjects of justice and human rights, not as mere objects.

First, the developing human being does not reach a level of maturity at which he or she performs a type of mental act that other animals do not perform—even animals such as dogs and cats—until at least several months after birth. A six-week-old baby lacks the *immediately exercisable* capacity to perform characteristically human mental functions. So if full moral respect were due only to those who possess immediately exercisable capacities for characteristically human mental functions, it would follow that six-week-old infants do not deserve full moral respect.[11] Thus, if human embryos may legitimately be destroyed to advance biomedical science, then it follows logically that, subject to parental approval, the body parts of human infants should be fair game for scientific experimentation. (This is no exaggeration; some philosophers have explicitly made these arguments.)[12]

Second, the difference between these two types of capacity is merely a difference between stages along a continuum. The immediately exercisable capacity for mental functions is only the development of an underlying potentiality that the human being possesses simply by virtue of the kind of entity it is. The capacities for reasoning, deliberating, and making choices are gradually developed, or brought toward maturation, through gestation, childhood, adolescence, and so on. But the difference between a being that deserves full moral respect and a being that does not (and can therefore legitimately be killed to benefit others) cannot consist only in the fact that, while both have some feature, one has *more* of it than the other. A *quantitative* difference (having more or less of the same feature, such as the development of a basic natural capacity) cannot by itself be a justificatory basis for treating different entities in radically different ways.[13]

Third, the acquired qualities that could be proposed as criteria for personhood come in varying degrees: developed abilities or dispositions, such as for self-consciousness or rationality, come in an infinite number of degrees. So if human beings were worthy of full moral respect only because of such qualities, then, because such qualities come in varying degrees, no account could be given of why human beings do not possess basic rights in varying degrees. The proposition that all human beings are created equal would be relegated to the status of a myth; since some people are more rational than others (that is, have developed that capacity to a greater extent than others), some people would be greater in dignity than others, and the rights of the superiors would trump those of the inferiors.[14]

So it cannot be the case that *some* human beings *and not others* are intrinsically valuable, by virtue of a certain degree of development. Rather, human beings are intrinsically valuable (in the way that enables us to ascribe to them equality and basic rights) in virtue of what kind of being they are—and *all* human beings are intrinsically valuable.

Since human beings are intrinsically valuable and deserve full moral respect in virtue of *what* they are, it follows that they are intrinsically and equally valuable *from the point at which they come into being*. Even in the embryonic stage of our lives, each of us was a human being and, as such, worthy of concern and protection. Embryonic human beings, whether brought into existence by union of gametes, SCNT, or other cloning technologies, should be accorded the respect given to human beings in other developmental stages.[15]

Parts and Wholes

Advocates of embryo-destructive research have advanced several arguments to cast doubt on the proposition that human embryos deserve to be accorded full moral status. For example, Ronald Bailey, a science writer for *Reason* magazine, has developed an analogy between embryos and somatic cells in light of the possibility of human cloning.[16] Bailey claims that every cell in the human body has as much potential for development as any human embryo. Embryos therefore have no greater dignity or higher moral status than ordinary somatic cells. Bailey observes that each cell in the human body possesses the entire DNA code; each has become specialized (as muscle, skin, and so forth) because most of that code has been turned *off*. In cloning, those portions of the code previously deactivated are reactivated. So, Bailey says, quoting Australian bioethicist Julian Savulescu: "If all our cells could be persons, then we cannot appeal to the fact that an embryo could be a person to justify the special treatment we give it." Since plainly we are not prepared to regard all our cells as human beings, we shouldn't regard embryos as human beings.

But Bailey's analogy between somatic cells and human embryos collapses under scrutiny. The somatic cell is something from which (together with extrinsic causes) a new organism can be *generated*; it is certainly not a distinct organism. A human embryo, by contrast, already is a distinct, self-developing, complete human organism.

Bailey suggests that the somatic cell and the embryo are on the same level because both have the "potential" to develop to a mature human being. The kind of "potentiality" somatic cells possess that might be used in cloning differs profoundly, however, from the potentiality of the embryo. A somatic cell has a potential only in the sense that something can be done to it so that its constituents (its DNA molecules) enter into a distinct whole human organism, which is a human being, a person. In the case of the embryo, by contrast, he or she already is actively, dynamically developing to the further stages of maturity of the distinct organism—the human being—he or she already is.

True, the whole genetic code is present in each somatic cell, and this code can be used to guide the growth of a new entire organism. But this point does nothing to show that the somatic cell's potentiality is the same as that of a human embryo. When the nucleus of an ovum is removed and a somatic cell is inserted into the remainder of the ovum and given an electric stimulus, this does more than merely place the somatic cell in an environment hospitable to its continuing maturation and development. It generates a wholly distinct, self-integrating, entirely new organism—it generates an embryo. The entity—the embryo—that this process brings into being is quite radically different from the constituents that entered into its generation.

Agata Sagan and Peter Singer have attempted to rescue Bailey's argument. They insist that the enucleated ovum, or ovular cytoplasm, is only environment (and so the fusion of a stem cell with it does not produce a new entity). If the nucleus of a stem cell were transferred to a different egg with different cytoplasm, this would not result (in their judgment) in a different embryo.[17] They conclude—comparing embryos to stem cells rather than to somatic cells (à la Bailey)—that "it would seem that if the human embryo has moral standing and is entitled to protection in virtue of what it can become, then the same must be true of human embryonic stem cells."[18]

So the question is: Is the ovular cytoplasm merely a suitable environment enabling an already existing organism (the somatic cell or stem cell) to develop capacities already within it (the claim of Bailey, Sagan, and Singer), or, on the contrary, is it a cause (or co-cause) that produces a substantial change resulting in the coming to be of a new organism, the embryo (my view)?

Notice, first, that a new organism might be generated by the interaction of two causes or by two different co-causes. Consider the case (discussed by Aristotle) of division of a flatworm. If a flatworm is split, the resulting parts have the potential to become a whole flatworm. But any of various mechanical forces might produce two flatworms and thus be the cause of the coming to be of new substances. Therefore, the fact—if it is a fact, and that is not clear—that the same embryo could be produced by cloning with this enucleated ovum or with that one does not show that the enucleated ovum is mere environment.

Moreover, in the transformation of a stem cell into a whole organism when it is fused with ovular cytoplasm, the cytoplasm is more than just suitable environment, and the change is a coming to be of a new organism. This is obvious for two reasons. First, the stem cell was not a whole organism prior to this fusion. Before its fusion, the cell functioned together with the other parts of a larger organism for the survival and flourishing of *that* organism, not of itself. After the fusion, there is a new and complete (i.e., whole) organism, not just a part. Second, something that qualifies as "merely environmental" does not enter into an organism and modify its internal parts, resulting in an entity with a new developmental trajectory. But the ovular cytoplasm does just that in regard to the somatic cell or stem cell (or its nucleus) placed within it. The cytoplasm, or factors in the cytoplasm, *reprogram* the nucleus of the cell (whether somatic or stem) fused with it. The crucial fact that undermines Sagan and Singer's effort to rescue Bailey's argument is that factors of the cytoplasm *change the epigenetic state* of what was hitherto a somatic cell or stem cell (or its nucleus). These factors modify the genes in various ways— for example, subtracting methyl groups from key molecules in the somatic or stem cell's DNA—so that it becomes dedifferentiated. That is to say, it ceases to be a somatic cell or a stem cell (a part of a larger organism); a new whole organism is produced (an embryo).

In the context of cloning, then, somatic cells are analogous not to embryos but to the gametes whose union results in the generation of an embryo in the case of ordinary sexual reproduction. You and I were never either a sperm cell or an ovum. Nor would a person who was brought into being by a process of cloning have been once a somatic cell. To destroy an ovum or a skin cell whose constituents might have been used to generate a new and distinct human organism is not to destroy a new and distinct human organism—for no such organism exists or ever existed. But to destroy a human embryo is precisely to destroy a new, distinct, and complete human organism—an embryonic human being.[19]

Personhood and the Brain

Michael Gazzaniga, a distinguished scholar of cognitive science at the University of California, Santa Barbara, and my colleague on the President's Council on Bioethics, has proposed a different argument. While agreeing that a human embryo is an entity possessing a human genome, he suggests that a human being in the sense of a "person" comes into being only with the development of a brain; that prior to that point, he says, we have a human organism, but one lacking the dignity and rights of a person.[20] Human beings in the earliest stages of development may therefore legitimately be treated as we would treat organs available for transplantation (assuming, as with transplantable organs, that proper consent for their use was given). In presenting his case, Dr. Gazzaniga observes that modern medicine treats the death of the brain as the death of the person—authorizing the harvesting of organs from the remains of the person, even if some physical systems are still functioning. If a human being is no longer a person with rights once the brain has died, then surely, he argues, a human being is not yet a person prior to the development of the brain.

This argument suffers, however, from a damning defect. Under prevailing law and medical practice, the rationale for "brain death" is not that a brain-dead body is a living human organism but no longer a "person." Rather, brain death is accepted because the irreversible collapse of the brain is believed to destroy the capacity for self-directed integral organic functioning of human beings who have matured to the stage at which the brain performs a key role in integrating the organism. In other words, at brain death there is no longer a unitary organism at all. By contrast, although an embryo has not yet developed a brain, it is clearly exercising self-directed integral organic functioning and so *is* a unitary organism—an embryonic human being. Its capacity to develop a brain is inherent and developing, just as the capacity of an infant to develop its brain sufficiently for it to actually *think* is inherent and developing.

Unlike a corpse—the remains of what was once a human organism but is now dead, even if particular systems may be artificially sustained—a human organism in the embryonic stage of development is a complete, unified, self-integrating human individual. It is not dead but very much alive, even though its self-integration and organic functioning are not brain directed at this stage. Its future lies ahead of it, unless it is cut off or not permitted to develop its inherent capacities. Thus it is that I and other defenders of embryonic human life insist that the embryo is not a "potential life" but rather a life *with potential*. It is a potential *adult*, in the same way that fetuses, infants, children, and adolescents are potential adults. It has the potential for agency, just as fetuses, infants, and small children do. But, like human beings in the fetal, infant, child, and adolescent stages, human beings in the embryonic stage are already, and not merely potentially, *human beings*.[21]

Acorns and Embryos

In an essay in the *New England Journal of Medicine*, the eminent Harvard political theorist Michael Sandel, another former Bioethics Council colleague, claims that human embryos are different *in kind* from human beings at later developmental stages. This argument truly takes us to the heart of the matter: is a human embryo a human being? At its core is an analogy:

> Although every oak tree was once an acorn, it does not follow that acorns are oak trees, or that I should treat the loss of an acorn eaten by a squirrel in my front yard as the same kind of loss as the death of an oak tree felled by a storm. Despite their developmental continuity, acorns and oak trees are different kinds of things.

So Sandel maintains that, just as acorns are not oak trees, embryos are not human beings. But this argument fails, and it fails in a way that highlights the basic error in supposing that human embryos lack fundamental worth or dignity and may therefore legitimately be relegated to the status of disposable research material.

Professor Sandel's argument begins to go awry with his choice of analogates. The acorn is analogous to the embryo and the oak tree (he says) is analogous to . . . the "human being." But in view of the developmental continuity that science fully establishes, and Sandel concedes, the proper analogate of the oak tree is the *mature* human being—that is, the adult. Sandel's analogy has its apparent force because we really do feel a sense of loss when a mature oak is felled. But while it is true that we do not feel the same sense of loss at the destruction of an acorn, it is also true that we do not feel the same sense of loss at the destruction of an oak *sapling*. Clearly the oak tree does not differ in kind from the oak sapling. This shows that we value oak trees not because of the kind of entity they are but rather because of their magnificence. Neither acorns nor saplings are magnificent, so we do not experience a sense of loss when they are destroyed.

The basis for our valuing human beings is profoundly different. As Sandel concedes, we value human beings precisely because of the *kind* of entities they are. Indeed, that is why we consider all human beings to be equal in basic dignity and human rights. We most certainly do not consider that especially magnificent human beings— such as Michael Jordan or Albert Einstein—are of greater *fundamental and inherent* worth and dignity than human beings who are physically frail or mentally impaired. We would not tolerate the killing of a Down syndrome child or a person suffering from, say, brain cancer in order to harvest transplantable organs to save Jordan or Einstein.

And we do not tolerate the killing of infants, which on Sandel's analogy would be *precisely* analogous to the oak saplings whose destruction in forest management we do not regret. Managers of oak forests freely kill saplings, just as they might destroy acorns, to ensure the health of the more mature trees. No one gives it a second thought. This is precisely because we do not have reason to value members of the oak species—as we value human beings—because of the *kind* of entity they are. If we did value oaks for the kind of entity they are, and not for their magnificence, then we would have no less reason to regret the destruction of saplings and even acorns than oak trees. Conversely, if we valued human beings in a way analogous to that in which we value oak trees, then we would have no reason to object to killing human infants or even mature human beings who were severely "defective."

Sandel's defense of embryo killing on the basis of an analogy between embryos and acorns collapses the moment one brings into focus the profound difference between our ground for valuing oak trees and our ground for ascribing intrinsic value and dignity to human beings. We value oaks for their accidental properties and the instrumental value they provide. But we value human beings because of the intrinsic worth and dignity they possess in virtue of the kind of entity they are.[22]

Twinning and Implantation

A final claim from defenders of embryo-destructive research is that, given the phenomenon of monozygotic twinning, the embryo in the first several days of its gestation is not a human individual. Some claim that as long as twinning can occur—that is, as long as the embryo can divide, giving rise to "identical" twins—what exists is not yet a unitary human being but only a mass of cells. Each cell, in this view, is "toti-potent," which is to say that if it is detached from the whole, it can become a distinct organism, one that develops to maturity as distinct from the embryo from which it was detached.

It is true that a cell or group of cells detached at an early stage of embryonic development can sometimes become a distinct organism and has the potential to develop to maturity. But this does nothing to show that before detachment the cells within the human embryo constituted only an incidental mass. The fact that a human individual in the embryonic stage can divide or be divided into two individuals is no cause for doubting that the individual is a human being. Consider the parallel case of the flatworm again. Parts of a flatworm have the potential to become a whole flatworm when isolated from the present whole of which they are part. Yet no one would suggest that prior to the division, the original flatworm was not a unitary individual, not a whole living member of the species. Likewise, at the early stages of human embryonic development, before cell specialization has progressed very far, the cells or groups of cells can become whole organisms if they are divided and have an appropriate environment after the division. But that fact does not in the least indicate that prior to the twinning event the embryo is other than a unitary, self-integrating, actively developing human organism. It certainly does not show that the embryo is a mere "clump of cells."

Although there remains a bit of uncertainty as to what typically causes the phenomenon of monozygotic twinning in humans and nonhuman animals, the evidence increasingly suggests that twinning of this sort is a natural form of cloning. Embryo A does not disappear while giving rise to embryos B and C. Rather, embryo B is a clone of embryo A, which continues to exist. Of course, Alan and Andrew or Jennifer and Jessica never know which of the two of them is A and which is B. But as a practical matter, who cares? To have destroyed embryo A (Jennifer, let us assume) prior to the emergence of embryo B (Jessica) would not have been to have destroyed Jessica (who, after all, never exists in this scenario), but it would have been to have destroyed Jennifer at a very early stage of her development.

In the first two weeks, the cells of a developing embryonic human being already manifest a degree of specialization and differentiation. From the very beginning, even at the two-cell stage, the cells differ in the cytoplasm received from the original ovum. Also they are differentiated by their position within the embryo. Even in the unfertilized ovum, there is already an "animal" pole and a "vegetal" pole.[23] After the initial cleavage, the cell coming from the "animal" pole is probably the primordium of the nervous system and the other senses, and the cell coming from the "vegetal" pole is probably the primordium of the digestive system.

Now, some people have claimed that the human embryo does not become a human being until implantation, because (they assume) the embryo cannot establish a basic body plan until it receives external, maternal signals at implantation; only then is it a self-directing human organism. According to this view, these signaling factors somehow transform what was hitherto a mere bundle of cells into a unitary human organism.

But does such maternal signaling actually occur? As embryologist Hans-Werner Denker observes, new evidence has led to a revision in thinking. It was once assumed that in mammals, in contrast to amphibians and birds, polarity in the early embryo depends on some external signal, since no clear indications of bilateral symmetry had been found in oocytes, zygotes, or early blastocysts. But, writes Denker, embryologists at both Oxford and Cambridge have found indications "that in mammals the axis of bilateral symmetry is indeed determined (although at first in a labile way) by sperm penetration, as in amphibians." He adds that "bilateral symmetry can already be detected in the early blastocyst and is not dependent on implantation." These findings show that polarity exists even at the two-cell stage.[24] Helen Pearson summarized this surprising shift in embryological thinking in an article in the scientific journal *Nature* entitled "Your Destiny, from Day One." That title says it all: your life began on the day you were conceived. From the earliest embryonic stage of your development, you were a complete organism, a living member of the species *Homo sapiens*. You did not begin as a nonhuman or prehuman creature and only later become a human being. You were a human being from the beginning.

Moreover—and here is the most important point—even if it were the case, as was once supposed, that polarity does not emerge until a maternal signal is received at implantation, that would *not* provide any evidence that such a signal transformed a bundle of cells into a unitary, multicellular human organism. Just as the lungs begin to breathe at birth only in response to certain external stimuli, so it would make sense (if the older view was true) that differentiation into the rudiments of the distinct body parts (basic bilateral polarity) would begin only in response to some external stimuli. And this is exactly how embryology texts interpreted such signals, which were speculated to occur in mammalian embryos, before the Oxford and Cambridge embryologists published their findings.

There is much evidence that the human embryo is from day one onward—even before implantation—a unitary organism, never a mere bundle of cells. Development in the embryo is complex and coordinated, including compaction, cavitation, and other activities in which the embryo is preparing itself for implantation.

The clearest evidence that the embryo in the first two weeks is not a mere mass of cells but is a unitary organism is this: if the individual cells within the embryo before twinning were each independent of the others, there would be no reason why each would not regularly develop on its own. Instead, these allegedly independent, noncommunicating cells regularly function together to develop into a single, more mature member of the human species. This fact shows that interaction is taking place between the cells from the very beginning, restraining them from individually developing as whole organisms and directing each of them to function as a relevant part of a single, whole organism continuous with the zygote.

So the fact of twinning does not show that the embryo is an incidental mass of cells. Rather, the evidence clearly indicates that the human embryo, from the zygote stage forward, is a unitary, human organism.[25]

The Stain on Our National Conscience

President Obama's decision to use federal taxpayer dollars to fund embryo-destructive research makes it certain that the debate about the value of embryonic human life will continue. But if that debate is informed by serious attention to the facts of embryogenesis and early human development, and to the profound, inherent, and equal dignity of human beings, then we, as a nation, will in the end reverse the course the president has put us on and reject the deliberate taking of embryonic human life, regardless of the promised benefits.

Does this mean we must sacrifice such benefits altogether? The answer to that question, I believe, is no. Scientists have already made tremendous progress toward the goal of producing fully pluripotent stem cells by non-embryo-destructive methods. Were such methods pursued with vigor, the future might see the promise of stem-cell science fulfilled, with no stain on our national conscience.

18

THE PERSONAL AND
THE POLITICAL

Some Liberal Fallacies

W E HAVE ALL heard the refrain: a politician claims to be "personally opposed" to abortion and embryo-destructive research but nevertheless supports keeping the practices legal so as not to "impose" his or her views on others. Among those to espouse this position are Vice President Joe Biden, Senator John Kerry, and former New York governor Mario Cuomo.[1] Cuomo may be the best-known exponent of this position. He famously articulated the view in a speech at the University of Notre Dame in 1984. Cuomo revisited the issue in 2002, speaking at a forum on "Politics and Faith in America."

The former governor is also a former law professor. He is a student of history, philosophy, and theology, and his speeches and writings reflect a range of intellectual interests. But something went wrong in Cuomo's 2002 speech.

The address is littered with fallacies—fallacies that need to be corrected, as they are often injected into the public debate over life issues. Arguments like Cuomo's, if successful, not only justify support for legal abortion and embryo-destructive research but actually *require* the legal right to engage in these practices despite their admitted moral wrongfulness.

Spectacular Fallacies

Things begin going wrong in Cuomo's speech almost right off the bat. In setting up his analysis of the question of religious faith in politics, Cuomo evidently forgets a basic principle of logical argumentation: one cannot employ as a premise the very proposition one is marshaling an argument to prove. The former governor asserts that holders of public office—including Catholic officeholders like him—have a responsibility "to create conditions under which all citizens are reasonably free to act according to their own religious beliefs, even when those acts conflict with Roman Catholic dogma regarding divorce, birth control, abortion, stem cell research, and even the existence of God." According to Cuomo, Catholics should support legalized abortion and embryo-destructive research, as he himself does, because in guaranteeing these rights to others, they guarantee their own right "to reject abortions, and to refuse to participate in or contribute to removing stem cells from embryos."

But Cuomo's idea that the right "to reject" abortion and embryo-destructive experimentation entails a right of others, as a matter of religious liberty, to engage in these practices is simply—and spectacularly—fallacious. The fallacy comes into focus immediately if one considers whether the right of a Catholic (or Baptist, or Jew, or member of any other faith) to reject infanticide, slavery, and the exploitation of labor entails a right of others who happen not to share these "religious" convictions to kill, enslave, and exploit.

By the expedient of classifying pro-life convictions about abortion and embryo-destructive experimentation as "Roman Catholic dogmas," Cuomo smuggles into the premises of his argument the controversial conclusion he is trying to prove. If pro-life principles were indeed merely dogmatic teachings—such as the teaching that Jesus of Nazareth is the only begotten Son of God—then according to the Church herself (not to mention American constitutional law), they could not legitimately be enforced by the coercive power of the state. The trouble for Cuomo is that pro-life principles are not mere matters of "dogma," nor are they understood as such by the Catholic Church (whose beliefs Cuomo claims to affirm) or by pro-life citizens, whether they happen to be Catholics, Protestants, Jews, Muslims, Hindus, Buddhists, agnostics, or atheists. Rather, pro-life citizens understand these principles and propose them to their fellow citizens as *fundamental norms of justice and human rights* that can be understood and affirmed even *apart* from claims of revelation and religious authority.

If Cuomo would like to persuade us to adopt his view that people have a right to destroy nascent human life, it is incumbent on him to present a rational argument in defense of his position. It will not do to suggest, as Cuomo seems to do, that the sheer fact that the Catholic Church (or some other religious body) has a teaching against these practices, and that some or even many people reject this teaching, means that laws prohibiting the killing of human beings in the embryonic and fetal stages violate the right to freedom of religion of those who do not accept the teaching. If that were anything other than a fallacy, then laws against killing infants, owning slaves, exploiting workers, and many other grave forms of injustice really would be violations of religious freedom. Surely Cuomo would not wish to endorse that conclusion.

Yet he provides no reason to distinguish those practices putatively falling within the category of religious freedom from those falling outside it. So we must ask: If abortion is immunized against legal restriction on the ground that it is a matter of religious belief, how can it be that slavery is not similarly immunized? If today abortion cannot be prohibited without violating the right to religious freedom of people whose religions do not object to abortion, how can Cuomo say that the Thirteenth Amendment's prohibition of slavery did not violate the right to religious freedom of those in the nineteenth century whose religions did not condemn slaveholding? Cuomo cannot respond to this challenge by asserting that, religious teachings aside, slaveholding really is an unjust practice and abortion is not; he takes pains to assure us that he believes abortion is nothing less than the unjust taking of innocent human life. Although the former governor says that the Catholic Church "understands that our public morality depends on a consensus view of right and wrong," in the mid-nineteenth century no social consensus existed on the question of slaveholding. Still, it would be scandalous to argue that Catholics should have opposed a constitutional amendment abolishing slavery in the nineteenth century—or legislation protecting the civil rights of the oppressed descendants of slaves in the mid-twentieth century—on the ground that "prudence" or "realism" requires respect for "moral pluralism" where there is no "consensus" on questions of right and wrong.

Cuomo presents another fallacy when he suggests that laws against abortion and embryo-destructive research would force people who do not object to such things to practice the religion of people who do. No one imagines that the constitutional prohibition of slavery forced those who believed in slaveholding to practice the religion of those who did not. Would Cuomo have us suppose that laws protecting workers against what he, in line with the solemn teaching of every pope from Leo XIII to Benedict XVI, considers to be exploitation and abuse have the effect of forcing non-Catholic factory owners to practice Catholicism?

At another point, in denying that he displayed any inconsistency as governor with his willingness to act on his anti-death-penalty views but not on his anti-abortion views, Cuomo claims that when he speaks of the death penalty, he never suggests that he considers it a "moral issue." Then, in the very same paragraph, he condemns the death penalty in the most explicitly, indeed flamboyantly, moralistic terms: "I am against the death penalty because I think it is bad and unfair. It is debasing. It is degenerate. It kills innocent people." He does not pause to consider that these are precisely the claims pro-life citizens make against the policy of legal abortion and its public funding—a policy that Cuomo defends in the name of religious liberty.

The fact is that pro-life citizens of every faith oppose abortion and embryo-destructive research for the same reason we oppose post-natal homicide: because these practices involve the deliberate killing of innocent human beings. Our ground for supporting the legal prohibition of abortion and embryo-destructive research is the same ground on which we support the legal prohibition of infanticide, for example, or the principle of noncombatant immunity even in justified wars. We subscribe to the proposition that all human beings are equal in worth and dignity and cannot be denied the right to protection against killing on the basis of age, size, stage of development, or condition of dependency.

Thus the claim that one can be "personally opposed" to abortion or embryo-destructive research yet support their legal permission and even public funding collapses—though many politicians, of both parties, make this very claim. By supporting abortion and embryo-destructive research, one unavoidably implicates oneself in the grave injustice of these practices.

Of course, it is possible for a person wielding public power to use that power to establish or preserve a legal right to abortion while at the same time *hoping* that no one will exercise the right. But this does not let such a person off the moral hook. For someone who acts to protect legal abortion necessarily *wills* that abortion's unborn victims be denied the elementary legal protections against deliberate homicide that one favors for oneself and for those whom one considers to be worthy of the law's protection. Thus one violates the most basic precept of normative social and political theory, the Golden Rule. One divides humanity into two classes: those whom one is willing to admit to the community of the commonly protected and those whom one wills to be excluded from it. By exposing members of the disfavored class to lethal violence, one deeply implicates oneself in the injustice of killing them—even if one sincerely hopes that no woman will act on her right to choose abortion. The goodness of what one *hopes* for does not redeem the grave injustice—the evil—of what one *wills*. To suppose otherwise is to commit yet another fallacy.

Principled Opposition or Hypocrisy?

If my analysis so far is correct, then the question arises: What should the leaders of the Catholic Church do about people who claim to be in full communion with the church yet promote gravely unjust policies that expose the unborn to the violence and injustice of abortion?

In the run-up to the 2004 presidential election, Archbishop Raymond Burke of St. Louis offered an answer. He declared that public officials who support abortion and other unjust attacks against innocent human life may not be admitted to Holy Communion, the preeminent sacrament of unity. Pro-life citizens of every religious persuasion applauded the archbishop's stand.

Critics, however, were quick to condemn Archbishop Burke. They denounced him for "crossing the line" separating church and state. But this is silly. In acting on his authority as a bishop to discipline members of his flock who commit what the church teaches are grave injustices against innocent human beings, Archbishop Burke is exercising his own constitutional right to the free exercise of religion; he is not depriving others of their rights. Freedom is a two-way street. No one is compelled by law to accept ecclesiastical authority. But Archbishop Burke—and anyone else in the United States—has every right to exercise spiritual authority over anyone who chooses to accept it. There is a name for people who accept the authority of Catholic bishops. They are called "Catholics."

In many cases, it is not only silly but also hypocritical to charge that bishops who exclude pro-abortion politicians from Communion are "crossing the line separating church and state." A good example of this hypocrisy comes from the *Bergen Record*, a prominent newspaper in my home state of New Jersey. John Smith, the bishop of Trenton, did not go as far as Raymond Burke had gone in forbidding pro-abortion Catholic politicians from receiving Communion. Bishop Smith did, however, in the words of the *Bergen Record*, "publicly lash" Governor James McGreevey, a pro-abortion Catholic, for his support of abortion and embryo-destructive research. In an editorial, the *Record* accused the bishop of jeopardizing the delicate "balance" of our constitutional structure. The paper contrasted Bishop Smith's position unfavorably with President John F. Kennedy's assurance to a group of Protestant ministers in Houston in 1960 that he, as a Catholic, would not govern the nation by appeal to his Catholic religious beliefs.

Since the *Record* had seen fit to take us back to 1960 for guidance, I thought I would invite its editors to consider a case that had arisen only a few years earlier than that. In a letter to the editor, I proposed a question that would enable readers to determine immediately whether the editors of the *Bergen Record* were persons of strict principle or mere hypocrites.

I reminded readers that in the 1950s, in the midst of the political conflict over segregation, Archbishop Joseph Rummel of New Orleans publicly informed Catholics that support for racial segregation was incompatible with Catholic teaching on the inherent dignity and equal rights of all human beings. Archbishop Rummel said that "racial segregation is morally wrong and sinful because it is a denial of the unity and solidarity of the human race as conceived by God in the creation of Adam and Eve." He warned Catholic public officials that support for segregation placed their souls in peril. Indeed, Rummel took the step of publicly excommunicating Leander Perez, one of the most powerful political bosses in Louisiana, and two others who promoted legislation designed to impede desegregation of diocesan schools. So I asked the editors of the *Bergen Record*: Was Archbishop Rummel wrong? Or do Catholic bishops "cross the line" and jeopardize the delicate constitutional balance only when their rebukes to politicians contradict the views of the editors of the *Record*? To their credit, the editors published my letter—but I am still waiting for them to reply to my question.[2]

The *Bergen Record* was hardly alone in expressing anger, even outrage, at Catholic bishops for teaching that the faithful must never implicate themselves in unjust killing by supporting legal abortion and embryo-destructive research. The editors of the *New York Times*, for example, also scolded the bishops, insisting that "separation of church and state" means that *no* religious leader may presume to tell public officials what their positions may and may not be on matters of public policy. But when Archbishop Rummel excommunicated the segregationist politicians in the 1950s, far from condemning the archbishop, the editors of the *New York Times* praised him. They were right then; they are wrong now.

19

A RIGHT TO LIFE DENIED OR A RIGHT TO DIE HONORED?

THERE IS A spectrum of positions on end-of-life issues, and on life issues generally. But a crucial line of division exists between those who affirm, and those who deny, that the life of each human being possesses inherent and equal worth and dignity, irrespective not only of race, ethnicity, age, and sex but also of stage of development, mental or physical infirmity, and condition of dependency.

People who deny this proposition frequently distinguish what they describe as "mere biological human life" from the life of a person. It is personal life, they say, that has value (even intrinsic value) and dignity; "mere biological life" does not. And personal life is the life of a being that possesses self-consciousness and, perhaps, developed capacities for characteristic human mental activity, such as conceptual thinking, deliberation, and choice.[1]

So some people argue that there are human beings who are not yet persons—namely, those in the embryonic, fetal, and at least early infant stages of development—and other human beings who will never become, or are no longer, persons: the severely retarded, the seriously demented, those in permanent comas or persistent vegetative states.[2] For people who hold this view, the question is not when does the life of a human being begin or end but when does a human being qualify as a person and therefore a creature with a serious right to life. Those human beings whom they regard as nonpersons, human individuals possessing merely biological life, do not possess such a right; however, depending on a variety of possible factors, it may be wrong to kill them for some reason other than respect for the inherent dignity of persons—for example, without the consent of their parents or others who have a claim to them.

Princeton philosopher Peter Singer crystallized this general point that not all human beings have a right to life in a letter to the editor to the *New York Times*. Replying to an op-ed by Mario Cuomo, Singer wrote, "The crucial moral question is not when human life begins, but when human life reaches the point at which it merits protection."[3] Singer, of course, believes that some human beings do not merit protection—namely, those in the embryonic, fetal, and infant stages of development,[4] as well as those who have not developed or who have irretrievably lost the capacities Singer identifies with personhood.

In contemporary discourse, this view is often allied with a sweeping belief in the value of autonomy as a core right of persons. Centrally, the right of autonomy immunizes individual choice against interference by others, including the state, in matters having to do with how one leads one's own life, especially where one's actions do not directly impinge negatively on the interests or rights of others. So, the thought goes, if a woman wishes to abort a fetus, or parents wish to terminate the life of a severely disabled newborn, or a person wishes to end his own life with the assistance of other willing persons, respect for autonomy demands that others, including public officials acting under color of law, refrain from interfering with these choices, and perhaps even take positive steps to facilitate them.[5]

Now, those of us who oppose abortion, infanticide, assisted suicide, euthanasia, and other forms of direct killing reject the idea that there are or can be prepersonal or postpersonal human beings, or human nonpersons of any description. We also reject the sweeping view of the value of autonomy. We defend a doctrine of inherent and equal dignity that affirms all living human beings as persons who merit protection, that excludes the direct killing of innocent human beings, and that demands respect for every individual's right to life. Most of us also believe that the law should honor the principle of the inherent and equal dignity of every member of the human family and not privilege the belief in autonomy over it. We view human life, even in developing or severely mentally disabled conditions, as inherently and unconditionally valuable, and though we regard individual autonomy as an important value, we understand it to be an instrumental and conditional one—one that is morally bounded by a range of ethical considerations, including but not limited to others' autonomy.[6] Many of our opponents take precisely the opposite view: autonomy has intrinsic worth; so-called biological life is of instrumental or conditional value.[7]

In this book and elsewhere, I have detailed my reasons for believing that the life of every human being has inherent and equal worth, and for rejecting the proposition that some living human beings are not persons and therefore lack a right to life.[8] The core of my argument identifies the arbitrariness of treating only immediately exercisable capacities, as opposed to basic natural capacities, for characteristically human mental functions as the ground of dignity and basic rights. I point out that human embryos, fetuses, and infants do possess, albeit in root form, a capacity or potentiality for such mental functions. Human beings possess this radical capacity precisely in virtue of the kind of entity they are—a being with a rational nature. Although human embryos and fetuses cannot immediately exercise these capacities, each human being—unlike, say, a canine or feline embryo—comes into existence possessing the internal resources and active disposition to develop the immediately exercisable capacity for higher mental functions. Only the adverse effects of extrinsic causes will prevent this development.

I have also stated, at book length, my reasons for rejecting the doctrine of the priority of autonomy and the political principles following from it.[9] In my view, theories of morality that treat autonomy as intrinsically valuable, or seek to derive a sweeping right to autonomy (or "privacy" or "moral independence") from the value of equality or some other putatively fundamental normative principle, enmesh themselves in contradictions and conundrums that cannot be resolved without adjusting the theories to limit significantly the scope of autonomy.

All these issues came to the fore in the Terri Schiavo case. The national debate that swirled around the question of whether to withhold food and fluids from Schiavo, who was in a minimally conscious state, offered a clear reminder that the issues at stake in theories of morality are anything but abstract.

"Always to Care, Never to Kill"

For an indication of what I believe someone on my side of the debate on these matters ought to think about, it is useful to consult a statement the Ramsey Colloquium of the Institute on Religion and Public Life issued entitled "Always to Care, Never to Kill: A Declaration on Euthanasia."[10] This statement sets forth the position that we are to maintain solidarity with those in disabled conditions, seeking to heal their afflictions when we can and making every effort to relieve their suffering and discomfort. At the same time, we should bring encouragement to anyone who is tempted to regard his life, currently or prospectively, as valueless or burdensome to himself or others, and discourage such a person from committing suicide or regarding his life as worthless. We should certainly not cooperate in suicidal choices or support the practice of assisted suicide or euthanasia.

Does this imply "vitalism"—that is, the view that human life is not only inherently valuable but is also the supreme value that trumps all others? Does it mean that we must struggle to keep dying patients alive at all costs?

No.

The key distinction is not between "killing" and "letting die," though I have come to think that this distinction (properly understood) is not always morally meaningless. Nor is the distinction between killing by a positive act and killing by not acting when one could act to preserve life (which is sometimes run together with the distinction between "killing" and "letting die"). Nor, strictly speaking, is the crucial distinction between the use of "ordinary" as opposed to "extraordinary" means of life support, at least where "ordinary" and "extraordinary" are defined in terms of the complexity or novelty of the technologies employed.

Rather, the key is the distinction between what traditionally has been called "direct killing," where death (one's own or someone else's) is sought either as an end in itself or as a means to some other end, and accepting death (or the shortening of life) as a foreseen side effect of an action (or omission) whose object is something other than death—some good (or the avoidance of some evil) that in the circumstances cannot be achieved in ways that do not result in death or the shortening of life.[11] Of course, the norm against the direct killing of innocent human beings is not the only norm that can be relevant to end-of-life decisions. Other norms, such as obligations of fairness and equity, apply even in cases of accepting death as a side effect. To show that an act which causes death or shortens life is not an act of direct killing is not necessarily to show that it is a morally legitimate act.

There are some classic examples of this crucial distinction. A soldier jumps on a grenade in a life-sacrificing effort to save the lives of his comrades in arms. Because his own death, though foreseen and accepted, is outside the scope of his intention, no one regards this as a suicide or an act of direct self-killing. The soldier's objective is not his own death but rather saving the lives of his comrades. Should he somehow miraculously survive the blow of the grenade while muffling its force, he will have fully achieved his aim. His surviving would in no way frustrate his objectives.

Perhaps more obviously relevant to the issues here under discussion is the case of a patient suffering from a painful condition who takes palliative drugs that he knows will result in his dying sooner than he would otherwise. Again, death, though foreseen and accepted, is not the object of the patient's act. His intention is solely to relieve the pain of his disease, and, we may assume, his willingness to accept death is not incompatible with any obligation he may have to others. (The moral equation changes if it is incompatible with any such obligation, such as an obligation to children or other family members.)

Now, people in extremis, or who anticipate being in extremis, may have many reasons for declining life support that do not implicate the person in willing his own death either as an end in itself or as a means to some other end. Particular forms of life support may be painful, burdensome, and expensive. When they are, people can certainly choose to forego them without willing their own deaths. So someone who thinks as I do may support, as I in fact support, giving people broad latitude to decide whether to accept life support and whether to continue it once accepted. This is one of the places where respect for autonomy makes a valid claim in the ethical framework I have sketched. Of course, it is to be expected that, given this latitude, some people will act on it for reasons that are not morally legitimate within that framework; this is a foreseeable, but acceptable, bad side effect of a good policy. The policy itself has as its aim something perfectly good and legitimate—respecting people's autonomy to choose among morally acceptable (even if tragic) but incompatible options bearing on their lives and futures. Although this freedom may be misused to choose morally wrongful options, it is not the intent of the policy to enable those choices. The intent is to allow choice among the many morally legitimate options.

But this does not mean we should accept a right to assisted suicide. Nor should we conceive the right to decline life support (or lifesaving medical care generally) as a right to commit suicide or to receive assistance in committing suicide. Policies or practices that are implicitly premised on belief in a right to suicide or assisted suicide or euthanasia should be roundly rejected.

Terri Schiavo died of dehydration. Her death was not the result of brain damage or any other affliction. It was chosen as the precise object of a decision to deny her fluids. She was not "allowed to die," for she was not dying; she was not, as I heard Al Franken claim on television, "brain dead"; she was not even terminally ill. The choice to deny her fluids was a choice to cause her death. Those who supported that choice said it was right either because she wasn't really a person anymore or because death was what she herself wanted, as she allegedly made clear in comments her husband later recalled and placed into evidence.[12] Either way, the killing of Terri Schiavo cannot be justified under the moral understanding I defend and that has traditionally governed medical ethics, whatever erosions it has suffered in recent years. Under that understanding, Terri was a person with a right to life; she was neither a nonperson ("mere biological life," a "vegetable") nor a person with a right to commit suicide. The obligation of others toward her was "always to care; never to kill."[13]

Does this mean that it is never morally acceptable to withhold fluids or food from a patient? Is it never right for a patient or individuals making medical decisions on behalf of a patient to decline food and fluids?

Some people on my side of the debate have argued that food and fluids must always be administered—that they are "hospitality" rather than life support and are part of "ordinary" care rather than extraordinary means. I agree that food and fluids are in most cases (or, as Pope John Paul II put it in his allocution on the subject, "in principle")[14] part of ordinary care, but in some cases, I believe, they can be legitimately not administered. That is because there can be cases in which the reason for not administering them is some goal or purpose other than the desire to bring about death. These are cases, comparatively rare to be sure, in which food and fluids cannot be administered without causing harm to the patient. Sometimes the problem will be in the administration of the food and fluids, and sometimes it will be a consequence of the food and fluids themselves. In either type of case, where the administration of food and fluid will cause or contribute to morbidity or hasten death, plainly a decision to withhold them need not be a choice to kill.

Obviously, what I have in mind here was not part of the picture in the Schiavo case. The point of withholding food and fluids from Terri Schiavo was precisely to bring about her death. The problem was not that she could not tolerate the food and fluids or that the administration of them would further damage her health. On the contrary, food and water would sustain her in life—a life that some judged to be in itself burdensome, both to Terri herself and to others, and that she, they contend, would have wanted to end were she in a position to decide the question. From the perspective of those who supported removing her feeding tube, doing so was a means of ending her life; it was not a side effect of a choice whose object was something else. It was a choice to kill, a choice the moral logic of which is indistinguishable from a choice to have ended her life more quickly by, for example, administering a lethal dose in an unambiguous act of euthanasia.

Nothing in my analysis is changed by the release of Terri Schiavo's autopsy results. Although many have touted the autopsy as vindication for Michael Schiavo and those who supported his efforts to remove nutrition and hydration, I do not think the results merit such a conclusion. Questions such as whether Terri was in a "persistent vegetative state" or not, whether she had the possibility of regaining consciousness or not, and whether her brain was "profoundly atrophied" or not were irrelevant to her status as a human person. What mattered was that Terri was alive, was not in the process of dying, and would continue to live unless someone chose to kill her, whether by dehydration or some more efficient means.

20

THE "RELICS OF BARBARISM," THEN AND NOW

with William L. Saunders

I N THE MIDDLE of the nineteenth century, a new political party
emerged dedicated to two great moral struggles. The Republican
Party pledged to fight the "twin relics of barbarism": slavery and
polygamy.

By then, slavery was deeply entrenched in the culture of the American South. What some had regarded as a "necessary evil" that would
gradually die out had been given a new lease on life by technological
developments and by the emergence of profitable overseas markets for
cotton. An entire social and economic system was built on slavery. No
longer was it reasonable to hope that the "peculiar institution," and
with it the moral controversy convulsing the nation, would quietly
fade away. Powerful interests had a stake not only in maintaining the
slave system but also in extending it into the western territories of the
United States.

So the Republicans faced a daunting challenge. Pro-slavery Democrats condemned them as "fanatics" and "zealots" who sought to
impose their religious scruples and moral values on others. Slavehold-
ers demanded that they "mind their own business" and stay out of the

"domestic" and "private" affairs of others. Defenders of a "right" to own slaves pointedly invited northern abolitionists to redirect their moral outrage toward the "wage slave" system in the North. "If you are against slavery," they in effect said, "then don't own a slave."

By the mid-1850s, polygamy, which had originally been the largely secret practice of the Mormon elite, had come out of the closet.[1] Polygamists claimed that attacks on "plural marriage" were violations of their right to religious freedom. Later, some would bring lawsuits asking judges to invalidate laws against polygamy as unconstitutional. One of these cases would make it all the way to the Supreme Court. Apologists for polygamy denied that plural marriage was harmful to children and challenged supporters of the ban on polygamy to prove that the existence of polygamous families in American society harmed their own monogamous marriages. They insisted that they merely wanted the right to be married in their own way and left alone.

But the Republicans stood their ground, refusing to be intimidated by the invective being hurled against them. They knew that polygamy and slavery were morally wrong and socially corrosive. And they were prepared to act on their moral convictions.

For the Republicans, the idea that human beings could be reduced to the status of mere "objects" to be bought and sold and exploited for the benefit of others was a profound violation of the intrinsic dignity of creatures made in the image and likeness of God. Similarly, the idea that marriage could be redefined to accommodate a man's desire for multiple sexual partners was, as they saw it, deeply contrary to the meaning of marriage as joining a man and a woman in a permanent and exclusive bond.

In the great moral struggles of the nineteenth century, the Republicans sought advantage in every morally legitimate and available way. Where appropriate, they would accept strategic compromises on the road to victory, but they would not compromise away their principles.

When in the *Dred Scott* decision the Supreme Court of the United States announced its discovery of what amounted to a constitutional right of slaveholding, Lincoln and other leading Republicans refused to treat the case as a binding precedent. They would not bow to judicial usurpation. When Utah sought admission as a state, the Republican-controlled Congress made statehood conditional upon incorporation of a prohibition of polygamy into the state constitution.

Republicans would do well to remember their moral heritage. The twin relics of barbarism have returned in distinctively modern garb. Abortion and embryo-destructive research are premised on the proposition that some human beings—those in the embryonic and fetal stages of development—may legitimately be reduced to objects that can be created and destroyed for the benefit of others. At the same time, the ideology of sexual liberationism threatens to undercut the traditional understanding of marriage as the permanent and exclusive union of one man and one woman.

A familiar mantra of "pro-choice" politicians is that abortion should be "safe, legal, and rare." Now, however, they seek to validate and fund a massive industry that would create human beings for the precise purpose of destroying them during the embryonic stage of development in biomedical research. What happened with slavery is now happening with embryo killing: the people who used to defend it as a "necessary evil" to be resisted or lessened by means other than legal prohibition now promote it as a social good—something that law and government should not only tolerate but embrace and even promote.

At the same time, the sexual-liberationist movement seeks to undermine traditional understandings of the meaning and significance of human sexuality. The attempt to abolish the legal concept of marriage as the one-flesh union of a man and a woman is part of a larger effort to "liberate" people from what the cultural-political Left regards as outmoded and repressive ideas about the centrality of procreation and the moral requirement of fidelity in human sexual relationships. Even some leading "conservative" advocates of "same-sex marriage" have announced their moral acceptance of promiscuity; one has gone so far as to proclaim the "spiritual value" of "anonymous sex." Increasingly, critics of traditional morality are willing explicitly to invoke the authority of ancient pagan civilizations in which practices (including abortion, infanticide, and homosexual conduct) condemned by the Judeo-Christian ethic sometimes flourished.

Critics of the Republican stand in defense of marriage and the sanctity of human life—including some within the party—echo the arguments of nineteenth-century apologists for the relics of barbarism. They accuse pro-life and pro-family Republicans of being "religious fanatics" who disrespect people's liberty and seek to "impose their values" on others. "If you are against abortion," they say, "then don't have an abortion." They maintain—often disingenuously—that legal recognition of the "marriages" of same-sex partners will not harm or weaken traditional marriages.

These arguments fare no better as defenses of human-embryo killing and the redefinition of marriage than they did of slavery and polygamy. Justice requires that all human beings irrespective of race or color, but also irrespective of age, or size, or stage of development, be afforded the protection of the laws. The common good requires that the laws reflect and promote a sound understanding of marriage as uniting one man and one woman in a bond founded on the bodily communion made possible by their reproductive complementarity.

An influential minority in the Republican Party proposes abandoning, or at least soft-pedaling, the party's commitments to the sanctity of human life and the dignity of marriage and the family. They say that social issues are "too divisive." They suppose that the easy road to Republican electoral success is as the party of low taxes and low morals. They counsel capitulation to judges who usurp the constitutional authority of the American people and their elected representatives.

Let Republicans be mindful of their heritage. It was moral conviction—and the courage to act on moral conviction—that gave birth to the Republican Party and made it grand. Now it is old but need not be any less grand. By summoning the moral courage that enabled their party to stand proudly against the twin relics of barbarism in the nineteenth century, Republicans can bring honor upon themselves in the great moral struggles of our own day.

Part IV

GOOD GUYS AND . . . NOT-SO-GOOD GUYS

21

HARRY BLACKMUN

Improbable Liberal Icon

A S A THEORY of political morality and a practical political philosophy, liberalism is nearly exhausted. Despite decades of hegemony in academic political theory, the leading theologians of the liberal faith, including most notably the late John Rawls of Harvard, have failed to produce an intellectually plausible defense of its dogmas. Most Democrats and all Republicans refuse to accept the term "liberal" as a label for their views; those unwilling or unable to be classified as "conservatives" proclaim themselves to be "progressives" or, more commonly, "moderates."

Still, there are true believers in that old-time religion of liberalism. For them the story of Harry Blackmun, as recounted by *New York Times* Supreme Court reporter Linda Greenhouse, is a wondrous tale of redemption.

Harry, you see, was a boring guy. In fact, he was worse than a boring guy. He was a square. He was a Republican.

He was from the Midwest. He went to Harvard on a scholarship from the Harvard Club of Minnesota. He took summer jobs installing windows and delivering milk. He worried about finances.

He went to Harvard Law School, where he ranked 120th in a class of 451. He returned to Minnesota to clerk for a judge and then practice law with a corporate firm in Minneapolis–St. Paul. He wore dark suits and skinny ties. He worked in the firm's tax department. His first car was a Ford coupe with a rumble seat, for which he paid $702.14. He named it "Mignon." He married a girl he met on the tennis court. They had three children.

Did I mention that Harry was a Republican?

One of Harry's clients was the Mayo Clinic. It was filled with rich doctors. Harry did their tax work and provided estate-planning advice. They liked him so well that the clinic offered him a position as its resident counsel. He accepted.

Harry's best friend was Warren E. Burger—another square, another Republican. When Burger became a federal appeals-court judge, he worked through his Republican cronies to help engineer a similar appointment for his pal Harry. Harry sat on the bench and followed precedent.

Burger was appointed chief justice of the United States by the evil Nixon. Soon Harry would be nominated by "Tricky Dick" to join his boyhood friend on the Supreme Court. Harry was so boring that his nomination was confirmed in the Senate by a vote of 94–0. It was 1970.

But the Lord works in mysterious ways His wonders to perform!

In 1972, the Supreme Court took up *Roe v. Wade*, a case challenging the authority of states to prohibit abortions. The chief justice assigned the case to his friend Harry, who, after all, knew a lot about medical matters since he had represented the Mayo Clinic. And abortion is a medical matter . . . sort of . . . isn't it?

Harry got in touch with librarians at the Mayo Clinic who helped him gather information on the history of abortion. Before completing his opinion for the court, he went to the Mayo library to do some research. He asked his wife and daughters what they thought about abortion. He studied the latest Gallup poll on the question.

Harry produced a long opinion, filled with references to history and precedent. He and six of his colleagues had discovered a fundamental right to abortion in the due process clause of the Fourteenth Amendment. This right to "terminate a pregnancy," as he delicately described the practice of intentional feticide, was part of a generalized "right to privacy" that the court a few years earlier (before Harry joined) had found lurking in penumbras formed by emanations.

The reasoning was . . . how does one say this politely? . . . weak. Harry made a complete hash of the legal history of abortion, and the absence in his opinion of anything resembling a constitutional argument was embarrassing. Even some devout liberals in the world of legal scholarship—such as Professors Archibald Cox and John Hart Ely—pronounced *Roe v. Wade* indefensible. But no matter. The truest of liberal true believers were confident that the law professoriate would somehow supply the deficiency of argument in *Roe*. The important—and amazing—thing was that boring old Republican Nixon-appointed Harry had delivered the biggest prize of all to the liberal faithful: a virtually unrestricted, constitutionally guaranteed right to abortion! Amens and hallelujahs arose from the congregation.

Of course, Harry would be vilified by conservative Christians and other fuddy-duddies. But this would serve only to confirm his belief in the rightness of what he had done and open his mind more generally to the righteousness of liberal doctrine. From now on, he would no longer be boring old Harry the square Republican. He would be a full-fledged *jurist*, indeed a lion of liberal jurisprudence, right up there with William O. Douglas, William J. Brennan, and Thurgood Marshall. Harry was redeemed! He had become Justice Blackmun.

In telling this tale, Greenhouse does her best—until almost the very end—not to gush. Although no reader will be in doubt as to where her sympathies lie, the book does not descend into hagiography. It is for the most part a straightforward factual account, properly documented, of how Harry Blackmun went from being a square Republican tax lawyer in Minnesota to being what Greenhouse describes as an "improbable icon" of what it pleases her and others in the mainstream press to call "abortion rights." Naturally, the core of the book concerns *Roe*, since it was that ruling (in 1973) that transformed boring old Harry into Justice Blackmun. But Greenhouse includes discussions of Blackmun's liberal epiphanies in other areas, such as the death penalty. (He eventually discovered that the Constitution prohibits it. Who knew?)

Amid the mass of trivia establishing that Blackmun, prior to his redemption, had been boring, square, and Republican, Greenhouse has managed to produce some rather interesting factoids. For example, after *Roe* was handed down, Blackmun received a letter from a Catholic priest with whom he had been friends. Father Vern Trocinski was on the faculty of St. Teresa College in Winona, Minnesota. The priest said that, though he "treasured" his friendship with Blackmun, he was having "a very difficult time" with the *Roe* ruling and felt an "obligation church-wise and civil-wise to speak out in defense of the unborn." In reply, Blackmun professed his "abhorrence" for abortion. (Yes, you read that right: *abhorrence*.) He asked Father Trocinski to understand, however, that the decision did not address the rightness or wrongness of abortion. "The Court's task," he advised the priest, "is to pass only on the narrow issue of constitutionality."

Blackmun's claim that he and his colleagues were abstaining from moral judgments and merely ruling on a "narrow issue of constitutionality" is risible. As Cox, Ely, and other honorable liberal critics of *Roe* candidly observed, there is nothing in the text, logic, structure, or original understanding of the Constitution creating a right to take the life of a child in the womb. To establish the proposition that there is such a right, the justices needed to import into their "legal" reasoning an elaborate set of undeniably *moral* judgments about, for example, the meaning of liberty and the value of human life.

And then there is that business about Blackmun's finding abortion to be "abhorrent." What is abhorrent about it? We ordinarily don't regard medical procedures as abhorrent. There is nothing abhorrent about an appendectomy or tonsillectomy. In the case of abortion, could it be the little matter of hacking off limbs, suctioning out body parts, and reassembling them to make sure that no parts of the baby (oops! I mean fetus) are left inside the mother (oops! I mean woman) to cause infection? I suppose that really is abhorrent in ways that appendectomies and tonsillectomies are not. Then again, perhaps Justice Blackmun and I are just squeamish.

As Greenhouse points out, Blackmun in *Roe* seemed to vacillate between understanding the abortion right as the right of a woman to exercise a species of personal liberty and seeing it as the right of her doctor to make a decision about her health. His official, quasi-doctrinal statement in the opinion was that it is a right of the woman in consultation with her doctor. The pro-abortion feminists who came to lionize Justice Blackmun didn't much like the bit about the doctor. For them, abortion was a matter of liberty (or "autonomy"), not a medical matter. Eventually, they brought Blackmun round to their way of seeing things. This, too, was part of his redemption. In accepting their applause, he stopped talking about doctors. And he got very quiet indeed about his abhorrence of what is done to a human being developing in utero when women exercise the sacred right he vouchsafed unto them.

22

ANDREW SULLIVAN

A Walking Contradiction

He's a walking contradiction,
Partly truth and partly fiction,
Taking every wrong direction
On his lonely way back home.
   —Kris Kristofferson

ANDREW SULLIVAN NEVER tires of reminding readers that he is a Catholic, yet he is the rather odd sort of Catholic who proclaims the "spirituality"—I'm not kidding, the word is his—of sexual encounters between strangers who don't even bother to reveal to each other their names (what Sullivan calls "anonymous sex"). He also advertises himself as a conservative, but in this, too, he is a walking contradiction. His book *The Conservative Soul* mixes some important truths about what it means to be a conservative with some outrageous and even zany fictions. At some level, he really does seem to want to be a faithful member of his church and a true conservative, but he is managing to take just about every possible wrong direction on his lonely way back home.

Andrew Sullivan is a passionate writer. He forcefully asserts strong opinions—mostly liberal ones—on a range of hotly contested moral and political issues. Expressions of doubt are rare in his writings. And woe betide those who have the temerity to express opposing views. They are consigned to the category of "fundamentalists"—twisted and dangerous people who are psychologically incapable of dealing with ambiguity or uncertainty and are bent on tyrannically imposing their beliefs on others. Much of *The Conservative Soul* is devoted to demonizing Evangelical Protestants and traditional Catholics who have, he insists, succeeded in usurping authentic conservatism and robbing this great tradition of its soul. (Full disclosure: I am one of his principal targets, though in an amusing display of ineptness he manages to confuse my arguments on the foundations of sexual ethics with those of the philosopher Edward Feser. Although I have respect for Professor Feser's work, he and I disagree with each other on the very points on which Sullivan runs our thought together and criticizes what he imagines to be my views. What he in fact criticizes are Feser's views—or, more accurately, a caricature of his views. Professor Feser has ably defended himself in a detailed response on the blog *Right Reason*.)

In its more formal and donnish aspect, Sullivan's book contrasts "two rival forms of conservatism." The bad conservatism is the type that has gained control of the Republican Party and led it down the path to perdition: this type of conservatism he labels "fundamentalism." ("The most powerful Christian fundamentalist in the world is George W. Bush.") The good conservatism—the one whose rescue "means rejecting the current fundamentalist supremacy in almost every respect"—is what Sullivan describes as "the conservatism of doubt." He writes:

> As a politics, its essence is an acceptance of the unknowability of ultimate truth, an acknowledgment of the distinction between what is true forever and what is true for here and now, and an embrace of the discrepancy between theoretical and practical

knowledge. It is an anti-ideology, a non-program, a way of looking at the world whose most perfect expression might be called
inactivism.

Sullivan is at pains to show that the conservatism of doubt has a
distinguished intellectual pedigree. Its architects and defenders have
included such intellectual giants as Michel de Montaigne and, much
more recently, Michael Oakeshott.

Sullivan also wishes to show that the good conservatism—though
an "anti-ideology" and a "non-program"—has some concrete substantive implications for contemporary moral and political deliberation.
You won't have difficulty guessing what these implications centrally
include: a thoroughly liberal conception of sexual morality (especially
regarding homosexual conduct and relationships integrated around
such conduct) and the public recognition of same-sex sexual partnerships as "marriages."

Now how did you know that? You knew it because if you know
anything about Andrew Sullivan, you know that he is *certain* that
the teachings of his church and of the broader Western tradition of
thought about sexuality and marriage are profoundly and destruc-
tively wrong. Although earlier in his career he famously argued in
favor of same-sex "marriage" as an antidote to male homosexual promiscuity (an argument that established his credentials as a "conservative" gay-rights advocate), he has long since abandoned the critique of
sexual license. Hence his proclamation, well before the publication of
The Conservative Soul, of the "spiritual value" of "anonymous sex."

For some reason, though, Sullivan wishes to hang on to the label
"conservative," just as he wishes to remain at least formally a Catholic. So he redefines conservatism to make it accommodate "toleration" of what most conservatives regard, and have always regarded,
as serious sexual misconduct. And mere "toleration" isn't enough.
Nothing short of official approbation will do. So legal recognition of
same-sex marriages is essential (though no longer as an antidote to
promiscuity).

Sullivan supposes that people who continue to believe that licentious sexual behavior, and not the condemnation of it, is immoral and socially destructive—those who observe that the consequences of such behavior in our own society are measurable in broken relationships and ruined lives—are actually not conservatives (or at least not good conservatives) at all. They are fundamentalists, people belonging to a class that includes Osama bin Laden and Dostoyevsky's Grand Inquisitor.

Perhaps Sullivan's lowest attack on those who do not go along with his beliefs (especially on sex) is reserved for men who experience same-sex sexual desires but who, because of their conscientious moral convictions, decline to act on them. Evidently, Sullivan cannot abide the thought of such men, much less consider the possibility that they, rather than he, have grasped the truth about sexual morality and human dignity. In discussing these men, he immediately descends into amateur psychiatrist mode:

> But a gay man who decides to sublimate his entire sexual being into the maintenance of a rigid religious orthodoxy is often an ideal fundamentalist. His own chastity is a particularly onerous sacrifice for the sake of truth; and such a sacrifice in turn intensifies commitment to the orthodoxy. The longer he retains this sacrifice, the more insistent he is on its necessity. And so you have the well-documented phenomenon of repressed homosexual men being in the forefront of religious campaigns to suppress homosexual behavior in others.

It doesn't seem to occur to Sullivan that someone, whatever his experiences of sexual desire, might think carefully about issues of sexual morality, consider the arguments advanced by people on various sides (including those who draw on what they regard as the wisdom of their religious traditions), arrive at conclusions at variance with Sullivan's own, and do his best to resist sexual temptation and orient himself so as to live a life in line with what he believes the dignity of a human person requires.

One would think that a proponent of "the conservatism of doubt" would be more charitable toward his intellectual and political opponents. One would expect him carefully to consider the possibility that people who have reached conclusions at variance with his own might have arrived at, or gotten nearer, the truth. One would certainly expect him to regard them, in the absence of evidence to the contrary, as reasonable people of goodwill whose views ought to be given respect and thoughtful consideration. Yet when it comes to issues of sexuality and sexual morality, Sullivan's "conservatism of doubt" yields—*mirabile dictu*—nothing short of a liberalism (one might even say a libertinism) of absolute certainty. Dissenters are not reasonable people who happen to disagree. They are psychologically warped individuals—fundamentalists!—who perversely refuse to recognize truths (even truths about themselves and their own motivations) and who are bent on tyrannizing others.

When it comes to the dogmas of the sexual revolution, Sullivan is as true a believer as one can find. But his dogmatism extends beyond sexual liberalism, central though that is to his quasi-evangelical mission. He fervently and largely uncritically expresses unshakable beliefs in many other areas as well—from bioethics to the war in Iraq—all the while attacking those who hold opposing views as "fundamentalists." Advertising himself as "mildly" pro-choice, he virtually invites ridicule by invoking in support of legal abortion and against its "fundamentalist" opponents none other than St. Thomas Aquinas: "Aquinas reasoned that unborn life went through three stages—a vegetative period, an animal stage, and finally a rational moment when the basis for cognition and reason could be detected, and 'ensoulment' fully realized." Well, yes, Aquinas, while rejecting abortion, did believe that unborn life went through these stages. But that was because the great medieval philosopher was working with what we now know to be a profoundly flawed understanding of the basic facts of embryogenesis and early intrauterine human development. Since the discovery of the ovum in the nineteenth century, our knowledge of the embryological facts has advanced far beyond anything a thirteenth-century writer such as Aquinas could possibly have known. Medieval speculation about "vegetative," "animal," and "rational" stages has been replaced by knowledge of human development as a self-directed, gradual, and gapless process by which the newly conceived human being develops from the embryonic into and through the fetal, infant, child, and adolescent stages, and into adulthood with his or her distinctness, unity, determinateness, and identity fully intact.

Sullivan's posturing as a practitioner of "the conservatism of doubt" is, in the end, risible. As Jonah Goldberg has pointed out in a devastating review of *The Conservative Soul*, Sullivan "believes nothing if not the moral superiority of his own position." In labeling his opponents as "fundamentalists," he is, at best, a pot hurling epithets at the kettles.

There is an important truth in the idea of a "conservatism of doubt." It was expressed many years ago by the great conservative jurist Learned Hand: "The spirit of liberty is the spirit which is not too sure that it is right. The spirit of liberty is the spirit which seeks to understand the minds of other men and women." Yet Sullivan's presentation of himself as the champion of such a spirit is the purest fiction. His problem is not that he doubts too much but rather that he doubts too little. It is not that he is excessively self-critical; it is that he is insufficiently so. He cannot entertain an intellectual challenge on an issue he cares about without classifying his interlocutor as warped and potentially tyrannical. Much less can he bring himself to consider the possibility that his opponent might actually be right. He is filled with too much dogmatic certainty for that.

23

BERNARD NATHANSON

A Life Transformed by Truth

F EW PEOPLE, IF any, did more than Bernard Nathanson to undermine the right to life of unborn children by turning abortion from an unspeakable crime into a constitutionally protected liberty. Yet someday, when our law is reformed to honor the dignity and protect the right to life of every member of the human family, including children in the womb, historians will observe that few people did more than Bernard Nathanson to achieve that reversal.

Dr. Nathanson, the son of a distinguished medical practitioner and professor who specialized in obstetrics and gynecology, had his first involvement with abortion as a medical student at McGill University in Montreal, which his father had also attended. Having impregnated a girlfriend, he arranged and paid for her illegal abortion. Many years later, he would mark this episode as his "introductory excursion into the satanic world of abortion."

In the meantime, however, Nathanson would become a nearly monomaniacal crusader for abortion and campaigner for its legalization. And he would himself become an abortionist.

By his own estimate, he presided over more than sixty thousand abortions as director of the Center for Reproductive and Sexual Health in New York, personally instructed medical students and practitioners in the performance of about fifteen thousand more, and performed five thousand abortions himself. In one of those abortions, he took the life of his own son or daughter—a child conceived with a girlfriend after he had established his medical practice. Writing with deep regret in his moving autobiography, *The Hand of God* (1996), Nathanson confessed his own heartlessness in performing that abortion: "I swear to you, I had no feelings aside from the sense of accomplishment, the pride of expertise."

In the mid-1960s, with the sexual revolution roaring after Alfred Kinsey's fraudulent but influential "scientific" studies of sex and sexuality in America, Hugh Hefner's aggressive campaign to legitimize pornography, and, perhaps above all, the wide distribution of the anovulant birth control pill, Nathanson became a leader in the movement to overturn laws prohibiting abortion. He cofounded the National Association for the Repeal of Abortion Laws (NARAL), which later became the National Abortion Rights Action League (NARAL) and is now NARAL Pro-Choice America. The group's goals were to remove the cultural stigma on abortion, eliminate all meaningful legal restraints on it, and make it as widely available as possible across the nation and, indeed, the globe.

To achieve these goals, Nathanson would later reveal, he and fellow abortion crusaders pursued dubious and in some cases straightforwardly dishonest strategies.

First, they promoted the idea that abortion is a medical issue, not a moral one. This required persuading people of the rather obvious falsehood that a normal pregnancy is a natural and healthy condition if the mother wants her baby, and a disease if she does not. The point of medicine, to maintain and restore health, had to be recast as giving "health care" consumers what they happen to *want*, and the Hippocratic Oath's explicit prohibition of abortion had to be removed. In the end, Nathanson and his collaborators succeeded in selling this propaganda to a small but extraordinarily powerful group of men: in the 1973 case of *Roe v. Wade*, seven Supreme Court justices led by Harry Blackmun, former counsel to the Mayo Clinic, invalidated virtually all state laws providing meaningful protection for unborn children on the ground that abortion is a "private choice" to be made by women and their doctors.

Second, Nathanson and his friends lied—relentlessly and spectacularly—about the number of women who died each year from illegal abortions. Their pitch to voters, lawmakers, and judges was that women are going to seek abortion in roughly equal numbers whether it is lawful or not. The *only* effect of outlawing it, they claimed, is to limit pregnant women to unqualified and often uncaring practitioners, "back alley butchers." So, Nathanson and others insisted, laws against abortion are worse than futile: they do not save fetal lives; they only cost women's lives.

Now, some women did die from unlawful abortions, though factors other than legalization, especially the development of antibiotics such as penicillin, are mainly responsible for reducing the rate and number of maternal deaths. And of course, the number of unborn babies whose lives were taken shot up dramatically after Nathanson and his colleagues achieved their goals—and they achieved them, in part, by claiming that the number of illegal abortions was *more than ten times higher* than it actually was.

Third, the early advocates of abortion deliberately exploited anti-Catholic animus among liberal elites and (in those days) many ordinary Protestants to depict opposition to abortion as a "religious dogma" that the Catholic hierarchy sought to impose on others in violation of their freedom and of the separation of church and state. Nathanson and his friends recognized that their movement needed an enemy—a widely suspected institution that they could make the public face of their opposition; a minority, but one large and potent enough for its detractors to fear.

Despite the undeniable historical fact that prohibitions of abortion were rooted in English common law and reinforced and expanded

by statutes enacted across the United States by overwhelmingly Protestant majorities in the nineteenth century, Nathanson and other
abortion movement leaders decided that the Catholic Church was
perfect for the role of freedom-smothering oppressor. Its male priest-
hood and authority structure would make it easy for them to depict
the church's opposition to abortion as misogyny, for which concern
to protect unborn babies was a mere pretext. The church's real motive,
they insisted, was to restrict women's freedom in order to hold them
in positions of subservience.

Fourth, the abortion movement sought to appeal to conservatives
and liberals alike by promoting feticide as a way of fighting poverty.
Why are so many people poor? It's because they have more children
than they can afford to care for. What's the solution? Abortion.
Why do we have to spend so much money on welfare? It's because
poor, mainly minority, women are burdening the taxpayer with too
many babies. The solution? Abortion. Initially, Nathanson himself
believed that legal abortion and its public funding would reduce out-
of-wedlock childbearing and poverty, though (as he later admitted)
he continued to promote this falsehood after the sheer weight of evidence forced him to disbelieve it.

Within a year after *Roe v. Wade*, however, Nathanson began to
have moral doubts about the cause to which he had been so single-
mindedly devoted. In a widely noticed 1974 essay in the prestigious
New England Journal of Medicine, he revealed his growing doubts about
the "pro-choice" dogma that abortion was merely the removal of an
"undifferentiated mass of cells," not the killing of a developing human
being. Referring to abortions that he had supervised or performed, he
confessed to an "increasing certainty that I had in fact presided over
60,000 deaths."

Still, he was not ready to abandon support for legal abortion. It
was, he continued to insist, necessary to prevent the bad consequences
of illegal abortions. But he was moving from viewing abortion itself
as a legitimate solution to a woman's personal problem to seeing it as
an evil that should be discouraged, even if for practical reasons it had

to be tolerated. Over the next several years, while continuing to perform abortions for what he regarded as legitimate "health" reasons, Nathanson would be moved still further toward the pro-life position by the emergence of new technologies, especially fetoscopy and ultrasound, that made it increasingly difficult, and finally impossible, to deny that abortion is the deliberate killing of a unique human being—a child in the womb.

By 1980, the weight of evidence in favor of the pro-life position had overwhelmed Nathanson and driven him out of the practice of abortion. He had come to regard the procedure as unjustified homicide and refused to perform it. Soon he was dedicating himself to the fight against abortion and revealing to the world the lies he and his abortion movement colleagues had told to break down public opposition.

In 1985, Nathanson employed the new fetal-imaging technology to produce a documentary film, *The Silent Scream*, which energized the pro-life movement and threw the pro-choice side onto the defensive by showing in graphic detail the killing of a twelve-week-old fetus in a suction abortion. Nathanson used the footage to describe the facts of fetal development and to make the case for the humanity and dignity of the child in the womb. At one point, viewers see the child draw back from the surgical instrument and open his mouth: "This," Nathanson says in the narration, "is the silent scream of a child threatened imminently with extinction."

Publicity for *The Silent Scream* was provided by no less a figure than President Ronald Reagan, who showed the film in the White House and touted it in speeches. Like Nathanson, Reagan, who had signed one of the first abortion-legalization bills when he was governor of California, was a zealous convert to the pro-life cause. During his term as president, Reagan wrote and published a powerful pro-life book entitled *Abortion and the Conscience of the Nation*—a book that Nathanson praised for telling the truth about the life of the child in the womb and the injustice of abortion.

Nathanson, long an unbeliever, continued to profess atheism for several years after his defection from the pro-choice to the pro-life side. His argument against abortion was not, he insisted, religious; it was based on scientific facts and generally accepted principles of the rights and dignity of the human person. In this, his views were very much in line with those of the great pro-life convert Nat Hentoff, a distinguished civil libertarian who for many years wrote for the liberal and secularist newspaper the *Village Voice*. But unlike Hentoff, who remains unconvinced of the claims of religion, Nathanson was gradually drawn to faith in God and ultimately to Catholicism by the moral witness of the believers among his newfound comrades in the struggle for the unborn.

As Nathanson frequently observed, it was not that he became Catholic and then embraced the pro-life view because it was the church's teaching. If anything, it was the other way around. Having become persuaded of the truth of the pro-life position, he was drawn to Catholicism because of the church's witness—in the face of prejudice Nathanson himself had helped to whip up—to the inherent and equal value and dignity of human life in all stages and conditions.

Nathanson was baptized and received into the Catholic Church in 1996 by John Cardinal O'Connor in a ceremony at St. Patrick's Cathedral. He chose as his godmother Joan Andrews Bell, a woman revered among pro-lifers for her willingness to suffer more than a year of imprisonment for blockading abortion facilities. Reflecting on her godson's conversion, she said that Nathanson was "like St. Paul, who was a great persecutor of the Church, yet when he saw the light of Christ, he was perhaps the greatest apostle for the Gospel. Dr. Nathanson was like that after his conversion. He went all around the world talking about the babies and the evils of abortion."

There are many lessons in Bernard Nathanson's life for those of us who recognize the worth and dignity of all human lives and who seek to win hearts and change laws. Two in particular stand out for me.

First is the luminous power of truth. As I have written elsewhere, and as Nathanson's own testimony confirms, the edifice of abortion is built on a foundation of lies. Nathanson told those lies; indeed, he helped to invent them. But others witnessed to truth. And when he was exposed to their bold, unintimidated, self-sacrificial witness, the truth overcame the darkness in Nathanson's heart and convicted him in the court of his own conscience.

Bernie and I became friends in the early 1990s, shortly after my own pro-life writings came to his attention. Once, during the Q&A after a speech he gave at Princeton, I asked him: "When you were promoting abortion, you were willing to lie in what you regarded as a good cause. Now that you have been converted to the cause of life, would you be willing to lie to save babies? How do those who hear your speeches and read your books and articles know that you are not lying now?" It was, I confess, an impertinently phrased question, but also, I believe, an important one. He seemed a bit stunned by it, and after a moment said, very quietly, "No, I wouldn't lie, even to save babies." At the dinner he and I had with students afterward, he explained himself further: "You said that I was converted to the cause of life, and that's true. But you must remember that I was converted to the cause of life only because I was converted to the cause of truth. That's why I wouldn't lie, even in a good cause."

The second lesson is this: we in the pro-life movement have no enemies to destroy. Our weapons are chaste weapons of the spirit: *truth and love*. Our task is less to defeat our opponents than to win them to the cause of life. To be sure, we must oppose the culture and politics of death resolutely and with a determination to win. But there is no one—*no one*—whose heart is so hard that he or she cannot be won over. Let us not lose faith in the power of our weapons to transform even the most resolute abortion advocates. The most dedicated abortion supporters are potential allies in the cause of life. It is the loving, prayerful, self-sacrificing witness of Joan Bell Andrews and so many other dedicated pro-life activists that softens the hearts and changes the lives of people like Dr. Bernard Nathanson.

May he rest in peace in the presence of the God of Abraham, Isaac, and Jacob, and may he share in the redemption wrought by the one who said that He came not to call the righteous, but sinners to repentance.

24

HE THREW IT ALL AWAY

On the Greatness of Richard John Neuhaus

I N THE EARLY 1970s, Lutheran pastor Richard John Neuhaus was poised to become the nation's next great liberal public intellectual—the Reinhold Niebuhr of his generation. He had going for him everything he needed to be not merely accepted but lionized by the liberal establishment. First, of course, there were his natural gifts as a thinker, writer, and speaker. Then there was a set of left-liberal credentials that were second to none. He had been an outspoken and prominent civil rights campaigner, someone who had marched literally arm in arm with his friend Martin Luther King Jr. He had founded one of the most visible anti-Vietnam War organizations. He moved easily in elite circles and was regarded by everyone as a "right-thinking" (i.e., left-thinking) intellectual-activist operating within the world of mainline Protestant religion.

Then something happened: abortion. It became something it had never been before—namely, a contentious issue in American culture and politics. Neuhaus opposed abortion for the same reasons he had fought for civil rights and against the Vietnam War. At the root of his thinking was the conviction that human beings, as creatures fashioned in the image and likeness of God, possess a profound, inherent, and equal dignity. This dignity must be respected by all and protected by law. That, so far as Neuhaus was concerned, was not only a biblical mandate but also the bedrock principle of the American constitutional order. Respect for the dignity of human beings meant, among other things, not subjecting them to a system of racial oppression, not wasting their lives in futile wars, not slaughtering them in the womb.

It is important to remember that in those days it was not yet clear whether support for "abortion rights" would be a litmus test for standing as a "liberal." After all, the early movement for abortion included many conservatives, such as columnist James J. Kilpatrick, who viewed abortion not only as a solution for the private difficulties of a "girl in trouble" but also as a way of dealing with the public problem of impoverished (and often unmarried) women giving birth to children who would increase welfare costs to taxpayers.

At the same time, more than a few notable liberals were outspokenly pro-life. In the early 1970s, Senator Edward M. Kennedy, for example, replied to constituents' inquiries about his position on abortion by saying that it was a form of "violence" incompatible with his vision of an America generous enough to care for and protect all its children, born and unborn. Some of the most eloquent and passionate pro-life speeches of the time were given by the Reverend Jesse Jackson. In condemning abortion, Jackson never failed to note that he himself was born to an unwed mother who would likely have been tempted to abort him had abortion been legal and easily available at the time.

The liberal argument against abortion was straightforward and powerful: "We liberals believe in the inherent and equal dignity of every member of the human family. We believe that the role of government is to protect all members of the community against brutality and oppression, especially the weakest and most vulnerable. We do not believe in solving personal or social problems by means of violence. We seek a fairer, nobler, more humane way. The personal and social problems created by unwanted pregnancy should not be solved by offering women the 'choice' of destroying their children in utero; rather, as a society we should reach out in love and compassion to mother and child alike."

So it was that Pastor Neuhaus and many like him saw no contradiction between their commitment to liberalism and their devotion to the pro-life cause. On the contrary, they understood their pro-life convictions to be part and parcel of what it meant to be a liberal. They were "for the little guy"—and the unborn child was "the littlest guy of all."

In the period from 1972 to 1980, however, the liberal movement steadily embraced the cause of abortion—on demand, at any point in gestation, funded with taxpayer dollars. The conservative movement went in precisely the opposite direction. In 1973, the Supreme Court handed down its decisions in *Roe v. Wade* and its companion case of *Doe v. Bolton*, effectively wiping out state laws forbidding the killing of unborn children by abortion. Ironically, several of the justices responsible for these decisions were regarded (and regarded themselves) as conservatives. Evidently, they were conservatives in the mold of James J. Kilpatrick. But the larger conservative movement did not accept *Roe* and *Doe*. The movement rejected these decisions for two reasons: first, they represented the judiciary's unconstitutional (indeed, anticonstitutional) usurpation of powers that the Constitution placed or left in the hands of legislatures; second, they constituted a grave injustice against abortion's tiny victims. By contrast, the liberal movement circled the wagons around *Roe* and *Doe*, celebrating these decisions as victories for women's rights and individual liberties.

By 1980, when Ronald Reagan (who as governor of California in the 1960s had signed an abortion-liberalization bill) sought the presidency as a staunchly pro-life conservative, and Edward Kennedy, having switched sides on abortion, challenged the wishy-washy President Jimmy Carter in the Democratic primaries as a doctrinaire "abortion rights" liberal, things had pretty much sorted themselves out. "Pro-choice" conservatives were gradually becoming rarer, and "pro-life" liberals were nearly an endangered species. (Jesse Jackson was still hanging on to his pro-life convictions, but he, too, yielded to the liberal movement's pro-abortion orthodoxy when he decided to seek the Democratic nomination for president in 1984.)

Richard Neuhaus, however, stood by his convictions and refused to yield. If the pro-life position is to be counted as the "conservative" position on the question of abortion, then fidelity to the cause of the unborn is how Neuhaus became the conservative that he was. He didn't change. His principles didn't change. He believed in 1984 and beyond what he had believed in 1974 and 1964. For him, justice, love, and compassion all pointed to protecting every member of the human family, however young, small, and dependent. What society owed to pregnant women in need was not the ghoulish compassion of the abortionist's knife but the love, moral and spiritual support, and practical assistance they needed to take care of themselves and their children. As Father Neuhaus's great friend, and fellow Lutheran convert to Catholicism, Father Leonard Klein put it in a beautiful tribute, "Richard's politics changed precisely because his principles did not change."

On some issues, Neuhaus's political views shifted because he came to doubt the wisdom and efficacy of programs and policies he had once believed in. The liberal movement's capitulation to the abortion license and the conservative movement's resolution to fight it opened him up to a reconsideration of where he should be—which for him meant a reconsideration of where the truth was to be found—on a variety of questions. He grew more skeptical of the bureaucratized big-government programs by which liberals sought to fight poverty and other social ills. He began to see that most of these programs were not only ineffective but even counterproductive. For a variety of reasons, statist solutions to poverty tended to increase and entrench rather than diminish it. And not unrelatedly, governmental expansion tended to weaken the institutions of civil society, above all the family and the church, on which we rely for the formation of decent, honest, responsible, civic-minded, law-abiding citizens—citizens capable of caring for themselves, their families, and people in need.

Of course, Neuhaus famously fought the liberal movement as it increasingly associated itself with the cause of driving religion and religiously informed moral witness out of the public square and into the merely private domain. His book *The Naked Public Square* did far more than introduce a catchy phrase; it revolutionized the debate. Neuhaus easily saw through the dubious (and sometimes laughable) "interpretations" of the religion clause of the First Amendment by which ACLU lawyers and judges in their ideological thrall attempted to privatize religion and marginalize people of faith. What motivated him most strongly, however, was the perception of the indispensable roles that religious institutions and other mediating structures played in preserving a regime of ordered liberty against unjustified encroachments by the administrative apparatus of the state. The real danger, as Neuhaus rightly saw it, was not that religious groups would seize control of the state and establish a theocracy; it was that the state would undermine the autonomy and standing of those structures that provide credible sources of authority in people's lives beyond the authority of the state—structures that could, when necessary, prophetically challenge unjust or overweening state power.

For Neuhaus, the liberal movement had gone wrong not only on the sanctity of human life but also on the range of issues on which it had succumbed to the ideology of the post-1960s cultural Left. While celebrating "personal liberation," "diverse lifestyles," "self-expression," and "if it feels good, do it," all in the name of respecting "the individual," liberalism had gone hook, line, and sinker for a set of doctrines and social policies that would only increase the size and enhance the control of the state—mainly by enervating the only institutions available to provide counterweights to state power.

The post-1960s liberal establishment—from the *New York Times* to NBC, from Harvard to Stanford, from the American Bar Association to Americans for Democratic Action—having embraced the combination of statism and lifestyle individualism that defines what it means to be a "liberal" (or "progressive") today, could not understand Richard Neuhaus or, in truth, abide him. Far from being lionized, he was loathed by them, albeit with a grudging respect for the intellectual gifts they once hoped he would place in the service of liberal causes. Those gifts were deployed relentlessly—and to powerful effect—against them and all their works and ways.

And so Father Richard John Neuhaus did not go through life, as it once seemed he would, collecting honorary degrees from the most prestigious universities, giving warmly received speeches before major professional associations and at international congresses of the great and the good, being a celebrated guest at social and political gatherings on the Upper West Side, or appearing on the Sunday network news shows as spiritual guarantor of the moral validity of liberalism's favored policies and practices.

His profound commitment to the sanctity of human life in all stages and conditions placed him on a different path, one that led him out of the liberal fold and into intense opposition. As a kind of artifact of his youth, he remained to the end a registered member of the Democratic Party. But he stood defiantly against many of the doctrines and policies that came to define that party in his lifetime. He was, in fact, their most forceful and effective critic—the scourge of the post-1960s liberals. He was not, as things turned out, their Niebuhr, but their nemesis.

25

A PRACTICAL PHILOSOPHER
IN EVERY WAY
G. E. M. Anscombe

"**E**ACH NATION THAT has 'liberal' abortion laws has rapidly become, if it was not already, a nation of murderers."
Who said that?

Operation Rescue's Randall Terry? The Reverend Jerry Falwell? Some fundamentalist preacher from the Ozarks?

No.

The person who spoke those words was one of the twentieth century's most eminent academic philosophers—indeed, a woman who might fairly have claimed (though it would never have occurred to her to make such a boast) to be the greatest philosopher of her sex in modern history: G. E. M. Anscombe.

Anscombe, a fellow of Somerville College, Oxford, who later succeeded her mentor, Ludwig Wittgenstein, in the chair in philosophy at the University of Cambridge, spoke those words in a lecture delivered in German and published for the first time (in English translation) in *Human Life, Action, and Ethics,* a superb collection of Anscombe's writings edited by her daughter Mary Geach—a fine philosopher in her own right—and Geach's husband, Luke Gormally.

The volume brings together essays ranging from her profoundly influential article "Modern Moral Philosophy" to the previously unpublished lecture "The Dignity of the Human Being," from which I quoted her "nation of murderers" line.

All the essays pertain to what philosophers, following Aristotle, call "practical reasoning." Most are about what people have reason to do and not do and what they ought to do and ought not to do. But not every essay is concerned with ethics, strictly speaking. Several focus on philosophical psychology and related subjects, elaborating and developing key ideas about how human acts are to be understood. (Of course, properly understanding human action is critical if we are to evaluate it intelligently from the ethical point of view.) It was work in this area—above all her 1957 book *Intention*—that established Anscombe as an intellectual giant. As Mary Geach observes in the introduction to *Human Life, Action, and Ethics*, "*Intention* changed the consciousness of Anglo-Saxon philosophy, making everyone aware that actions are intended under descriptions, and that they are at least to be judged under those."

Anscombe was a powerful and determined opponent of abortion, euthanasia, and the intentional killing of noncombatants in war (even in justified war). In considering these questions, she drew on the resources of Catholic philosophy (she was a convert to the faith, as was her husband, the distinguished philosopher Peter Geach, who survives her) and the history of philosophy generally. Yet she never hesitated to correct what she regarded as errors in traditional philosophical doctrines and ways of thinking or improve on ideas she drew from them. For example, though she did not dismiss the idea of "double effect," as some philosophers of her generation did, she carefully analyzed and cleaned up the parts of what turns out to be a rather complex philosophical doctrine to show that whether an act counts as "intentional killing" is one thing, but whether the act is justified even if it can be shown to qualify as the unintended causing of death is something else.

Anscombe coined the term *consequentialism* (which she introduced in "Modern Moral Philosophy") to name the view, widely held today even by people who reject the classic utilitarian identification of good with pleasure and evil with pain, that there is no act that cannot in certain circumstances be justified by its good consequences (or by the bad consequences that would likely follow from not performing the act). Consequentialism, in her opinion (and mine), has proved to be a profoundly destructive force, not only in ethics considered as a field of academic philosophy but also in the ethical lives of individuals and cultures. The conviction that a little evil may rightly be done for the sake of a greater good (however one defines "good"), or for the sake of preventing a greater evil, puts human beings on the path to losing their grip on good and evil altogether. We would not have gotten those "liberal" abortion laws in the first place were it not for the widespread adoption of an essentially consequentialist view of right and wrong.

Interestingly, Anscombe had doubts about whether the early human embryo is a human being. Because in the very early stages of development the embryo can divide, giving rise to monozygotic ("identical") twins, Anscombe was puzzled by the exact status of early embryonic human life. She wrestles with the problem in two essays reprinted in *Human Life*: "Were You a Zygote?" and "Embryos and Final Causes." Never, though, was Anscombe tempted to conclude that abortion—even early abortion—can be justified. As Mary Geach quotes her saying, "even if it were certain that, for example, a week-old conceptus is not a human being, the act of killing what is in the earliest stages of human life has evidently the same sort of malice as killing it later on when it is unquestionably a human, or more than one."

Anscombe herself allowed that the early embryo is a "living individual whole whose life is—all going well—to be the life of one or lives of more than one human being." That's certainly right. And this "living individual whole" is nothing less than a complete and distinct human organism possessing all the genetic material needed to inform and organize its growth, as well as an active disposition to develop using that information. The direction of its growth is not *extrinsically* determined but is in accord with the genetic information *within* it. The human embryo is not, then, something different in kind from a human being, nor is it merely a "potential human being," whatever that might mean; rather, the human embryo *is* a human being—a whole living member of the species *Homo sapiens*—in the embryonic stage.

Anscombe's "theoretical doubts," as she called them, did not erode what she called her "practical certainties" about the need to respect and protect by law human life at all stages and in all conditions. Nor did they induce in her any willingness to tolerate the dehumanization of the child in the womb. I was once at a conference where the theologian Lisa Sowle Cahill objected to an analogy proposed by another speaker, Russell Hittinger, between slavery and abortion. Cahill said that African Americans whose ancestors suffered the horrors of slavery could reasonably take offense at Hittinger's comparing them to embryos. Anscombe, who was also in attendance, immediately intervened to say: "The lady should not say 'embryo,' but rather 'conceived child.'"

Late in her life, Anscombe and one of her daughters became active in the British equivalent of Operation Rescue. They got themselves arrested for blockading an abortion clinic in an effort to stop the abortions being performed there. She was in every way a practical philosopher.

THE ACHIEVEMENT OF JOHN FINNIS

"THERE ARE HUMAN goods that can be secured only through the institutions of human law, and requirements of practical reasonableness that only those institutions can satisfy."

With these words, John Finnis, while still in his late thirties, began his masterwork, *Natural Law and Natural Rights*—the book that would not only revive scholarly interest in the venerable, but deeply misunderstood, idea of natural law and natural rights but also challenge dominant ways of thinking among philosophers of law and moral and political philosophers in the analytic tradition.[1]

Future intellectual historians will no doubt present the book, together with Professor Finnis's other philosophical writings, as part of the broad revival in more or less Aristotelian approaches to moral and political thinking that gained prominence beginning in the late 1970s. And they will be right to do so. Like Elizabeth Anscombe, David Wiggins, Philippa Foot, Alasdair MacIntyre, and many others, Finnis adopted or adapted Aristotelian methods to overcome the defects of utilitarian and other consequentialist approaches to ethics, on the one side, and Kantian or purely "deontological" approaches, on the other.

Like utilitarians, and unlike Kantians, these thinkers (who can be called neo-Aristotelians) hold that ethical thinking must be deeply linked to considerations of human well-being or flourishing—Aristotle's *eudaimonia*. But such thinking, they maintain, cannot treat the human good as subject to aggregation and calculation in a way that could somehow render coherent and workable a norm directing people to choose the option (or act on the rule) that will, for example, produce the "greatest happiness of the greatest number" or the "net best proportion of benefit to harm overall and in the long run." So, like Kantians, they reject the belief that ethics is a matter of technical reasoning (or "cost-benefit analysis") aimed purely and simply at producing the best possible consequences. Unlike Kantians, however, they also reject the idea of a purely deontological ethics, with its reduction of moral thinking to the domain of logic. To be sure, they accept the idea of morality as a matter of rectitude in willing, but they argue that morally wrongful choosing is not merely a matter of inconsistency in thought. Rather, immorality consists in choosing (and thus willing) in ways that are contrary to the good of human persons.

A critical moment—one might say *the* critical moment—in Finnis's intellectual biography occurred when, nearly fifteen years before the publication of *Natural Law and Natural Rights*, he encountered the work of Germain Grisez. It was Grisez's "re-presentation and very substantial development" of Aquinas's understanding of the first principles of practical thinking, the understanding articulated in the "treatise on law" of the *Summa Theologiae*, that made it possible for Finnis to deploy with the rigor rightly demanded in the analytical tradition of philosophy an Aristotelian approach to problems in philosophy of law and moral and political philosophy.[2] According to Grisez and Finnis, Aquinas correctly understood that the underived (*per se nota* and *indemonstrabilia*) first and most basic principles of practical reason direct human choosing and acting toward intelligible human goods—the various irreducible aspects of human well-being and fulfillment that provide more than merely instrumental reasons for action—and away from their privations. These first principles (and the basic human goods to which they refer in directing our choosing and acting—friendship, knowledge, critical aesthetic appreciation, skillful performances of various types, etc.) are not themselves moral norms. (Knowledge of them is moral knowledge incipiently, but only incipiently.) Rather, they guide and govern *all* coherent practical thinking, whether it results in morally upright action (such as visiting an ailing colleague in the hospital simply as an act of friendship) or immoral action (such as telling a lie to protect the reputation of a friend who has done something disgraceful).

Moral norms, whether general ones, such as the Golden Rule ("do unto others as you would have them do unto you"), or more specific ones, such as the prohibition of lying even to protect the reputation of a friend, are specifications of the obligation to honor the dignity of all human persons (including oneself) by respecting human well-being in its fullness—that is, the basic goods of human persons considered integrally. And so what Grisez and Finnis, who (together with Joseph M. Boyle Jr.) would later collaborate extensively in developing the moral theory Grisez pioneered, call "the first principle of morality" enjoins us to choose and otherwise will in ways that are compatible with a will toward integral human fulfillment.[3] Just as the various "basic human goods" are specifications of the first and most general principle of practical reason, which Aquinas formulates as "good (*bonum*) is to be done and pursued and bad (*malum*) is to be avoided," the various moral norms that we strive to live by and transmit to our children are specifications of the first and most general principle of morality. These norms of morality governing human choosing are not mere projections of feeling or emotion, nor are they imposed on reason extrinsically; rather, they are the fruit of reasoning about the human good and its integral directiveness and are, in that sense, as Finnis says, requirements of (practical) *reasonableness*.

When Finnis arrived in Oxford in the early 1960s as an Australian Rhodes scholar holding an LLB from the University of Adelaide, he was fortunate to be able to write his doctoral dissertation (on the idea of judicial power) under the supervision of Herbert Hart, holder of the University of Oxford's Professorship of Jurisprudence and the preeminent Anglophone legal philosopher of his time. Hart had recently published his own masterwork, *The Concept of Law*.[4] Much of what Finnis would go on to achieve in legal and political philosophy would be rooted in critical engagement with Hart's thought. This was an engagement that Hart welcomed. Indeed, in his role as editor of the prestigious Clarendon Law Series of Oxford University Press, Hart would commission Finnis (who in the mid-1960s became his colleague on the Oxford law faculty) to write *Natural Law and Natural Rights*, even specifying the title. While resisting most of Finnis's criticisms of his work, Hart had a keen appreciation of the power of his young colleague's intellect and the force of his arguments.

Although Hart's sympathies tended to run in a moderate empiricist and to some extent utilitarian direction, there is a sense in which his work (especially *The Concept of Law*) prefigured the Aristotelian revival. Despite his firm commitment to what he regarded as "legal positivism"—which he understood as a strict commitment to the "conceptual separation of law and morality"—Hart was a severe critic of Jeremy Bentham's externalist and reductionist view of law (or the concept of law). Bentham supposed that the social phenomenon (or set of phenomena) we know as "law" is best understood on the model of "orders backed by threats"—orders issued by a sovereign who is habitually obeyed but who obeys no one. On this understanding, laws function as *causes* of human behavior. They do not create obligation, at least in the normal, normatively flavored sense of that word. Rather, they merely oblige—by way of threats of punishment for noncompliance. They oblige in the way that an armed bandit obliges a victim to turn over his wallet.

Now, Hart's objection to Bentham's account was not moralistic; rather, he argued that it failed *descriptively*—it did not "fit the facts."[5] In particular, it did not account for the ways in which laws characteristically function in the lives of citizens and officials as frequently providing certain types of intelligible *reasons* for action, what he would later describe as "content-independent peremptory reasons."[6] To "fit the facts," an account of law must pay attention to the practical point of laws and legal institutions, and draw the distinctions between various types of laws and their various functions. But this, in turn, requires the legal theorist, or descriptive sociologist[7] of law and legal systems, to adopt what Hart called "the internal point of view"—that is, the practical viewpoint of citizens and officials for whom the laws provide *reasons* for acting by, among other things, enabling them individually and/or collectively to pursue certain objectives and accomplish certain goals (for example, transporting themselves on the highway, getting married, creating a binding commercial contract, establishing a charitable trust).[8]

Having identified and adopted the internal point of view, Hart's "concept" (and philosophy) of law begins to move away from the voluntarism (law as will) that lies at the heart of Benthamite legal positivism and toward a recognition of law as *rationally* grounded—that is, as providing reasons that guide choosing. Law (and laws), according to Hart, cannot be reduced to *causes* of human behavior, nor can it accurately be described as the sheer imposition of *will* (of a sovereign). It is characteristically (though not always) reasoned and reasonable. At least, it is capable of being so, and will be so in the central or "focal" cases in which law functions in the ways that make it intelligible as a product of human deliberation and judgment in the first place. And yet Hart himself drew short of committing himself to any such conclusion. He wished to retain the core of legal positivism even while jettisoning Bentham's externalism (and strict voluntarism) and reductionism. It was precisely for this drawing short, this refusal to identify fully reasonable (i.e., just) law as the focal case of law and the point of view of the morally motivated legal official and citizen as the focal case of the internal point of view, that Finnis criticized the otherwise powerfully compelling philosophy of his teacher.

For Finnis, the focal case of a legal system is one in which legal rules and principles function as practical reasons for citizens as well as judges and other officials because of people's appreciation of their virtue and value—that is, their *point*. Aquinas's famous *practical* definition of law as an ordinance of reason directed to the common good by the persons and institutions having responsibility for the care of the community here has its significance in *descriptive* legal theory. Finnis observes:

> If we consider the reasons people have for establishing systems of positive law (with power to override immemorial custom), and for maintaining them (against the pull of strong passions and individual self-interest), and for reforming and restoring them when they decay or collapse, we find that only the moral reasons on which many of those people often act suffice to explain why such people's undertaking takes the shape it does, giving legal systems the many features they have—features which a careful descriptive account such as H. L. A. Hart's identifies as characteristic of the central case of positive law and the focal meaning of "law," and which therefore have a place in an adequate concept (understanding and account) of positive law.[9]

But Hart himself refused to distinguish central from peripheral cases of the internal point of view. Thus, he treated cases of obedience to law by virtue of "unreflecting inherited attitudes" and even the "mere wish to do as others do" as indistinguishable from morally motivated fidelity to law.[10] These "considerations and attitudes," like those that boil down to self-interest or the avoidance of punishment, are, Finnis argues, "diluted or watered-down instances of the practical viewpoint that brings law into being as a significantly differentiated type of social order and maintains it as such. Indeed, they are parasitic upon that viewpoint."[11]

This is not to suggest that Finnis denies any valid sense to Hart's insistence on the "conceptual separation" of law and morality.[12] It is merely to highlight the ambiguity of the assertion of such a separation and the need to distinguish, even more carefully and clearly than

Hart did, between the respects in which such a separation obtains and those in which it does not. Still less is it to suggest that belief in natural law or other forms of moral realism entails the proposition that law and morality are connected in such a way as to confer upon judges plenary authority to enforce the requirements of natural law or to legally invalidate provisions of positive law that they judge to be in conflict with these requirements. The scope and limits of judicial power is a separate issue—one that was the focus of criticism of Hart's jurisprudence by another of his eminent former students, the late Ronald Dworkin, who faulted Hart's positivism for excessively narrowing the authority of judges and other officials to bring moral judgments to bear in the enterprise of legal interpretation.[13] Finnis has not signed on to Dworkin's critique of Hart's jurisprudence—a critique that is sometimes regarded as proceeding from a natural-law vantage point of its own—and parts of Finnis's work suggest reasons for believing that Dworkin's critique is in important ways misguided. For Finnis, the truth of the proposition *lex iniusta non est lex* (an unjust law is no law at all) is a moral truth—namely, that the moral obligation created by authoritative legal enactment (that is to say, by positive law) is conditional rather than absolute. The prima facie moral obligation to obey the law is *defeasible*. Finnis does not claim that unjust laws are in no legitimate sense laws,[14] nor does he argue that judges enjoy as a matter of natural law some sort of plenary authority to invalidate or even to subvert or ignore laws that they regard (even reasonably regard) as unjust.

We see, then, that Finnis takes on board Hart's key insights deriving from his critical engagement with Benthamite legal positivism and pushes them to their logical conclusions—conclusions that move legal philosophy beyond legal positivism, even in its comparatively modest Hartian iteration, into a recognition of law as, in a meaningful sense, connected with reason's quest for justice and the common good (law as reason and not merely will). In the process, he strikes a blow against a familiar caricature of natural law whose wide acceptance (including, incidentally, by Hart himself as well as by Hans

Kelsen and others) had provided apparent grounds for scholars to dismiss it.

The achievement of John Finnis goes well beyond his signal contributions to philosophy of law. It includes his work with Grisez and Boyle in developing the understanding of practical reasoning and moral judgment that has come to be known, problematically, as the "new" natural law theory.[15] It also includes his critical writings against moral skepticism, utilitarianism and other forms of consequentialism in ethics, and ethical theories that purport to lay aside considerations of human well-being in identifying norms of conduct for the moral life.[16] It includes, too, significant work in political philosophy, some of it directed to pulling the rug out from under the most influential forms of "liberal" political theory of our time—namely, those "antiperfectionist" theories (often underwriting an ideology of expressive and/or possessive individualism), such as the theory of justice and "political liberalism" that the late John Rawls advanced. According to Rawls's theory, political decisions may not legitimately be based on controversial ideas of what makes for or detracts from a valuable and morally worthy way of life. Rawls also proposed that in decisions pertaining to constitutional essentials and matters of basic justice, liberty may not legitimately be limited except on the basis of "public reasons" (where the concept of a public reason strictly excludes reasons drawn from "comprehensive" philosophical and religious views— however reasonable those "comprehensive" views may be).[17]

Finnis's contributions in political philosophy go beyond his criticism of major works by influential contemporary liberal thinkers, such as Rawls, Dworkin, and the late Robert Nozick. *Natural Law and Natural Rights*, especially chapters 6–11, constitutes a major affirmative contribution to thought about (1) justice and its requirements; (2) the content (and scope) of the political common good; (3) rights, including human rights, and their identification; (4) the rational grounds for honoring legal and political authority and recognizing legal and political obligation; and (5) the nature and social functions of law. In all these areas, Finnis's analysis and prescriptions are notable not only for their analytical rigor and precision but also for their attention to the complexities of the subject matter. Taken together, *Natural Law and Natural Rights* and later essays represent an important and distinctive contribution to the contemporary debate about the selection of political principles and the proper design and healthy functioning of political institutions.[18]

In normative ethics and political theory, Finnis has been a force second to none in defending the moral inviolability of human life in all stages and conditions and the norm against making the death or injury of a human being the precise object of one's choosing. He has written powerfully against abortion, infanticide, euthanasia, and the intentional (including the conditional) willingness to kill or maim noncombatants (including captured or subdued enemy soldiers) even in justified wars. Similarly, he has been a leading voice in defense of the historic understanding of marriage as a conjugal partnership—the union of husband and wife. In many cases, his views have put him at odds with the socially liberal orthodoxy prevailing in the universities and other intellectual sectors of the culture; in a few, they have placed him in dissent from what are regarded today as conservative positions. Like his hero Socrates, in an analogy his commendable humility would cause him vehemently to reject, he has followed arguments wherever they lead and has never hesitated to state and defend a view because it flies in the face of the intellectual, moral, or political dogmas of the day. The accolades and honors that have come his way were not purchased by conformity to allegedly enlightened opinion or by silence in regard to what he judges to be its grave defects. His powerful and very public dissent could hardly have been contrived to gain him a personal chair in Oxford or election as a Fellow of the British Academy. In this, as in so many other ways, he has always been an inspiration to those of us fortunate enough to have been his students and to young scholars in the various fields of his interest and influence who know his work and the witness to the unconditional pursuit of truth it represents.

And this takes us to one last area of his interest and influence, an area in which the truths pursued are truths about ultimate things. While still a young philosopher, in a milieu dominated by secularism—one that was already showing signs of hostility to dissent—he made the move from secularism to (Catholic) Christianity, under the influence of classic philosophers as well as Christian saints. It was not that he came to faith and therefore saw the world differently. If anything, the reverse was true. The closed horizon of secularism artificially constrained the questions that, pursued with Socratic relentlessness, undermine secularism itself and inaugurate a journey of faith that might well lead to the rational affirmation of spiritual realities and an openness to entering into some form of communication and friendship with a transcendent source of meaning, value, and indeed all that there is. It was, in other words, reflection on the world—and the manifold orders of intelligibility (the natural, the logical, the moral, the technical) in which it presents itself to us and yields to our questioning and investigating—that led John Finnis to conclude that there are more things to be understood (and engaged) than can be immediately perceived with the senses or accounted for by empirical inquiry or technical analysis. Like so many other notable modern philosophers who have made the journey from secularism to Catholicism—Elizabeth Anscombe, Alasdair MacIntyre, Michael Dummett, Peter Geach, Nicholas Rescher—it was reason and reasoning that brought him to faith.

Faith was not to be, for Finnis, purely a matter of personal piety detached from his exertions as a philosopher. It could not be, since the lines of questioning that must be pursued in practical philosophical disciplines—ethics, political philosophy, philosophy of law—will, unless for no adequate reason we choose to cut them off, take us to the deepest questions of meaning and value. Reason itself, if it is anything more than a computational power, is a spiritual capacity, one that is not reducible solely to material and efficient causes. And reason cannot be a merely computational power if it is indeed capable of grasping more than merely instrumental reasons for action (and their integral directiveness)—reasons (including moral norms) that are capable of guiding choices that are truly free. And if we are indeed

rational and free creatures—that is, *persons*, beings whose fundamental makeup (nature) is oriented to deliberation, judgment, and
choice—then we are not merely material but also spiritual creatures,
creatures whose integral good includes not only our bodily (biological) health but our intellectual, moral, and spiritual well-being too.
Obviously, these anthropological facts, if facts indeed they are, cannot
but be highly relevant to questions of ethics, political philosophy, and
philosophy of law, as well as to theology (including, centrally, moral
theology).

Finnis's work in moral theology prompted the highest authorities
of the Catholic Church to summon him to service on its most important theological council, the International Theological Commission.
There he worked especially on the philosophical and theological cur-
rents that were washing away the concept of intrinsically morally
wrongful acts. In his own voice, and not purporting to speak for the
commission, he published a small but lastingly valuable book on the
subject entitled *Moral Absolutes*.[19] Here, in my view, we have a supreme
example of the value of rigorous philosophical work marshaled in
the causes of understanding the data of revelation and illuminating
and enriching the teachings of faith. The work vindicates the claim
famously advanced by Pope John Paul II in the opening sentence of
his encyclical letter *Fides et Ratio*: "Faith and reason are like two wings
on which the human spirit ascends to contemplation of truth." The
truth-seeking achievements of John Finnis have been made possible
by his willingness to use both wings.

27

ELIZABETH FOX-GENOVESE
A Life Well Lived

E LIZABETH FOX-GENOVESE WAS a scholar as notable for her bravery as for her brilliance. After what she described as her "long apprenticeship" in the world of secular liberal intellectuals, it was careful reflection on the central moral questions of our time that led her first to doubt and then to abandon both liberalism and secularism. Needless to say, this did not endear her to her former allies.

At the heart of her doubts about secular liberalism (and what she described as "radical, upscale feminism") was its embrace of abortion and its (continuing) dalliance with euthanasia. At first, she went along with abortion, albeit reluctantly, believing that women's rights to develop their talents and control their destinies required its legal availability. But Betsey (as she was known by her friends) was not one who could avert her eyes from inconvenient facts. The central fact about abortion is that it is the deliberate killing of a developing child in the womb. For Betsey, euphemisms such as "products of conception," "termination of pregnancy," "privacy," and "choice" ultimately could not hide that fact. She came to see that to countenance abortion is not to respect women's "privacy" or liberty; it is to suppose that some people have the right to decide whether others will live or die. In a statement that she knew would inflame many on the Left and even cost her valued friendships, she declared that "no amount of past oppression can justify women's oppression of the most vulnerable among us."

Betsey knew that public pro-life advocacy would be regarded by many in the intellectual establishment as intolerable apostasy—especially from one of the founding mothers of "women's studies." She could have been forgiven for keeping mum on the issue and carrying on with her professional work on the history of the American South. But keeping mum about fundamental matters of right and wrong was not in her character. Though she valued her standing in the intellectual world, she cared for truth and justice more. So she spoke out ever more passionately in defense of the unborn.

And the more she thought and wrote about abortion and other life issues, the more persuaded she became that the entire secular liberal project was misguided. Secular liberals were not deviating from their principles in endorsing killing whether by abortion or euthanasia in the name of individual "choice"; they were following them to their logical conclusions. But this revealed a profound contradiction at the heart of secular liberal ideology, for the right of some individuals to kill others undermines any ground of principle on which an idea of individual rights or dignity could be founded.

Even in her early life as a secular liberal, she was never among those who disdained religious believers or held them in contempt. As a historian and social critic, she admired the cultural and moral achievements of Judaism and Christianity. As her doubts about secularism grew, she began to consider seriously whether religious claims might actually be true. Reason led her to the door of faith, and prayer enabled her to walk through it. As she herself described her conversion from secularism to Catholicism, it had a large intellectual component, but it was, in the end, less her choice than God's grace.

Betsey continued her scholarly labors, especially in collaboration with her husband, Eugene Genovese, our nation's most distinguished historian of American slavery. Not long ago, Cambridge University Press published their masterwork, *The Mind of the Master Class*. Soon after Betsey's own religious conversion, Gene (who had long been an avowed Marxist but who had gradually moved in the direction of cultural and political conservatism) returned to the Catholic faith of his boyhood under the influence of his beloved wife.

As if she had not already antagonized the intellectual establishment enough, Betsey soon began speaking out in defense of marriage and sexual morality. Her root-and-branch rejection of the ideology of the sexual revolution—an ideology that now enjoys the status of infallible dogma among many secular liberal intellectuals—was based on a profound appreciation of the centrality of marriage to the fulfillment of men and women as sexually complementary spouses; to the well-being of children, for whom the love of mother and father for each other and for them is literally indispensable; and to society as a whole, which depends on the marriage-based family for the rearing of responsible and upright citizens. If her pro-life advocacy angered many liberal intellectuals, her outspoken defense of marriage and traditional norms of sexual morality made them apoplectic.

Betsey's marriage to Gene was one of the great love stories of our time. They were two very different personalities, perfectly united. He was the head of the family; she was in charge of everything. Their affection for each other created a kind of force field into which friends were drawn in love for both of them. Although unable to have children of their own, they lavished parental care and concern on their students and younger colleagues, who in turn worshipped them.

Betsey leaves us many fine works of historical scholarship and social criticism—works admired by honest scholars across the political spectrum. Even more important, her life provides an unsurpassed example of intellectual integrity and moral courage. Her fervent witness to the sanctity of human life and the dignity of marriage and the family will continue to inspire. May the living God who drew her to Himself grant her a full share in His divine life.

28

EUGENE GENOVESE

Truth Teller

E UGENE DOMINICK GENOVESE, the eminent historian of
slavery and the American South who died on September 26,
2012, at his home in Atlanta, was legendary not only for the
brilliance of his scholarship but also for his intellectual integrity and
his utter loathing of hypocrisy and cant.

Although I am not a historian and I never sat in his classroom, I
cannot help but think of Gene as an esteemed teacher and of myself as
one of his students. Gene and his late wife, Elizabeth Fox-Genovese,
an equally distinguished historian and his coauthor on many important works, were my dear friends. I learned much from them not only
about the historical subjects to which they devoted themselves so
fruitfully but also, and more important, about what it means—and
what it takes—to be a scholar.

Gene's place in the pantheon of American historians was fixed by
his pathbreaking study of slavery in antebellum America titled *Roll,
Jordan, Roll: The World the Slaves Made*. Though hardly an apologia for
slavery—indeed, Gene was still a devout Marxist revolutionary when
he wrote the book and would remain one for many years—it stressed

how slaves retained their humanity, in part with the de facto cooperation of owners and their families, with whom slaves were in unmistakably human (albeit unequal and profoundly unjust) relationships. And it showed that the slaves were able, despite the injustice and horrors of slavery, to "make a world" for themselves. They were actors, not merely inert creatures being acted upon by others (or by "forces" of history or society).

In *Roll, Jordan, Roll* and other works, Gene demonstrated the value for the social historian of sympathetically adopting the perspectives of those whose lives are studied. He was able to convey a sense of how things really were in the days of American slavery by reproducing the points of view of slaves, their masters in the planter class, nonslaveholding white southerners, and others.

Gene's skills as a researcher and writer, his brilliance, and his acumen were obvious. They jumped off the pages of any book or article he wrote. One perceives further virtues, however, when one looks at the corpus of his work as a whole. One cannot but be impressed by the analytical rigor of his scholarship, his impeccable intellectual honesty, and his willingness to assess evidence and draw fair conclusions, however ideologically uncongenial. By example and not merely by precept, Gene taught all of us who read his writings, students or otherwise, to follow the evidence and the arguments wherever they lead, whatever our prior commitments.

The practice of these virtues could not have been easy for Gene Genovese, for he was a man of strong passions. On this point, his friends and admirers and his foes and detractors will be in perfect agreement. The dispassion of his historical scholarship was remarkable for a man whose moral and political passions were so formidable.

When I look back over Gene's long life as a scholar and controversialist, two passions stand out above the others: his passion for justice and his passion for truth.

A passion for justice is, to be sure, a good thing, but it can sometimes lead people badly astray. That happened in Gene's case. It was his passion for justice that led him as a boy of fifteen into Marxism and the Communist Party. Although by age twenty he had managed to get himself expelled from the party—he "zigged," as he would later explain, when the party line was to "zag"—he remained an avowed and faithful communist for many decades after that.

The question could be asked of Gene, as of so many other brilliant people: "How could someone so intellectually gifted—and honest—have fallen hook, line, and sinker for a view (let's face it) as absurd as Marxism and stuck with it for all those years?"

Here is how. Born in 1930, Gene grew up during the Great Depression in a working-class household in the Bensonhurst section of Brooklyn. His father was a wood caulker. Because of his circumstances, he witnessed not only poverty and despair but also disgusting episodes of exploitation and abuse. When in the late 1930s Gene's father lost his job, Gene got a personal taste of suffering. After his communist faith finally collapsed, he reflected on the experience in an interview that is worth quoting at length:

I . . . spent my first eight or nine years in the worst depression in American history. My father knew nothing of left-wing ideology, and like so many other workers, was a New Deal Democrat. Roosevelt was his god. Those were rough years, especially 1938, when my father was out of work for six months and too proud to go on relief, as welfare was then called. It is not enjoyable to watch your parents stint themselves on food so that you and your brother can get a proper meal. Take my word for it, it's bad for the digestion.

In any case, I grew up in a class-conscious home. Class-conscious, but by no means ideologically driven. I hated the bourgeoisie with the terrible passion that perhaps only a child can muster. When I came across the communists at age 15, and read *The Communist Manifesto*, and some other pamphlets, I suddenly had a precise focus for my hatred. I would have happily sent the bastards to firing squads in large numbers, and their wives and children along with them.

Yet something always bothered me about my father. No one could've hated the bosses more intensely than he, but unlike the son [i.e., Gene himself], he was selective in his hatred. He admired old Mr. Cadell, who had begun as a worker and built the small shipyard in which Dad worked. He regarded Mr. Cadell as a decent man, who had worked hard for what he had earned, and tried to treat his workers decently. It was Cadell, Junior, who took over the business, who incurred Dad's wrath and whom he would have shot. I cannot imagine my father, who was a hard man, ever agreeing to shoot anyone's wife and children.

The last sentence, of course, is the punch line. Gene is there distinguishing himself as a communist from his father, who was a New Deal Democrat. Then he goes on:

In particular, my father was enraged by the sight of Junior's flunkies throwing his dogs steaks, while his unemployed workers were begging for a day's work. I know that Dad did not make up that story, or the story of the foreman who was even worse than his employer, and wound up with his head crushed by a caulker's mallet. The workers, including my father, told the police that they had seen nothing and knew nothing. They did know that they were not about to pass judgment on him.

Gene grew up in an Italian Catholic family. Of course, Christianity had a criticism of exploitation and injustice. It had a story—one rooted deeply in the Bible and especially the prophets—about the need to oppose injustice. But it didn't have something that communism offered the youthful and passion-filled Eugene Genovese—namely, *a program*. So young Gene, enthralled by the program, abandoned Christianity and joined the communists.

But Gene's passion for truth, throughout his entire life, even at the most intense moments of his communist period, was powerful.

And it would, in the end, win out. That extraordinary intellectual and personal integrity was his hallmark.

Nowhere was Gene's integrity, rooted in his passion for truth, more evident than in his stand against the politicization or instrumental-ization of scholarship. No end, however much he personally cherished it, could justify that in his eyes. In the mid-1960s, at the height of the Cold War, when Gene was teaching at Rutgers University, he publicly called for the victory of Ho Chi Minh and the North Vietnamese over the Americans. The Vietnam War had not yet become widely unpopu-lar, so Gene's comments were regarded as outrageous, even treason-ous. Politicians, including future president Richard Nixon, called for Rutgers to fire him. It became a very public issue.

What received far less publicity was this: not too long after that episode, Gene fought a lonely battle in the American Historical Asso-ciation against a resolution, similar to ones passed by other academic and professional associations, to condemn American involvement in the war in Vietnam. Why would a Marxist historian who favored a North Vietnamese victory do that? The answer is simple: a deep com-mitment to the integrity of scholarship and an equally deep aversion to its politicization. As colleagues clamored for passage of the resolu-tion, Gene warned them that going down that road would lead to the corruption of intellectual life. He noted that what bound them together as members of a professional academic association was not a common set of political beliefs; it was, rather, a shared commitment to the pursuit of knowledge and the attainment of truth. Political "party lines" had no place in the association, even when the line in question was one to which he personally hewed.

You see, Eugene Genovese, even as a Marxist, knew that a passion for justice could pose a grave danger to the cause of truth. And he was keenly aware that he was personally far from immune to the dan-ger. Here are his own words: "My biggest problem as an historian has always been, I suppose, the conscious effort to rein in my hatred"—that is, his hatred of exploitation, his hatred of injustice—"and not let it distort my reading of the historical record. I'm sure that it's taken a toll, but I hope I have kept that toll to a minimum."

Readers who knew Gene personally will recognize the word that was, by his own lights, the worst thing he could call a person— especially if that person was a fellow academic. He could hiss this word: *faker.* By a "faker," Gene meant someone who pretends to be something he is not—someone, in particular, who merely pretends to intellectual integrity and honest scholarship. Gene despised intellec- tual conformism and loathed "political correctness." He had a special contempt for those who tolerated or went along with these vices for careerist reasons, or to get attention, or (for that matter—and there is more of this in the academy than nonacademics know) to get girls. They were "fakers."

But there's another word that Gene favored, and it was the best thing he could call someone. That word is *brave.* Gene knew that it takes bravery—in any age, not just ours—to have integrity, to exem- plify it in one's work, especially in one's work as a scholar. To say what one believes to be true, even when it's unpopular or goes against the grain, takes bravery. And often it takes a certain kind of bravery to contradict what one has previously thought and published and say, "I was wrong about that."

Gene (like his wife, Betsey) exemplified magnificently the bravery he valued so highly and praised in others. If, as I believe, it was the passionate love of truth that was the anchor of Gene's extraordinary integrity, it was courage that enabled him to be so faithful to that object of his passion.

Some of Gene's critics, including his Marxist critics, had a point when they claimed that he was a rather unorthodox Marxist, even at periods when he would have prided himself on his Marxist orthodoxy. Here was the core of his unorthodoxy: Gene never accepted Marxism's utopian view of human nature. He was always, even at the height of his communist atheism, a firm believer in original sin. One might say he represented the Calvinist school of Marxism. He believed in the total depravity of man.

Something else Gene never accepted about orthodox Marxism was its strict economic determinism. He knew that the economic explanation of human conduct and the practices and institutions partially constituted by that conduct could get one only so far. It could be only part of the story. He thought it was usually an important part, but he simply couldn't buy the determinism. On this, he was not a Calvinist. He believed people could act, and sometimes did act, freely. That made him a pretty bad Marxist, but it fitted him out well for his eventual return to Catholicism.

And there is a third element of Marxist orthodoxy that Gene rejected—namely, its Hegelian teleology. Now, if someone claiming to be a Marxist rejects *that* element of the story, it's not quite clear how he is a Marxist. To me it's like saying, as Jefferson did, that he would be a Christian but without the miracles, when one of those miracles is the Incarnation.

So perhaps Gene wasn't really a Marxist after all, though he certainly believed he was one. There was always in his scholarship and thinking about politics and other human activities a sense of the contingency and openness of things. Indeed, it was a sense of human freedom that enabled him so brilliantly to enter into the minds and lives of the people about whom he wrote, to understand them "from the inside"—that is, *as they understood themselves*. When one reads Eugene Genovese's accounts of the past, it's not as if one is looking in from the outside. He brings one into the world that he is writing about—for example, the world the slaves and planters and other southerners made.

I suppose it's not really surprising that Gene was, at best, an unorthodox Marxist. He was always suspicious, if not downright hostile, to intellectual or political dogmas of any type. And that is because he knew that groupthink is toxic to the love of truth.

It is important to note that even after he formally abandoned communism as a philosophical idea and a political movement, Gene was willing to acknowledge certain virtues in it as an approach to the explanation of social reality. "The Marxist focus on social struggles," he said, "primarily but not entirely class-based, has proven salutary to historians of the right, as well as the left, at least when shorn of its implicit Hegelian teleology."

So Gene was not the kind of ex-Marxist who insists that everything about it was wrong. It's probably fair to say, or at least not too unfair to say, that we could finally classify Gene as a cultural conservative, a pedagogical liberal (especially in his openness to debate and hostility to intellectual orthodoxies), and something of an analytical Marxist.

Yet as a lover of truth and, above all, a teller of truth, Gene publicly and fully acknowledged that Marxism was, in political practice, an unfathomable catastrophe. Here's what Gene said in an article he wrote for the left-wing journal *Dissent* in 1994: "In a noble effort to liberate the human race from violence and oppression we broke all records for mass slaughter, piling up tens of millions of corpses in less than three-quarters of a century." That was Gene's confession. Notice that he said "we," not "they." *We* did it. We Marxists. He did not exclude or excuse himself or other Western intellectuals who embraced or condoned communism or regarded anticommunism as a greater threat to liberty. Gene always believed in personal responsibility, and he was honest and brave enough not only to acknowledge his own responsibility for supporting Stalinism and post-Stalinist Soviet ideology and Soviet policy but also to confront the entire Left—Marxists, democratic socialists, and left liberals—with its culpability.

In that article in *Dissent*, Gene put to himself and his longtime allies a pair of questions that he feared many were simply too polite to ask him, for he loved truth too much to avoid them: given the "piling up [of] tens of millions of corpses in less than three-quarters of a century," he asked, "what did we know, and when did we know it?"

And he answered the questions:

What did we know? "Everything." It wasn't hidden. It wasn't some surprise. We knew. Or, if we didn't know, we didn't know because we didn't want to know. We knew about the gulag, about the disappearances, about the murders, about the massacres. We knew everything.

When did we know it? "From the beginning." But drunk on our ideology and our hatred of exploitation and economic injustice, we thought it was justified. That was our error. We "preached the need to break eggs to make omelets." To defeat exploitation and oppression, we had to murder some innocent people—"some," as in eighty million.

Gene said, "We spent three-quarters of a century in building socialisms that cost tens of millions of lives, created hideous political regimes, and could not even deliver a decent standard of living. The essential ingredient in a proper evaluation would have to be a frank assessment of the extent to which the assumptions that underlay the whole left, social democratic and liberal groups, as well as the Stalinist left, have proven untenable, not to invoke a harsher word."

Gene Genovese was indeed a teller of truth, even when the truth to be told was ugly, embarrassing, humiliating. He told the truth, even when it meant confessing complicity in world-historical crimes. And even at the height of his passionate attachment to communism, he was equally passionate about telling the truth and avoiding any politicization or corruption of scholarship.

Betsey was her husband's peer in devotion to truth, and no less brave about truth telling. This shared commitment to truth and truth telling, and the courage that Gene and Betsey reinforced in each other, help to explain the extraordinary bond between two people who were, in so many other ways, unlike each other. And extraordinary it was. Their marriage was, as I said in my tribute to Betsey in the previous chapter, one of the great love stories of our time. And as in all truly great love stories, their devotion to each other created a kind of force field into which others were drawn. I was blessed to be among them.

Gene and Betsey were united in love for each other and for the many friends who loved them; they were united in the love of truth and in the willingness to speak the truth whatever the cost; and, in the end, they were united in faith. Drawn by the moral witness of the Catholic Church to the sanctity of human life and the dignity of marriage and the family, Betsey in midlife abandoned the secularism in which she had been reared and began a journey of thought and prayer that led her into Catholicism. Under her influence, Gene, having lost faith in dialectical materialism, returned to the sacraments. Twenty-six years after their secular wedding, they were sacramentally married as faithful—and joyful—Catholics.

Eugene Dominick Genovese was laid to rest next to his beloved Betsey after a funeral in Christ the King Cathedral in Atlanta. If it were left to me, the grave marker would bear this simple legend: *Here lie Eugene Genovese and Elizabeth Fox-Genovese: truth tellers.*

Notes

Chapter 2: The Limits of Constitutional Limits

1 See Alexander Hamilton, *Federalist Papers*, Number 84.
2 See, e.g., Jeremy Waldron, "The Core of the Case against Judicial Review," *Yale Law Journal* 115 (2006): 1345–1406.
3 See, e.g., *United States v. Lopez*, 514 U.S. 549 (1995).
4 *National Federation of Independent Business v. Sebelius*, 567 U.S. ___ (2012).
5 John Adams, *Message to the Officers of the First Brigade of the Third Division of the Militia of Massachusetts* (1798).

Chapter 6: Some Hard Questions about Affirmative Action

1 See, e.g., *Adarand Constructors, Inc. v. Pena*, 515 U.S. 200, 227 (1995).
2 *Gratz v. Bollinger*, 123 S. Ct. 2411, 2417 (2003); *Grutter v. Bollinger*, 123 S. Ct. 2325, 2331 (2003).
3 *Gratz*, 123 S. Ct. at 2427; *Grutter*, 123 S. Ct. at 2337–38.
4 *Gratz*, 123 S. Ct. at 2427; *Grutter*, 123 S. Ct. at 2339.
5 *Gratz*, 123 S. Ct. at 2427–28.
6 *Grutter*, 123 S. Ct. at 2342.
7 See *Gratz*, 123 S. Ct. at 2445 (Ginsburg, J., dissenting); *Grutter*, 123 S. Ct. at 2349 (Scalia, J., concurring in part and dissenting in part).
8 *Gratz*, 123 S. Ct. at 2446 (Ginsburg, J., dissenting).
9 *Grutter*, 123 S. Ct. at 2343.

10 See ibid. at 2340 (describing military and business leaders' support for treating diversity as compelling government interest).

11 Ibid. at 2348–49 (Scalia, J., concurring in part and dissenting in part).

12 Why this is the case is disputed. In my opinion, it has nothing to do with genetics.

13 The absence of diversity of opinion among academics manifests itself in many areas, not least on the question of racial and ethnic preference policies in university admissions. Many intelligent people of goodwill in the United States question whether it is prudent, just, and constitutionally legitimate to grant preferences to members of certain racial and ethnic groups. Yet among contemporary academics in law and the social sciences, there is little diversity of opinion. It is easy to find scholars who favor the policies in question; it is not so easy to find scholars who oppose them. Case in point: when this essay originally ran as part of a *Columbia Law Review* symposium on *Grutter* and *Gratz*, it was the only one in the whole issue written by someone critical of racial and ethnic preference policies.

14 See *Grutter*, 123 S. Ct. at 2351 (Thomas, J., concurring in part and dissenting in part) (reviewing precedents defining compelling government interest as involving "pressing public necessity").

15 See *Korematsu v. United States*, 323 U.S. 214, 216 (1944). The standard announced in *Korematsu* was right, though the court's application of the standard and thus the outcome of the case were mistaken.

16 *Adarand*, 515 U.S. 200 at 237.

17 *Grutter*, 123 S. Ct. at 2333.

18 Peter Kirsanow, "Michigan Impossible," *National Review Online*, July 1, 2003, www.nationalreview.com/comment/comment-Kirsanow070103.asp.

19 *Regents of the University of California v. Bakke*, 438 U.S. 265 (1978).

20 Nat Hentoff, "What the Supreme Court Left Out: The Smoking Gun in *Grutter v. Bollinger*," *Village Voice*, July 16, 2003, 34.

21 *Grutter v. Bollinger*, 137 F. Supp. 2d 821, 849 (E.D. Mich. 2001), revised in part and vacated in part, 288 F.3d 732 (6th Cir. 2002), affirmed, 123 S. Ct. 2325 (2003).

22 Ibid. at 853.

23 Hentoff, "What the Supreme Court Left Out" (quoting Jacques Steinberg, "The New Calculus of Diversity on Campus," *New York Times*, February 2, 2003).

24 Ibid.

Chapter 8: Natural Law, God, and Human Dignity

1 See Bernard J. F. Lonergan, *Insight: A Study of Human Understanding* (London: Longman's, 1955).

2 Inasmuch as the first and most basic practical principle directing human choosing toward what is intelligibly worthwhile and away from its privations is foundational to the identification of moral knowledge, there is a sense in which knowledge of this principle is *incipiently* moral knowledge.

3 St. Thomas Aquinas, *Summa Theologiae*, I-II, Q. 94, A. 2.

4 On the first principle of morality and its specifications, see John Finnis, Joseph M. Boyle Jr., and Germain Grisez, *Nuclear Deterrence, Morality, and Realism* (Oxford: Clarendon Press, 1987), 281–87.

5   By the phrase *our humanity*, I refer more precisely to the nature of humans as rational beings. The nature of human beings is a rational nature. So in virtue of our human nature, we human beings possess a profound and inherent dignity. The same would be true, however, of beings other than humans whose nature is a rational nature, if indeed there are such beings. In the case of humans, even individuals who have not yet acquired the immediately exercisable capacities for conceptual thought and other rational acts, and even those who have temporarily or permanently lost them, and, indeed, even those who do not possess them, never possessed them, and (short of a miracle) never will possess them, possess a rational nature.

6   Having said this, I do not want to suggest a sharper difference than can be justified between positive and negative rights. Even in the case of negative rights, it is sometimes relevant to ask how a right should be honored and who, if anyone, has particular responsibility for protecting it. Moreover, it can be the case that there is not a uniquely correct answer to questions about what place the protection of the right should occupy on the list of social priorities. Consider, for example, the right not to be subjected to assault or battery. Although it is obvious that individuals have an obligation to respect this right, and equally obvious that governments have an obligation to protect persons within their jurisdiction from those who would violate it, different communities reasonably differ not only as to the means to protect persons from assault and battery but also as to the level of resources they allocate to protect people against violations of the right. I am grateful to Allen Buchanan for this point.

7   See, e.g., Yves R. Simon, *A General Theory of Authority* (Chicago: University of Chicago Press, 1962); John Finnis, *Natural Law and Natural Rights*, 2nd ed. (Oxford: Oxford University Press, 2011), 59–127.

8   David Hume, *A Treatise of Human Nature* (Oxford: Clarendon Press, 1888 [1739]), bk. 2, pt. 3, sec. 3, at 415.

9   Thomas Hobbes, *Leviathan*, ed. Edwin Curley (London: Hackett Publishing Company, 1994 [1651]), 41.

10   I offer a detailed critique of Humean skepticism, and a defense of my own view of the relationship of reason to feeling, emotion, and the like, in Robert P. George, *In Defense of Natural Law* (Oxford: Oxford University Press, 1999), ch. 1. See also John Finnis, *Reason in Action* (Oxford: Oxford University Press, 2011), ch. 1 ("Practical Reason's Foundations").

11   See, e.g., John Finnis, *Religion and Public Reasons* (Oxford: Oxford University Press, 2011), esp. ch. 1 ("Darwin, Dewey, Religion, and the Public Domain").

12   See Thomas Aquinas, *Summa Theologiae* I–II, Q. 91, art. 2, Q. 100, art. 1, at 997.

13   See John Finnis, *Moral Absolutes: Tradition, Revision, and Truth* (Washington, DC: Catholic University of America Press, 1991), 26n50.

14   Second Vatican Council, *Declaration on Religious Liberty: Dignitatis Humanae*, secs. 2–3 (1965), reprinted in *Vatican Council II: The Conciliar and Post-Conciliar Documents*, ed. Austin Flannery, OP, rev. ed. (Northport, NY: Costello, 1988), 800–801.

15   See Finnis, *Natural Law and Natural Rights*, 33–48.

16   In defense of freedom of choice (or freedom of the will) as described here, see Joseph M. Boyle Jr., Germain Grisez, and Olaf Tollefsen, *Free Choice: A Self-Referential Argument* (Notre Dame, IN: University of Notre Dame Press, 1976).

17   Although the distinction between intending bad side effects and accepting them
     is often pertinent to moral evaluation on a natural-law account, one should not
     suppose that it is impossible to violate moral norms in accepting side effects.
     On the contrary, one may behave *unjustly*, for example, in accepting bad side
     effects, even where one has not run afoul of the norm against intending, say,
     the death or injury of an innocent human being. See, e.g., George, *In Defense of
     Natural Law*, 106.
18   See, e.g., Aristotle, *Nicomachean Ethics, supra* note 4, at 1113b5–13.

Chapter 10: Two Concepts of Liberty . . . and Conscience

1   John Stuart Mill, *On Liberty and Other Essays* (Oxford: Oxford University Press,
     1991), 13–14.
2   H. L. A. Hart, *Law, Liberty, and Morality* (Oxford: Oxford University Press, 1963).
3   Mill, *On Liberty*, 15.
4   See, e.g., Robert P. George, *Making Men Moral: Civil Liberties and Public Morality*
     (Oxford: Clarendon Press, 1993).
5   See John Finnis, *Fundamentals of Ethics* (Oxford: Oxford University Press, 1983),
     ch. 3.
6   John Henry Newman, *Certain Difficulties Felt by Anglicans Considered . . . A Letter
     Addressed to the Duke of Norfolk* (London: Longmans, Green, 1897), 250.
7   *Planned Parenthood v. Casey*, 505 U.S. 833 (1992) (plurality opinion by Justices
     Sandra Day O'Connor, Anthony Kennedy, and David Souter).
8   See John Finnis, *Natural Law and Natural Rights*, 2nd ed. (Oxford: Oxford Univer-
     sity Press, 2011), 89–90.
9   See George Weigel, *Witness to Hope: The Biography of Pope John Paul II* (New York:
     HarperCollins, 1999).

Chapter 11: Religious Liberty

1   See John Finnis, *Natural Law and Natural Rights*, 2nd ed. (Oxford: Oxford Univer-
     sity Press, 2011), chs. 3–4.
2   Germain Grisez, "The First Principle of Practical Reason: A Commentary on
     the *Summa Theologiae*, 1–2, Question 94, Article 2," *Natural Law Forum* 10 (1965):
     168–96.
3   Ibid.
4   Finnis, *Natural Law and Natural Rights*, 450–52.
5   Martin Luther King, *Letter from Birmingham Jail* (New York: HarperCollins,
     1994). The letter was written and originally published in 1963.
6   John Rawls, "On the Priority of Right and Ideas of the Good," *Philosophy and
     Public Affairs* 17, no. 4 (1988): 251–76.
7   John Finnis, Joseph M. Boyle Jr., and Germain Grisez, *Nuclear Deterrence, Moral-
     ity, and Realism* (Oxford: Clarendon Press, 1987), 304–9.
8   On religion as a basic human good, see Finnis, *Natural Law and Natural Rights*,
     89–90.

9   For a deeply informed and sensitive treatment of similarities and differences in the world historical religions, see Augustine DiNoia, *The Diversity of Religions: A Christian Perspective* (Washington, DC: Catholic University Press, 1992).

10 See Kevin J. Hasson, *The Right to Be Wrong: Ending the Culture War over Religion in America* (New York: Encounter Books, 2005).

11 *Dignitatis Humanae*, 2–3.

12 On natural law and religious freedom in the Jewish tradition, see David Novak, *In Defense of Religious Liberty* (Wilmington, DE: ISI Books, 2009). (Rabbi Novak kindly dedicated this fine work to me. Inasmuch as this is the first time I've had occasion to cite it in a publication, I am happy to have the opportunity publicly to thank him for what I consider to be a high honor.)

13 John Rawls, *Political Liberalism*, expanded ed. (New York: Columbia University Press, 1993), 137.

14 *Nostra Aetate*, 2–4.

Chapter 12: What Marriage Is—and What It Isn't

1   This section draws heavily from material in the book I coauthored with Sherif Girgis and Ryan Anderson. See Sherif Girgis, Ryan T. Anderson, and Robert P. George, *What Is Marriage? Man and Woman: A Defense* (New York: Encounter, 2012), 68–70.

2   Elizabeth Brake, "Minimal Marriage: What Political Liberalism Implies for Marriage Law," *Ethics* 120 (2010): 303.

3   See Maggie Gallagher, "(How) Will Gay Marriage Weaken Marriage as a Social Institution: A Reply to Andrew Koppelman," *University of St. Thomas Law Journal* 2, no. 1 (2004): 62.

4   "Beyond Same-Sex Marriage: A New Strategic Vision for All Our Families and Relationships," BeyondMarriage.org, July 26, 2006, beyondmarriage.org/full_statement.html.

5   Jessica Bennett, "Only You. And You. And You: Polyamory—Relationships with Multiple, Mutually Consenting Partners—Has a Coming-Out Party," *Newsweek*, July 29, 2009, www.newsweek.com/2009/07/28/only-you-and-you-and-you.html.

6   "Three-Person Civil Union Sparks Controversy in Brazil," BBC News, August 28, 2012, www.bbc.co.uk/news/world-latin-america-19402508.

7   "Mexico City Proposes Temporary Marriage Licenses," *The Telegraph*, September 30, 2011, www.telegraph.co.uk/news/worldnews/centralamericaandthecaribbean/mexico/8798982/Mexico-City-proposes-temporary-marriage-licences.html.

8   "Toronto School District Board Promotes Polygamy, Group Sex to Children," *Blazing Cat Fur*, September 2012, blazingcatfur.blogspot.com/2012/09/tdsb-promotes-polygamy-group-sex-to.html.

9   E. J. Graff, "Retying the Knot," in Andrew Sullivan, ed., *Same-Sex Marriage: Pro and Con: A Reader* (New York: Vintage Books, 1997), 134, 136.

10 Ibid., 137.

11 Andrew Sullivan, *Virtually Normal: An Argument about Homosexuality* (New York: Vintage Books, 1996), 202–3.

12 Ari Karpel, "Monogamish," *The Advocate*, July 7, 2011, www.advocate.com/Print_Issue/Features/Monogamish/.

13   Victoria A. Brownworth, "Something Borrowed, Something Blue: Is Marriage
      Right for Queers?" in Greg Wharton and Ian Philips, eds., *I Do/I Don't: Queers on
      Marriage* (San Francisco: Suspect Thoughts Press, 2004), 53, 58–59.
14   Michelangelo Signorile, "Bridal Wave," *Out* 42 (December–January 1994): 68, 161.

Chapter 15: Conscience and Its Enemies

1   President Obama made the remark at a town hall meeting in Johnstown, Penn-
     sylvania, on March 29, 2008. So there can be no doubt that I am treating him
     fairly, I will provide the quotation in its full context: "When it comes specifi-
     cally to HIV/AIDS, the most important prevention is education, which should
     include—which should include abstinence education and teaching the children—
     teaching children, you know, that sex is not something casual. But it should also
     include—it should also include other, you know, information about contracep-
     tion because, look, I've got two daughters. Nine years old and six years old. I
     am going to teach them first of all about values and morals. But if they make a
     mistake, I don't want them punished with a baby. I don't want them punished
     with an STD at the age of sixteen. You know, so it doesn't make sense to not
     give them information." See blogs.cbn.com/thebrodyfile/archive/2008/03/31/
     obama-says-he-doesnt-want-his-daughters-punished-with-a.aspx.

Chapter 16: When Life Begins

1   For a useful summary of the scientific studies in this area, see the white paper
     produced by Maureen L. Condic, "When Does Human Life Begin? A Scientific Per-
     spective" (Westchester Institute for Ethics and the Human Person, October 2008).
2   In 2008, Biden told NBC's Tom Brokaw, "It's a personal and private issue. For
     me, as a Roman Catholic, I'm prepared to accept the teachings of my church. . . .
     I'm prepared as a matter of faith to accept that life begins at the moment of
     conception. But that is my judgment. For me to impose that judgment on every-
     one else who is equally and maybe even more devout than I am seems to me is
     inappropriate in a pluralistic society." During the 2012 vice-presidential debate,
     Biden said, "I accept my church's position on abortion. . . . Life begins at con-
     ception in the church's judgment. I accept it in my personal life. But I refuse to
     impose it on equally devout Christians and Muslims and Jews, and I just refuse
     to impose that on others."

Chapter 17: Embryo Ethics

1   For what it is worth, I should point out that the Catholic Church does not try
     to draw *scientific* inferences about the humanity or distinctness of the human
     embryo from *theological* propositions about ensoulment. In fact, it works the
     other way around. Someone who wanted to talk the pope into declaring that
     the human embryo is "ensouled"—which is something that up to this point the

Catholic Church has never declared—would have to prove his point by marshaling (among other things) the scientific facts. The *theological* conclusion would be drawn on the basis of (among other things) the findings of *science* about the self-integration, distinctness, unity, and determinateness of the developing embryo. So things work *exactly the opposite* of the way some advocates of embryo-destructive research who think they know what the Catholic Church says about "ensoulment" imagine they work.

2 My point in saying this is not to make light of, much less to denigrate, the important witness of many traditions of faith to the profound, inherent, and equal dignity of all members of the human family. Faith can, and many traditions of faith do, reinforce ethical propositions that can be rationally affirmed even apart from faith.

3 Thus, "recollecting (at her birth) his appreciation of Louise Brown as one or two cells in his petri dish, [Robert] Edwards [said]: 'She was beautiful then and she is beautiful now.'" John Finnis, "Some Fundamental Evils in Generating Human Embryos by Cloning," in Cosimo Marco Mazzoni, ed., *Etica della Ricerca Biologica* (Florence: Leo Olschki, 2000), 115-23, at 116 (quoting Robert Edwards and Patrick Steptoe, *A Matter of Life* (London, 1981). Edwards and his coauthor accurately describe the embryo as "a microscopic human being—one in its very earliest stages of development" (p. 83). They say that the human being in the embryonic stage of development is "passing through a critical period in its life of great exploration: it becomes magnificently organised, switching on its own biochemistry, increasing in size, and preparing itself quickly for implantation in the womb" (p. 97).

4 Keith Moore and T. V. N. Persaud, in *The Developing Human: Clinically Oriented Embryology*, perhaps the most widely used of the standard embryology texts, make the following unambiguous statement about the beginning of a new and distinct human individual: "Human development begins at fertilization when a male gamete or sperm (spermatozoon) unites with a female gamete or oocyte (ovum) to form a single cell—a zygote. This highly specialized, totipotent cell marked *the beginning of each of us as a unique individual*" (p. 16, emphasis added).

5 A human embryo (like a human being in the fetal, infant, child, or adolescent stage) is not properly classified as a "prehuman" organism with the mere potential to become a human being. No human embryologist or textbook in human embryology known to me presents, accepts, or remotely contemplates such a view. The testimony of leading embryology textbooks is that a human embryo *is*—already and not merely potentially—a new individual member of the species *Homo sapiens*. His or her potential, assuming a sufficient measure of good health and a suitable environment, is to develop by an internally directed process of growth through the further stages of maturity on the continuum that is his or her life. Nor is there any such thing as a "pre-embryo." That is a concept invented, as Lee Silver has pointed out, for political, not scientific, reasons (Lee Silver, *Remaking Eden* [New York: Avon Books, 1997], 39).

6 Is a cloned human embryo a subhuman organism? The answer is surely no. Just as fertilization, if successful, generates a human embryo, cloning produces the same result by combining what is normally combined and activated in fertilization—that is, the full genetic code plus the ovular cytoplasm. Fertilization produces a new and complete, though immature, human organism. The same is true of

successful cloning. Cloned embryos therefore ought to be treated as having the same moral status, whatever that might be, as other human embryos.

7   The first one or two divisions, in the first thirty-six hours, occur under the direction of the messenger RNA acquired from the oocyte, and thereafter the cleavages are guided by the embryo's DNA. See, among other sources, Ronan O'Rahilly and Fabiola Mueller, *Human Embryology and Teratology* (New York: John Wiley & Sons, 2000), 38. Still, these cleavages do not occur if the embryo's nucleus is not present, and so the nuclear genes also control these early changes.

8   For a fuller explanation, see Patrick Lee and Robert P. George, "The First Fourteen Days of Human Life," *New Atlantis*, no. 13 (2006).

9   I will leave unaddressed here the question whether embryonic stem cells are likely to be used anytime soon—or ever—in therapies to treat human diseases and afflictions.

10   For an entity to have a rational nature is for it to be a certain type of substance; having a rational nature, unlike, say, being tall, or Croatian, or gifted in mathematics, is not an accidental attribute. Each individual of the human species has a rational nature (even if disease or defect blocks its full development and expression in some individuals—if the disease or defect could somehow be corrected, it would perfect the individual as the kind of substance he is; it would not transform him into an entity of a different nature). Having a rational nature is, in Jeff McMahan's terms, a "status-conferring intrinsic property." So my argument is not that every member of the human species should be accorded full moral respect based on the fact that the more mature members have a status-conferring intrinsic property, as Professor McMahan interprets the "nature-of-the-kind argument." See his "Our Fellow Creatures," *Journal of Ethics* 9 (2005): 353–80. Rather, my proposition is that having a rational nature is the basis for full moral worth, and *every* human individual possesses that status-conferring feature.

11   Unsentimental believers that full moral respect is due only to those human beings who possess immediately exercisable capacities for characteristically human mental functions do not hesitate to draw the inference that young infants do not deserve full moral respect. See, e.g., Peter Singer, "Killing Babies Isn't Always Wrong," *The Spectator*, September 16, 1995, 20–22.

12   My Princeton colleague Peter Singer was asked whether there would be anything wrong with a society in which children were bred for spare parts on a massive scale. "No," he replied. (See "Blue State Philosopher," *World Magazine*, November 27, 2004.)

13   Michael Gazzaniga has suggested that the embryo is to the human being what a Home Depot store is to a house—that is, a collection of unintegrated components. According to Dr. Gazzaniga, "It is a truism that the blastocyst has the potential to be a human being. Yet at that stage of development it is simply a clump of cells. . . . An analogy might be what one sees when walking into a Home Depot. There are the parts and potential for at least 30 homes. But if there is a fire at Home Depot, the headline isn't 30 homes burn down. It's Home Depot burns down." Quoted as "Metaphor of the Week" in *Science* 295, no. 5560 (March 1, 2002): 1637. Dr. Gazzaniga gives away the game, however, in conceding, as he must, that the term *blastocyst* refers to a *stage of development* in the life of a determinate, enduring, integrated, and, indeed, self-integrating entity. If an analogy to a Home Depot is

to be drawn, it is the gametes (or the materials used to generate an embryo by a process of cloning), not the embryo, that constitute the "parts and potential."

14 This conclusion would follow no matter which of the acquired qualities proposed as qualifying some human beings (or human beings at some developmental stages) for full respect were the one selected.

15 For a more complete presentation of this argument, see Patrick Lee and Robert P. George, "The Wrong of Abortion," in Andrew I. Cohen and Christopher Wellman, eds., *Contemporary Debates in Applied Ethics* (New York: Blackwell Publishers, 2005), 13–26.

16 Ronald Bailey, "Are Stem Cells Babies?" *Reason*, July 11, 2001.

17 Agata Sagan and Peter Singer, "The Moral Status of Stem Cells," *Metaphilosophy* 38 (2007), 264–84.

18 Ibid., 269.

19 Patrick Lee and I replied to Bailey at great length in a series of exchanges on *National Review Online*. Lee and I replied to similar arguments advanced by Lee Silver in his book *Challenging Nature*.

20 President's Council on Bioethics, transcript of meeting of Friday, January 18, 2002, session 5, www.bioethics.gov/transcripts/jan02/jan18session5.html.

21 Patrick Lee and I have replied to other arguments that identify the human "person" as the brain or brain activity, and the human "being" as the bodily animal, in "Dualistic Delusions," *First Things*, no. 150 (2005).

22 Patrick Lee and I have provided a full reply to Sandel in our article "Acorns and Embryos," *New Atlantis*, no. 7 (2005): 90–100

23 Werner A. Muller, *Developmental Biology* (New York: Springer Verlag, 1997), 12ff.; O'Rahilly and Mueller, *Human Embryology and Teratology*, 38–39.

24 Denker refers specifically to the work of Magdalena Zernicka-Goetz and her colleagues at the University of Cambridge and that of R. L. Gardner at Oxford University. See Hans-Werner Denker, "Early Human Development: New Data Raise Important Embryological and Ethical Questions Relevant for Stem Cell Research," *Naturwissenschaften* 91 (2004): 21ff.

25 Patrick Lee and I have presented this information at length in "The First Fourteen Days of Human Life."

Chapter 18: The Personal and the Political

1 Vice President Biden has said, "I accept my church's position on abortion. . . . Life begins at conception in the church's judgment. I accept it in my personal life. But I refuse to impose it on equally devout Christians and Muslims and Jews, and I just refuse to impose that on others" ("2012 Vice-Presidential Debate: Vice President Biden and Rep. Paul Ryan's remarks in Danville, Ky., on Oct.11 [running transcript]," *Washington Post*, October 11, 2012). Senator Kerry has stated, "I am actually personally opposed to abortion. But I don't believe that I have a right to take what is an article of faith to me and legislate it to other people" (*Meet the Press*, NBC, January 30, 2005).

2 Some good and sincere people have expressed concern that bishops are guilty of a double standard when they would deny Communion to politicians who

publicly support abortion and embryo-destructive research but not to those who support the death penalty, which Pope John Paul II condemned in all but the rarest of circumstances, and the U.S. invasions of Iraq, of which the pope and many other Vatican officials were sharply critical. But neither the pope nor the *Catechism of the Catholic Church* places the death penalty on a par with abortion and other forms of direct killing of the innocent. Moreover, the status of the church's teaching on the death penalty differs from that of the teaching on abortion. As John Paul II made clear in the great encyclical *Evangelium Vitae*, the teaching on abortion (as well as all other forms of direct killing of the innocent) is infallibly proposed by the ordinary and universal magisterium of the church; the same is plainly not true of the developing teaching on the death penalty—that is, opposition to the death penalty has *not* achieved the status of a definitively settled moral teaching of the church. Regarding the U.S. invasions of Iraq, neither Pope John Paul II nor Pope Benedict XVI has asserted that opposition to the war is binding on the consciences of Catholics. John Paul II's statements opposing the use of force in the run-up to both invasions plainly questioned the *prudential judgments* of political leaders who, in the end, had and have the right and responsibility (according to the *Catechism* and the entire tradition of Catholic teaching on war and peace) to make judgments as to whether force is in fact necessary. That is why the pope and the bishops did not say that Catholic soldiers may not participate in the war. This contrasts with their clear teaching that Catholics may not participate in abortions or other forms of embryo killing or support the use of taxpayer monies for activities involving the deliberate killing of innocent human beings.

Chapter 19: A Right to Life Denied or a Right to Die Honored?

1   See, e.g., Peter Singer, *Practical Ethics*, 2nd ed. (Cambridge: Cambridge University Press, 1993) (especially ch. 6); Ronald Dworkin, *Life's Dominion: An Argument about Abortion, Euthanasia, and Individual Freedom* (New York: Alfred A. Knopf, 1993); Michael Tooley, *Abortion and Infanticide* (Oxford: Clarendon Press, 1983); Michael Tooley, "Abortion and Infanticide," *Philosophy and Public Affairs* 2, no. 1 (1972): 37; Mary Ann Warren, "On the Moral and Legal Status of Abortion," *The Monist* (January 1973): 43.
2   Ibid.
3   Peter Singer, Letter to the Editor, "Science, Religion and Stem Cells (5 Letters)," *New York Times*, June 23, 2005, www.nytimes.com/2005/06/23/opinion/123cuomo.html?_r=0.
4   When Singer was interviewed by *World Magazine*, the interviewer asked: "What about parents conceiving and giving birth to a child specifically to kill him, take his organs, and transplant them into their ill older children?" Singer replied: "It's difficult to warm to parents who can take such a detached view, [but] they're not doing something really wrong in itself." The interviewer then asked: "Is there anything wrong with a society in which children are bred for spare parts on a massive scale?" Singer's reply: "No." Marvin Olasky, "Blue State Philosopher," *World Magazine*, November 27, 2004, www.worldmag.com/articles/9987.

5 See Dworkin, *Life's Dominion*.

6 See Germain Grisez and Joseph Boyle, *Life and Death with Liberty and Justice: A Contribution to the Euthanasia Debate* (Notre Dame, IN: University of Notre Dame Press, 1979), and Patrick Lee, *Abortion and Unborn Human Life* (Washington, DC: Catholic University Press, 1996). For a discussion of dualism, see David Braine, *The Human Person: Animal and Spirit* (Notre Dame, IN: University of Notre Dame Press, 1992). On issues of political theory and autonomy, see Robert P. George, *Making Men Moral* (Oxford: Clarendon Press; New York: Oxford University Press, 1993). On issues of moral philosophy, see Robert P. George, *In Defense of Natural Law* (Oxford: Clarendon Press, 1999).

7 See, e.g., Singer, *Practical Ethics*; Dworkin, *Life's Dominion*; Tooley, *Abortion and Infanticide*; and Warren, "On the Moral and Legal Status of Abortion."

8 See George, *In Defense of Natural Law*; Patrick Lee and Robert P. George, "The Wrong of Abortion," in Andrew I. Cohen and Christopher Wellman, eds., *Contemporary Debates in Applied Ethics* (New York: Blackwell Publishers, 2005); and Robert P. George and Patrick Lee, "Acorns and Embryos," *New Atlantis*, no. 7 (Fall 2004/Winter 2005): 90.

9 See George, *Making Men Moral*.

10 See Hadley Arkes et al., "Always to Care, Never to Kill: A Declaration on Euthanasia," *First Things* (February 1992): 45, www.firstthings.com/ftissues/ft9202/articlestdocumentation.html. An abbreviated version of the declaration appeared in the *Wall Street Journal* on November 27, 1991.

11 See Patrick Lee, "Personhood, Dignity, Suicide, and Euthanasia," *The National Catholic Bioethics Quarterly* (Autumn 2001): 329; Chris Tollefsen, "Euthanasia and the Culture of Life," www.princeton.edu/~prolife/articles/tollefsen.pdf.

12 See, e.g., Arthur Caplan, "The Time Has Come to Let Terri Schiavo Die," MSNBC, March 18, 2005, www.msnbc.msn.com/id/7231440/.

13 See my interview with *National Review Online*, "Always to Care, Never to Kill," *National Review Online*, March 21, 2005.

14 See the address Pope John Paul II gave on March 20, 2004, to the participants in the International Congress, "Life-Sustaining Treatments and Vegetative State: Scientific Advances and Ethical Dilemmas," http://www.vatican.va/holy_father/john_paul_ii/speeches/2004/march/documents/hf_jp-ii_spe_20040320_congress-fiamc_en.html.

Chapter 20: The "Relics of Barbarism," Then and Now

1 It is important to note that the Church of Jesus Christ of Latter-Day Saints has long since rejected polygamy and is today a leading force in defending the institution of marriage as the monogamous union of husband and wife.

Chapter 26: The Achievement of John Finnis

1 John Finnis, *Natural Law and Natural Rights* (Oxford: Clarendon Press, 1980); 2nd ed. published in 2011.

2   Germain Grisez, "The First Principle of Practical Reason: A Commentary on the *Summa Theologiae*, 1–2, Question 94, Article 2," *Natural Law Forum* 10 (1965): 168–96. In the preface to *Natural Law and Natural Rights*, Finnis acknowledges his intellectual debt to Grisez, noting that "the ethical theory advanced in Chapters III–IV and the theoretical arguments in sections VI.2 and XIII.2 are squarely based on my understanding of his vigorous re-presentation and very substantial development of the classical arguments on these matters."

3   This development is discussed intensively in Joseph Boyle's essay herein, in Finnis's response to it, and in Grisez's essay too. In *Natural Law and Natural Rights*, Finnis did not formally articulate the first principle of morality—something he accounts as a "failure" in the postscript to the book's second edition (see p. 419). This was, however, soon rectified in his writing, as a result of collaboration with Grisez and Boyle in the refinement and development of their "new" natural law theory. As Finnis points out, he accorded "openness to integral fulfillment" the status of the "master principle of morality" in *Fundamentals of Ethics* (Oxford and Washington, DC: Oxford University Press and Georgetown University Press, 1983), 70–74, 120–24, and 1511–52. A more formal articulation of the principle first appears in Germain Grisez, Joseph M. Boyle Jr., and John Finnis, "Practical Principles, Moral Truth, and Ultimate Ends," *American Journal of Jurisprudence*, 32 (1987): 126–29.

4   H. L. A. Hart, *The Concept of Law* (Oxford: Clarendon Press, 1961); 2nd edition published in 1994.

5   Ibid., 78.

6   H. L. A. Hart, *Essays on Bentham* (Oxford: Clarendon Press, 1982), ch. 10.

7   On the very first page of *The Concept of Law*, Hart invites the reader to regard the book as an exercise in "descriptive sociology."

8   As Finnis points out, Hart in *The Concept of Law* "gives descriptive explanatory priority to those who do not 'merely record and predict behavior conforming to rules,' or attend to rules 'only from the external point of view as a sign of possible punishment,' but rather '*use* the rules as standards for appraisal of their own and others' behavior.'" See Finnis, *Natural Law and Natural Rights*, 12, quoting Hart, *The Concept of Law*, 95–96.

9   John Finnis, "The Truth in Legal Positivism," in Robert P. George, ed., *The Autonomy of Law: Essays on Legal Positivism* (Oxford: Clarendon Press, 1996), 195–214, at 204.

10   Hart, *The Concept of Law*, 198.

11   Finnis, *Natural Law and Natural Rights*, 14.

12   See generally Finnis, "The Truth in Legal Positivism."

13   Dworkin set forth his critique of the "positivism" of Hart and Joseph Raz in *Taking Rights Seriously* (Cambridge, MA: Harvard University Press, 1977). Finnis comments on Dworkin's critique in an illuminating endnote to chapter 2 of *Natural Law and Natural Rights*, arguing that the debate "miscarries" because Dworkin "fails to acknowledge that their theoretical interest is not, like his, to identify a fundamental 'test for law,' in order to identify (even in the most disputed 'hard cases') where a judge's legal (moral and political) duty really lies, in a given community at a given time. Rather, their interest is in describing what is treated (i.e., accepted and effective) as law in a given community at a given

time, and in generating concepts that will allow such descriptions to be clear and explanatory, but without intent to offer solutions (whether 'right answers' or standards which if properly applied would yield right answers) to questions disputed among competent lawyers."

14 Finnis, *Natural Law and Natural Rights*.

15 The substance of the account of natural law offered by Finnis et al. is hardly new. Its core can be found in Aquinas, and much of that, in turn, Aquinas draws from Aristotle. It is true that Finnis, Grisez, and others have developed the Thomistic theory of natural law in various ways and have articulated the theory in a modern philosophical idiom. But to develop a theory is not to reject it. It is, rather, to accept its substance and draw out its further implications. That is what they have done by, for example, showing how reflection on the integral directiveness or prescriptivity of the principles of practical reason that Aquinas presents enables us to identify moral principles and norms that distinguish options for choice that are fully in line with all that reasonableness demands from options that, in one way or another, fall short or afoul of the full demands of practical reasonableness.

16 See especially Finnis, *Fundamentals of Ethics*.

17 See John Rawls, *A Theory of Justice* (Cambridge, MA: Harvard University Press, 1971); John Rawls, *Political Liberalism* (New York: Columbia University Press, 1993); Robert Nozick, *Anarchy, State, and Utopia* (Oxford: Oxford University Press, 1974); Ronald Dworkin, *A Matter of Principle* (Cambridge, MA: Harvard University Press, 1985).

18 Finnis expanded, deepened, and in various ways enriched what he originally presented in *Natural Law and Natural Rights* in papers he subsequently published, most of which are included in the five volumes of *Collected Essays of John Finnis* (Oxford: Oxford University Press, 2011).

19 Finnis, *Moral Absolutes: Tradition, Revision, and Truth*.

Acknowledgments

I T IS A pleasure to acknowledge the many people to whom I owe debts of gratitude. The list begins with Luis Tellez, president of the Witherspoon Institute, to whom this book is dedicated. Gabrielle Speach, Michael Liccione, and Jed Donahue provided excellent editing and commentary. Then there are the many friends and colleagues who in countless conversations helped me think through the issues addressed in the book: William C. Porth; William L. Saunders; Ryan Anderson; Sherif Girgis; Daniel Mark; Melissa Moschella; Dermot Quinn; Hadley Arkes; John Finnis; Daniel Robinson; William Hurlbut; John DiIulio; Mary Ann Glendon; Rabbi David Novak; Bradford Wilson; Matthew Franck; John Londregan; David Tubbs; Germain Grisez; Gerard V. Bradley; Yuval Levin; James Kurth; Joseph M. Boyle Jr.; Carter Snead; Patrick Lee; Christopher Tollefsen; Maggie Gallagher; Christian Brugger; Helen Alvare; Frank Cannon; Jeffrey Bell; George Weigel; William Kristol; Edward Whelan; Michael Horowitz; James Stoner; Russell Moore; Monsignor Thomas Mullelly; David Oakley; Stephen Whelan; Donald Drakeman; Mark O'Brien; George Will; Janet Madigan; Eric Cohen; the late Father Richard John Neuhaus; Rabbi Meir

275

Soloveichik; Leonard Leo; Peter Ryan, SJ; Stephen Hutchens; Charles Kesler; James Hitchcock; Kevin Flannery, SJ; Anthony Esolen; William Allen; Father Patrick Reardon; William Mumma; Maria Maddalena Giungi; James Kushiner; Shaykh Hamza Yusuf; Jennifer Bryson; Carlos Cavalle; John Keown; David Mills; Kristina Arriaga; Larry Arnn; Benjamin Carson; R. R. Reno; José Joel Alicea; Patrick Langrell; Donald Landry; Leon Kass; Gilbert Meilaender; John Eastman; Richard Land; Seamus Hasson; Frank Schubert; Cornel West; Archbishop Charles Chaput; Monsignor Stuart Swetland; Adam Keiper; John Haldane; Paul McHugh; Diana Schaub; Brian Brown; Maurizio Viroli; Paul Yowell; Matthew O'Brien; Roger Scruton; the late Elizabeth Fox-Genovese; Paul Mankowski, SJ; Maureen Condic; Ramesh Ponnuru; Jeremy Waldron; Christopher Wolfe; Stephen Macedo; Michael Skiles; George Dent; Michael Sandel; the late Alfonso Gomez-Lobo; Edmund Pellegrino; John Garvey; Kent Greenawalt; the late James Q. Wilson; Katrina Lantos Swett; Markus Grompe; and Jean Bethke Elshtain.

Although this book has been revised in many ways, many of these essays have appeared before in other places, including *First Things*, *Public Discourse*, *National Review* (both print and online), the *New Criterion*, and the *American Spectator*. I thank these publications. I also thank the Brookings Institution for permission to reprint the chapter "The Personal and the Political: Some Liberal Fallacies," which originally appeared as "Cuomological Fallacies" in E. J. Dionne Jr., Jean Bethke Elshtain, and Kayla M. Drogosz, eds., *One Electorate Under God? A Dialogue on Religion and American Politics* (2004); the *International Journal for Religious Freedom* for permission to reprint "Religious Liberty: A Fundamental Human Right," which originally appeared as "Religious Liberty and the Human Good" (vol. 5, no. 1); *Constitutional Commentary* for permission to reprint "A Right to Life Denied or a Right to Die Honored?," which originally appeared as "Terri Schiavo: A Right to Life Denied or a Right to Die Honored?" (vol. 22, no. 3); and *Columbia Law Review* for permission to reprint "Some Hard Questions about Affirmative Action," which originally appeared as "*Gratz* and *Grutter*: Some Hard Questions" (vol. 103, no. 6).

Index

INTERCOLLEGIATE
STUDIES INSTITUTE
Educating for Liberty